GRAMMAR EXPLORER 3

TEACHER'S GUIDE

Eleanor Barnes & Kristin Sherman

NATIONAL GEOGRAPHIC LEARNING | CENGAGE Learning

Australia • Brazil • Japan • Korea • Mexico • Singapore • Spain • United Kingdom • United States

NATIONAL GEOGRAPHIC LEARNING | CENGAGE Learning

Grammar Explorer 3 Teacher's Guide
Eleanor Barnes and Kristin Sherman

Publisher: Sherrise Roehr
Executive Editor: Laura Le Dréan
Managing Editor: Eve Einselen Yu
Senior Development Editor: Kim Steiner
Development Editor: Liz Henley
Associate Development Editor: Alayna Cohen
Assistant Editor: Vanessa Richards
Senior Technology Product Manager: Scott Rule
Director of Global Marketing: Ian Martin
Executive Marketing Manager: Ben Rivera
Sr. Director, ELT & World Languages:
Michael Burggren
Production Manager: Daisy Sosa
Content Project Manager: Andrea Bobotas
Senior Print Buyer: Mary Beth Hennebury
Cover Designer: 3CD, Chicago
Cover Image: Feng Wei Photography/Getty Images
Compositor: Cenveo® Publisher Services

© 2015 National Geographic Learning, a part of Cengage Learning

ALL RIGHTS RESERVED. No part of this work covered by the copyright herein may be reproduced, transmitted, stored, or used in any form or by any means graphic, electronic, or mechanical, including but not limited to photocopying, recording, scanning, digitizing, taping, Web distribution, information networks, or information storage and retrieval systems, except as permitted under Section 107 or 108 of the 1976 United States Copyright Act, or applicable copyright law of another jurisdiction, without the prior written permission of the publisher.

> For product information and technology assistance, contact us at
> **Cengage Learning Customer & Sales Support,**
> **1-800-354-9706**
>
> For permission to use material from this text or product,
> submit all requests online at **www.cengage.com/permissions.**
> Further permissions questions can be e-mailed to
> **permissionrequest@cengage.com.**

Teacher's Guide 3: 978-1-111-35113-7

National Geographic Learning
20 Channel Center Street
Boston, MA 02210
USA

Cengage Learning is a leading provider of customized learning solutions with office locations around the globe, including Singapore, the United Kingdom, Australia, Mexico, Brazil and Japan.

Cengage Learning products are represented in Canada by Nelson Education, Ltd.

Visit National Geographic Learning online at **ngl.cengage.com**

Visit our corporate website at **www.cengage.com**

Printed in the United States of America
Print Number: 01   Print Year: 2015

CONTENTS

From the Series Editors iv

Series Components v

General Guide to Teaching a Unit 2

Unit-Specific Teaching Tips and Answer Keys 9

    Unit 1 9

    Unit 2 19

    Unit 3 28

    Unit 4 37

    Unit 5 44

    Unit 6 53

    Unit 7 63

    Unit 8 73

    Unit 9 80

    Unit 10 90

    Unit 11 99

    Unit 12 111

    Unit 13 120

    Unit 14 130

    Unit 15 141

Audio Scripts A1

FROM THE SERIES EDITORS

Message from the Series Editors

As the series editors, we are pleased to introduce the exciting new **Grammar Explorer** series. Throughout the process of developing these materials, our goal has been to provide students and teachers with a solid and thorough grammar experience that is easy for teachers and engaging for learners.

We do not take the word *explorer* lightly. We want to provide students and teachers with fascinating global content that acknowledges the incredibly diverse world we live in. This content allows students to explore the world and discuss their roles in it through meaningful communication. Students also explore language. They encounter the grammar in rich listening, speaking, reading, and writing activities that focus on a wide variety of topics—from science and innovation to ancient history. Students develop communicative skills that will serve them beyond the classroom.

Rob Jenkins and Staci Johnson

Introduction to Grammar Explorer

Grammar Explorer is a three-level grammar series starting at high-beginning and moving through low-advanced. Each unit of *Grammar Explorer* has two to four well-structured lessons that introduce and practice the target grammar gradually, with control and *without* overwhelming students.

Each *Grammar Explorer* lesson will captivate students with its content and engage them with a series of thought-provoking activities. The lesson starts with a short high-interest text where students *discover* the grammar. It continues with controlled practice of the target grammar point, and gradually moves toward open-ended speaking and/or writing activities.

Students learn, construct meaning, and practice using **all four skills**, with the goal of communicating fluently while using the target grammar accurately and appropriately. Each activity serves a purpose and provides a step in the path to student success. Furthermore, the series assists teachers by providing well-thought-out lessons that make teaching and learning both more effective *and* more fun.

Why does Grammar Explorer work?

Real-World Content

Relevant up-to-date topics and photos capture students' attention and bring learning to life. Students immediately have a reason to communicate on themes that reflect the world they live in. Grammar discovered through interesting content, as it is throughout *Grammar Explorer*, provides a common starting place for all learners and eventually leads seamlessly to application.

Integrated Skills in Controlled Lessons

Every unit of *Grammar Explorer* provides numerous opportunities to read, write, listen, and speak. Charts are simple and do not provide more information than a student can grasp at one time. After warming up with the *Explore* section, students do the controlled practice in *Learn* to ensure that they have a sufficient understanding of the structure before moving on to more open-ended and communicative activities in *Practice*.

Application of Knowledge

Each lesson and unit in *Grammar Explorer* ends with an application exercise. Teachers everywhere know that students not only need to master rules but also try out those rules by speaking and writing on their own. Carefully designed application exercises aim to help students gain the confidence they need to successfully transfer what they have learned to real life. Application exercises ask students to **critically think** about a variety of topics, **synthesize** information they have learned in a lesson or unit, and **use English** to discuss and communicate their ideas.

Flexible Learning

1. **Flipped Classrooms:** The readings, controlled practice activities, and listening activities can be assigned as out-of-class work, allowing teachers to focus on interactive and productive activities in class, while students work at their own pace at home.

2. **Blended or Online:** The Online Workbook and interactive eBook provide options for teaching a blended or fully online course.

SERIES COMPONENTS

Grammar Explorer components support a variety of classrooms, including traditional, flipped, blended, and online.

For the Student

Student Book
Also available in:
- split editions
- eBooks

Audio CD
Students can listen to:
- all *Explore* readings
- all listening activities
- all pronunciation activities

eBook
eBooks give learners fully integrated online, downloadable, and mobile access to their programs. With eBooks you can:
- complete and save activities
- listen to embedded audio
- search for keywords or phrases
- skip to any section with a functional table of contents
- highlight text and make notes
- view on devices running Mac®, Windows®, iOS™, and Android™

Online Workbook
The Online Workbook has both teacher-led and self-study options and includes:
- extensive additional practice of grammar in each lesson
- review exercises, including a "Unit Challenge" game
- interactive, automatically-graded activities
- independent practice for self-study, or results reported to instructor in MyELT
- additional listening practice
- additional pronunciation practice

For the Teacher

Teacher's Guide
In addition to presenting a general guide for teaching a unit, the Teacher's Guide provides:
- detailed teaching notes and background information for each unit
- suggestions for online activities to engage students with lesson themes
- extension activities and alternative writing exercises
- tips for flipped classrooms: activities can be assigned as homework, allowing teachers to focus on interactive activities in class
- answer keys and audio scripts

Teacher's eResource
The Teacher's eResource can be used as a reference and a Classroom Presentation Tool. With the Teacher's eResource, instructors can:
- project the Student Book pages and reveal answers
- challenge students to provide new example sentences in customizable grammar charts
- play embedded audio in the classroom
- reference the complete Teacher's Guide in an electronic version

Assessment CD-ROM with ExamView®
Assessment CD-ROM with ExamView® is an easy-to-use test generating program that:
- provides pre-made test questions for every unit
- allows teachers to customize their tests or create quizzes in as little as three minutes

GENERAL GUIDE TO TEACHING A UNIT

Unit Opener

Each unit begins with an engaging National Geographic photo, the unit theme, and a list of the lessons and target grammar structures.

Using the Photo

- Direct students' attention to the photo and the photo caption. Ask them level-appropriate questions such as: *Who are the people? What do you see? Where is this? What is the theme of the unit? What does the photo say about the theme?*
- Ask students to write three questions about the photo. Then, if they have Internet access or are previewing at home, see if they can find answers to their questions online or in another reference.
- Read the Unit-Specific Teaching Tips to find background notes on the photo and theme-specific questions to ask.

Using the Table of Contents

- Draw students' attention to the table of contents in the box on the lower right. You may want to check their previous knowledge of the grammar by asking them: *Which grammar do you already know? What is an example?* Write any examples on the board and ask other students if they are correct. Don't provide any explanation at this point. This is a good way to get a sense of where your students are.
- If the grammar is new or if you want to be sure they understand the grammar-related language, you can preview the grammar terms that students will see in the unit. For your convenience, the Unit-Specific Teaching Tips provide a list of grammar terms and definitions for each unit. Also be sure to tell students to refer to the Glossary of Grammar Terms in the back of their Student Book any time they are unsure of a grammatical term.

Orienting Students to the Unit Theme

- Tell students to flip through the unit for one minute, looking at the pictures and reading any titles and captions. Then, ask students what they think the unit will be about and have them write their three guesses on a piece of paper. After they discuss their ideas with a group for two minutes, ask each group for their "best" answer.

- For three- or four-lesson units, tell students to flip through and look at the *Explore* readings at the beginning of each lesson in the unit. Ask them to rank the readings in order of interest. If possible, they can explain why.

Lessons

Each unit has two to four lessons.

- See the Unit-Specific Teaching Tips for student learning outcomes (SLOs) for each lesson. The **SLOs** help you and your students see more concretely what they will learn, or have learned. Write or project the SLOs on the board before you begin a new lesson and after you finish a lesson or a unit.

EXPLORE

1 READ.

This section provides a model reading in one of many genres, including magazine articles, websites, conversations, blog posts, radio shows, and others.

- Have students skim the text quickly and call out any words they don't understand. Write them on the board and, as a group, define each one using an example sentence or a drawing. **Option:** On the board, write only those words you feel are necessary for students to know. See if a student can provide a definition or an example sentence for each. Write your students' correct definitions or example sentences on the board. Write your own if they do not have any.
- See the Unit-Specific Teaching Tips for "Be the Expert," which provides background information on the content and often includes ideas on how to use the information in class.
- Play the audio as students follow along silently. Try stopping at the end of each paragraph and asking students comprehension questions.
- Play the audio again or have students read in pairs. Reading more than once will help students become more familiar with the content, vocabulary, and grammar.

Photo Tips: In addition to the unit opener, the Student Book features many photos. Some illustrate the text, while others provide context for listening activities.
- Direct students' attention to a photo and use it to illustrate any vocabulary.
- Use photos to recycle target grammar from previous lessons or units.
- Be sure to draw students' attention to captions as these will provide additional important information and provide context for the exercise.

General Reading Tips

The reading activities provide students with grammar in context, help them expand their vocabulary, and engage them with interesting content. While the Unit-Specific Teaching Tips offer information for individual passages, for further expansion and exploitation, you can also:
- have students create additional comprehension items about the passage;
- have students do paired readings of the passage to practice oral fluency;
- photocopy and cut up the passage into pieces for students to put in order, jigsaw-style:
    1. Cut the reading passage into three or four parts. If it's a conversation, consider cutting after each line or group of lines.
    2. Put students into groups of three or four (See *Tips for Grouping* on page 6) and give each student one part of the text.
    3. Students read their part and learn the general ideas. Then, they tell their groupmates what is in their part.
    4. As a group, they decide which part is first, second, and so on. This can be a good opportunity to point out discourse markers such as topic sentences, introductions, and conclusions.

General Vocabulary Tips

Both the reading passages and the audio inputs expose students to vocabulary that may be unfamiliar to them. Incorporating the following techniques into the classroom will help students acquire language better and develop study habits that will help them outside and beyond the classroom.
- Suggest that students keep a vocabulary notebook and add unfamiliar words as well as definitions and sentences. Tell them to write down sentences they hear or find online. This will help them see the common collocations and grammar patterns that often occur with certain words.
- Facilitate dictionary skills by having students look up new words.
- Help students acquire these words by suggesting that they practice them in speaking and writing activities.
- At lower levels, encourage students to make flashcards and practice them in pairs. Be sure to tell them to focus on commonly used words as opposed to highly specialized words. For beginners, for example, the word *mangrove* is not as important as *forest*.

Front

```
explore (verb)
/ɛksplôr/
```

Back

```
Translation: (students
first language)

Collocation: explore a
place/a topic/ideas

Other forms:
explorer (noun, person)
exploration (noun, idea)
```

GENERAL GUIDE TO TEACHING A UNIT

2 CHECK.

This section provides short comprehension questions about the reading.

- Have students complete the activity individually before checking their answers with a partner.
- For higher-level students or early finishers, write additional questions on the board to complete, or have them write their own additional questions.

3 DISCOVER.

These section activities guide students from noticing the target structure in the reading to identifying information about the structure. Exercise **A** generally provides a noticing exercise, and exercise **B** elicits rules or shows students important level-appropriate aspects of the form or function of the grammar.

- Have students complete exercise **A** alone or for more interactivity and support, in pairs.
- Have students complete exercise **B** individually. This will help them learn to notice patterns and infer rules. Then, provide an opportunity for peer or class discussion to clarify the usage of the grammar and explain or elicit rules.
- See the Unit-Specific Teaching Tips for ideas to help bridge the *Explore* section to the grammar charts in *Learn*.

FLIP IT!

Have students do the *Explore* section of a lesson at home.

1. Preview the reading in class and ask students to look at the photo and title and make predictions about the content.
2. Pre-teach unfamiliar vocabulary.
3. Students read and complete the *Explore* exercises at home.
4. Students compare their answers to exercises **2** and **3** with a partner as soon as they get to class.
5. Allow students to discuss any questions they have about the grammar. Encourage other students to explain the rule.

LEARN

Grammar Charts

- See the Unit-Specific Teaching Tips for information specific to the grammar in a unit and for ideas for presenting the grammar in class.

Presentation of Model Structures

Option 1: Read the sentences in the chart and have students repeat. If the chart poses questions and answers, call on students and ask the questions, eliciting the appropriate responses.

Option 2: Call on students to read the sentences in the chart. Ask questions to check comprehension (e.g., *What form of be do we use with* he? *What form of the main verb do we use in a question? What part of speech is this word/phrase?*).

Practice of Model Structures

Option 1: Write the parts of the sentence on different cards or sentence strips and have students come to the board and put them in order.

Option 2: Draw the outline of the grammar chart on the board or project the customizable chart in the Teacher's eResource. Include the grammar labels (e.g., *Noun, Verb,* . . .), but do not include the example sentences. Have students provide new examples sentences of their own.

Option 3: As in Option 2, provide the model structure, but with a new example filled in and the grammar labels missing. Have students choose or tell you the correct label for each part of the sentence.

Presentation of the Notes/Rules Chart

Option 1: Have students read the notes silently (or at home). Ask them to tell a partner another example sentence. Then, have some students write more examples sentences on the board. Answer any questions.

Option 2: With partners, ask students to cover the rule/note side of the notes chart and first read the examples, noticing the bold words. See if students can tell you the rule. Then, read the rule together and check.

Practice of the Notes/Rules Chart

Option 1: Either to review or as a follow up to home study, project the notes on the board and have students write examples of their own.

Option 2: Provide examples and have students identify the rule from their chart in their book.

> **BE A GRAMMAR EXPLORER!**
>
> Let students know that language and its rules are always changing. They may hear examples of language that there are no rules for, and they may find that native speakers often disagree on what is "correct." Encourage them to notice the language and explore it outside of their textbooks. Try the following.
> - Have a grammar *Show and Tell*. Tell students to find examples of the grammar they are studying and bring it to class. Let students figure out the grammar rule, if there is one. Guide them when necessary to a relevant chart. This can bring to light many unusual usages that they will not find rules for.
> - Have students keep a grammar journal, noting examples that they find in the real world.

General Tips for Controlled Activities
- Have students compare their answers in pairs before asking for the answers from individual students. This will help reduce anxiety and give students the confidence to speak.
- Use the Teacher's eResource to project the exercise with answers on the board and let students check their own work. You can also write answers as students say them, or ask students to come up and write the answers.
- When calling on students to check answers or demonstrate the language, be sure to surprise them by calling names randomly. This will keep them more focused on the task since they are never sure who will be next.
- Avoid letting stronger or more talkative students dominate the class. Check names as you call on them, so you are sure that everyone has a chance to participate.

PRACTICE

LISTEN Activities
- Set the context, provide background and cultural notes, and pre-teach essential vocabulary. You may want to write the vocabulary on the board. Instead of pre-teaching, elicit possible meanings of the words after students listen once.
- Play the audio once from beginning to end so that students have a chance to listen for overall comprehension. They should be able to get the gist of the input in one listening. If you are reading the script, read with expression and at a natural pace. Do not slow down or overarticulate. You can also photocopy the audio script and have students read along chorally.
- Play the audio again as students complete the task. You may want to stop at intervals to give students time to answer questions.

General Listening Activity Tips
- Before any listening, have students read through the items so that they know what to listen for.
- In many exercises, you can have students predict correct answers before they listen and check.
- The audio provides another kind of language input for students. Many students are intimidated by listening, so you may need to provide extra scaffolding. Allow students to listen to the audio first to achieve a more authentic experience. Then, if students have difficulty, let them read the audio script.

SPEAK Activities
- After students work with a partner and you monitor their work, call on a few students to model for the class, addressing any common errors.
- With free speaking that asks students to offer their own ideas, allow them to work with a partner. After a set amount of time (5–8 minutes), call on two or three pairs of students to share their ideas and/or tell the class about their partners.

General Speaking Activity Tips
- Model any controlled speaking activity. Ask a student to be your partner and demonstrate the first item to the class. Have students repeat any language they may need before they begin.
- Walk around and monitor students during any group activity. Help individual students with pronunciation or other aspects of their speaking as you walk around.

GENERAL GUIDE TO TEACHING A UNIT

WRITE Activities
- If students completed the activity for homework, put them in pairs to exchange work and provide feedback.
- As with freer speaking activities, call on students to share their ideas and/or tell the class about their partner's ideas.
- You may want to collect writing samples to use as an informal assessment. To help, have students exchange papers with a partner and provide feedback.

FLIP IT!
Have students complete the writing tasks at home. If you have a class website, blog, or LMS, let students post their work. Ask students to read each other's work and leave at least one positive comment and one comment that suggests an improvement.

EDIT Activities
- Display the corrected sentences on the board or with a projector, using the Teacher's eResource. Give students the opportunity to ask questions and discuss the corrections.
- You may want to display the EDIT activity without the answers and correct the errors as students say them or let students correct them on their own.

General Tip for Error Correction
If a student makes an error either in writing on the board or in a spoken exercise, be sure to give them a chance to correct themselves. Indicate that it is wrong with a facial expression or gesture of some kind. Give the student or her classmates a chance to identify and correct the error.

APPLY Activities
- To make the activity more interactive or to provide extra scaffolding for students, have them work in pairs or small groups to generate ideas and/or gather information.
- Students produce language in spoken or written form. After students have completed this part, provide an opportunity for them to share their work by speaking or reading to the class, a small group, or a new partner.
- Facilitate any interaction by encouraging students to get up and talk to five new classmates.

General Tips for Grouping
- To assure that students do not only talk to their friends, try assigning them to a different partner each time by using different techniques:
- Prepare cards from a deck with two of each type of card, e.g., aces, ones, twos, . . . (depending on the number of students). Hand them out and have students find their match.
- Try pairing lower-level students with higher-level students. Read their names and indicate where they should sit.
- For small groups (three to four students are best), tell students to count off in threes or fours (for classes of 12–21 students). Then, ask all number ones to raise their hands; then twos, threes, etc. Point to a part of the room and tell each group where to sit.

Review the Grammar

This section always includes an activity that combines the grammar from the lessons in a unit, a listening activity, and an editing activity. It can be used for assessment purposes by you or as a self-assessment for the students.

FLIP IT!
Have students do the controlled activities, EDIT, and LISTEN as an out-of-class assignment to allow them time to go back and review the unit as necessary.

Note: Students need the audio in order to complete the LISTEN exercise. They can find this on the Student Companion Site at NGL.Cengage.com/GrammarExplorer.

Connect the Grammar to Writing

Students first read and identify the grammar in a model. Then, they analyze the organization/content of the model text. After they brainstorm and organize their ideas, they write their own piece of writing. Students focus both on accurate usage of the target grammar and a new writing strategy or skill. The Writing Focus boxes are designed to build on each other throughout each book, giving students a toolbox for writing by the end of the series.

1 READ & NOTICE THE GRAMMAR.

> ### FLIP IT!
> Students can do the READ & NOTICE THE GRAMMAR activities at home. Then, let them check answers with a partner and brainstorm ideas for their own writing when they come to class.

- If you do this activity in class, have students preview the three parts of the activity.
- Have students read the text silently or follow along as you read it aloud. Put students in pairs to discuss answers to the grammar noticing activity.
- Have students read the Grammar Focus box and complete the task in exercise **B**.
- Have students compare the information in the graphic organizers in exercise **C** with a partner.
- Or project the graphic organizers, using the Teacher's eResource, and have students fill it in together. Discuss as a class, eliciting any corrections from students.

2 BEFORE YOU WRITE.

- After explaining the activity, provide students with enough time to generate ideas. Don't rush this part of the writing process. **Option:** Have students share their ideas in pairs or small groups. Encourage them to ask each other questions to clarify and get more information.
- Walk around the room to provide help as needed. **Option:** Have students generate ideas as an out-of-class assignment, and then share their ideas in the next class.
- See the Unit-Specific Teaching Tips for an alternative writing option that can be used for additional in-class writing or homework.

3 WRITE.

- Go over the instructions and the Writing Focus box. Have students complete the assignment in class or at home.
- See the Unit-Specific Teaching Tips for more activity ideas for practicing the Writing Focus box in class.

4 SELF ASSESS.

- Go over the checklist. Have students use the checklist to edit their own work. You may want to have students exchange their writing and use the checklist to edit each other's work and provide feedback.

> ### FLIP IT!
> Have students complete WRITE at home. If you have a class website, blog, or LMS, let students post their work. Ask students to read each other's work and leave at least one positive comment and one comment that suggests an improvement, or use the checklist and have students evaluate their own or each other's work in class.

Assessment

Grammar Explorer provides four different types of assessment:

1. **Formative Assessment within the Unit**
   Formative assessment is used to determine how learning is going and whether or not more explanation, practice, and general help are needed before continuing. The LEARN activities after the charts, the final exercises before the APPLY, and the Review the Grammar activities can serve as the formative assessment.

2. **Review the Grammar**
   By monitoring student success in these end-of-unit activities, instructors can determine if students are prepared to go on to the writing section; they can determine how much students have learned and what their problem areas might be.

3. **Connect the Grammar to Writing**
   This end-of-unit writing is another type of assessment. It will show your students' progress with the grammar of the current unit and all previous units. A rubric is a good way to evaluate students' work. Share the rubric with students before they write. You may want to start with a simple rubric, and then with each new unit add a writing focus and/or grammar review point from a previous unit or units. See page 8 for an example rubric.

4. **Assessment CD-ROM with ExamView®**
   - Create custom tests and quizzes. Teachers can choose the test questions they want and/or add their own items.
   - Can be used to create tests for various purposes that include:
     – creating a unit pretest to see what students already know;
     – creating a summative final test;
     – creating additional practice activities in the form of a quiz.

GENERAL GUIDE TO TEACHING A UNIT

Rubric to Assess Writing

Standard	3	2	1	0
Student writing is clear and easy to understand.	Writing is clear and requires little or no inferences.	Writing is somewhat clear and requires some inferences.	Writing is more unclear than clear and requires many inferences.	Writing does not relate to the assignment or is completely unclear.
Student uses [grammar points here] correctly.	90–100 percent of the time.	70–89 percent of the time.	Less than 70 percent but more than once or twice.	Rarely if ever.
[Writing Focus for the unit; add each new writing focus as you progress through the book.]	90–100 percent of the time.	70–89 percent of the time.	Less than 70 percent, but more than once or twice.	Rarely if ever.
[Add your own focus.]	90–100 percent of the time.	70–89 percent of the time.	Less than 70 percent, but more than once or twice.	Rarely if ever.

UNIT 1 Family

Present and Past: Simple and Progressive

Unit Opener

Photo: Read the photo caption to the students and say, *This is a grizzly bear and her four cubs. Male grizzly bears can be a danger to the cubs, so their mother raises them. She takes care of her cubs for two to three years. What do you think the mother teaches her cubs during this time?*

Location: Grizzly bears live in the northwest of the United States and in parts of Canada, including British Columbia and the Yukon.

Theme: This unit explores the daily lives and routines of the family life of both animals and people. It also discusses how families are changing.

Page	Lesson	Grammar	Examples
4	1	Simple Present and Present Progressive	I **eat** breakfast every day. What **is cooking** in the oven?
12	2	Stative Verbs	The baby **wants** the bottle now. The flowers **smell** wonderful! **Smell** this perfume. Do you like it?
18	3	Simple Past and Past Progressive	Jim **left** the party at 8:00 last night. Jim **was driving** home at 8:15. **While Don was talking on the phone,** Jim was eating lunch. Dave was playing soccer **when he hurt his foot**.
26	Review the Grammar		
28	Connect the Grammar to Writing		

Unit Grammar Terms

action verb: a verb that shows an action.
➢ The team **practices** every day.

clause: a group of words with a subject and a verb. (See *dependent* and *main clause*.)
➢ We watched the game. *(one clause)*
➢ We watched the game after we ate dinner. *(two clauses)*

past progressive: a verb form used to talk about an action that was in progress in the past.
➢ I'm **eating** dinner right now. I can't talk.
➢ She's **taking** English classes this summer.

simple past: a verb form used to talk about completed actions.
➢ Last night we **ate** dinner at home.

simple present: a verb form used to talk about habits or routines, schedules, and facts.
➢ She **teaches** at the university.

stative verb: (also called a *non-action* verb) a verb that does not describe an action. Stative verbs indicate states, senses, feelings, or ownership. They are not common in the progressive.
➢ I **remember** the party well.
➢ They **have** a new car.

time clause: a clause that tells when an action or event happened or will happen. Time clauses are introduced by conjunctions, such as *when, after, before, while,* and *since*.
➢ **While I was walking home,** it began to rain.

LESSON 1 — Simple Present and Present Progressive

Student Learning Outcomes
- **Read** an article about some researchers' observations of a gorilla family.
- **Analyze** and **use** the simple present and present progressive.
- **Listen** to someone describe her family.
- **Speak** about family trends in different cultures.
- **Find** and **edit** errors with the simple present and present progressive.
- **Write** about a family member or friend.

Lesson Vocabulary

| (v.) behave | (v.) feed | (v.) observe | (n.) researcher | (v.) survive |
| (v.) decline | (adv.) instantly | (adj.) permanent | (n.) shade | (adj.) temporary |

EXPLORE

1 READ, page 4 — 10 min.
- Ask students if they know what a rainforest is. (a tropical forest that has heavy rainfall and many trees)
- Tell students that many kinds of gorillas live in rainforests, and ask them what other animals live in tropical environments.

Be the Expert
- This reading is about a family of lowland gorillas that live in the Odzala National Park. Lowland gorillas are the largest of all gorillas. They can reach up to 6 feet in height (1.8m) and weigh from 400–600 lbs. (181–272 kg).
- Because lowland gorillas live in dense rain forests, it is difficult for scientists to accurately estimate how many are left in the wild. However, their population is decreasing due to poaching, disease, and destruction of their habitat.

2 CHECK, page 5 — 5 min.

1. F 2. T 3. T 4. F 5. T

- **Tip:** After students have completed exercise **2**, have them find the corresponding sentences in the reading and correct the statements that are false.

3 DISCOVER, page 5 — 10 min.
- **Tip:** Before you do the first example in exercise **A**, make sure students understand the meaning of *temporary* (not lasting a long time), *permanent* (forever), and *routine* (common tasks that you do regularly or everyday activities). These words are important unit vocabulary.

A 1. b   2. b   3. a

B

This verb form shows that the action is . . .	Simple Present	Present Progressive
1. permanent.	✓	
2. a routine or habit.	✓	
3. in progress now or over a current time.		✓

- **Expansion Tip:** Have students return to the reading on page 4 and notice which progressive forms express actions that are "happening now" and which express actions that are happening "over a period of time."

LEARN

Chart 1.1, page 6 — 10–15 min.
- **Notes 1 & 2:** Many languages express time, tenses, and the progressive aspect differently from English. For example, a speaker of such a language might say "I study now" or "I shopping now" to say that he's in the middle of studying.

4 pages 6–7 — 5 min.

1. do you find
2. I go
3. does it take
4. It usually takes
5. we don't/do not find
6. Are the trackers following
7. The trackers are spending
8. exploring
9. are you staying
10. I'm staying/I am staying
11. surprises
12. laugh
13. Do you follow
14. I'm doing/I am doing
15. makes
16. Young chimps and gorillas stay
17. Chimp fathers usually don't stay/Chimp fathers usually do not stay
18. rarely leave

10   PRESENT AND PAST: SIMPLE AND PROGRESSIVE

> **REAL ENGLISH, page 6**
>
> Tell students that *ever, usually, often,* and *sometimes* are called *frequency adverbs* because they describe how often something occurs. Other frequency adverbs are *occasionally, sometimes,* and *rarely*. Point out that *sometimes* can be placed before the main verb or at the beginning or end of a sentence without a change in meaning: I **sometimes** eat with chopsticks. / **Sometimes**, I eat with chopsticks. / I eat with chopsticks **sometimes**.

Chart 1.2, page 7   10 min.

- **Notes 1 & 2:** Another use of the present progressive is to refer to actions or events that are planned for the future; for example, *I'm going to Maine for the summer.* Usually a specific time phrase makes it clear that the action will occur in the future, as in *I'm going to travel for a year **after college**.*

5 page 7   5 min.
1. is growing
2. are getting
3. are growing
4. is increasing
5. always go
6. compare
7. always take care of
8. is always getting
9. is becoming
10. is always complaining

6 ANALYZE THE GRAMMAR, page 8   5 min.
1. A change over time: 1, 2, 3, 4, 9
2. An unwanted repeated action: 8, 10, or;
3. A regular or expected action: 5, 6, 7

PRACTICE

7 page 8   5 min.

8 page 8   10 min.
1. I'm enjoying
2. 'm staying/am staying
3. do
4. take
5. don't eat/do not eat
6. use
7. 'm getting /am getting
8. speaks
9. is improving
10. often laughs
11. doesn't bother/does not bother
12. often make OR 'm always getting/ am always making

A
1. Do you eat with chopsticks at every meal?
2. Does your family remove their shoes inside the house?
3. What are you getting better at?
4. Does anyone in your family speak English well?
5. What language do you speak at home?
6. Who do you live with?
7. Is your English improving day by day?
8. Do you ever laugh at your mistakes in English?

B *Answers will vary.*

9 page 9   10 min.

> **REAL ENGLISH, page 9**
>
> **Constantly** has almost the same meaning as *always* and can also be used with the present progressive to make complaints.

A
1. is always borrowing; not returning
2. are always checking; texting
3. is always complaining
4. are always making
5. is always talking
6. is always losing

10 page 10   10–15 min.
A
1. are living
2. is decreasing; is not increasing/isn't increasing
3. is not going up/isn't going up; is coming down/'s coming down
4. are getting; are waiting
5. are not having/ aren't having; are having/'re having
6. are continuing
7. are growing

11 LISTEN AND WRITE, page 10   10–20 min.
A 1. b   2. c   3. e   4. a   5. f   6. d

B *Answers will vary. Possible answers:*
Julia's grandmother never drives at night.
Julia's grandmother still drives.
Julia's father is standing next to her brother Alex.
Her twin sister Ana plays in an orchestra.
Her brother Lucas is studying in Scotland.
Her whole family doesn't get together too often.

12 EDIT, page 11   5 min.

This week I ~~visit~~ am visiting my twin sister. We ~~aren't getting~~ don't get together often because we live a couple of hours apart. We talk and text all the time, though, so we don't feel too far apart. We ~~are telling~~ tell each other our problems and try to help each other out. Another reason we don't see each other often is my sister's job. She is very busy. We often make plans, but she is ~~cancelling always~~ always cancelling our plans at the last minute. Sometimes this upsets me. It's almost summer, though, so her schedule ~~becomes~~ is becoming much less busy. This week, at least, we ~~do~~ are doing a lot together. It's great!

13 APPLY, page 11   10 min.

- **Alternative Writing:** Have students write a paragraph about their partner.

UNIT 1   LESSON 1   **11**

LESSON 2	**Stative Verbs**
Student Learning Outcomes	• **Read** an article about changes in family size in Brazil. • **Recognize** and correctly **use** stative and active verbs. • **Speak** about family size in your culture. • **Identify** verbs that have stative and active meanings. • **Express** temporary changes in behavior with *being* + adjective. • **Listen** to classmates describe their family. • **Write** about a family using stative verbs.
Lesson Vocabulary	(n.) aspect (v.) deny (n.) influence (n.) maximum (v) resemble (adj.) average (v.) design (n.) label (n.) popularity (n.) trend (n.) character

EXPLORE

1 READ, page 12   10 min.

- Have the students read the question above the article. Ask them why they think families in Brazil are getting smaller.
- Use the size of the letters in the title to elicit the meaning of *shrinking* (getting smaller).

Be the Expert

Until recently, the Brazilan family often included the husband and wife, their children, and extended family members. It was not unusual for grandparents to live in the same house with their sons or daughters and grandchildren. This situation is now changing, and you will find some reasons for this in the article.

2 CHECK, page 13   5 min.

1. don't want
2. are not having
3. is not only one/more than one
4. don't have

- **Tip:** After exercise **2**, elicit reasons from the article why Brazilian families are changing (women's education and novellas). Continue the discussion by asking students if similar changes are taking place in their countries.

3 DISCOVER, page 13   10 min.

A   1. is thinking   4. looks
    2. think   5. are having
    3. is looking   6. have

B   1. 1, 3   2. 2, 4, 5, 6

LEARN

Chart 1.3, page 14   15 min.

- **Note 2:** Explain that *stative* is the adjective form of *state* (the condition or situation that someone or something is in). Stative verbs describe an unchanging state.
- **Tip:** After reading chart 1.3 with students, have them close their books. Ask them to tell you the categories of stative verbs, i.e., the categories given in Note 2a–g., and write them on the board. Have students write a list of verbs that fall in each category without looking at their books. Then have them look again at Note 2a-g to check their answers.

4 page 14   5 min.

1. S   5. S
2. A   6. S
3. S   7. A
4. A   8. S

5 pages 14–15   5 min.

1. A: Do people have   B: Many families have
2. A: Do most people own   B: most people don't/do not own
3. A: Does it cost   B: Yes, it costs
4. A: do you think   B: I hope
5. A: Do you know   B: it seems
6. A: do you look like   B: I resemble

6 SPEAK, page 15   10 min.

Answers will vary.

Chart 1.4, page 15   10 min.

- **Notes 1 & 2:** Many teachers find that their students incorrectly use the present progressive

12   PRESENT AND PAST: SIMPLE AND PROGRESSIVE

form with a stative verb when the simple present is required, e.g., "Stefanie is smelling good because she has a new perfume."

One reason for this may be that there are many more active verbs in English than stative verbs. Students hear the present progressive form used frequently and use it with stative verbs.

- **Tip:** After reading chart 1.4, create the two-column chart shown below on the board. Write the headings only. Tell the students to close their books. Then have students work in pairs to complete the chart with as many stative verbs as they remember from charts 1.3 and 1.4. After students have finished, have them compare their answers with another pair of students.

Verbs with a stative meaning only	Verbs with stative and active meanings
believe, belong, like, look, own, prefer, understand, want	appear, feel, have, hear, look, see, smell, taste, think

REAL ENGLISH, page 16

Before doing exercise **7**, read the Real English box on page 16. Elicit a list of adjectives that describe character traits. Write them on the board. Then have students give the opposite of each trait. (e.g., serious ≠ funny, shy ≠ outgoing, rude ≠ polite, quiet ≠ talkative, etc.) On the board, write:

She/he's being so _____. She/he's usually so _____. She/he isn't being very _____. She/he's usually so _____.

Have students work in pairs to write a sentence for each pair.

7 pages 15–16   10 min.
1. a. has   b. is having
2. a. think   b. am thinking
3. a. weighs   b. is weighing
4. a. isn't being b. is
5. a. doesn't see b. is seeing
6. a. is looking b. looks
7. a. am smelling b. smells
8. a. is coming   b. comes

PRACTICE

8 page 16   5 min.
1. A: are you tasting   B: It doesn't smell/does not smell
2. A: Do you have   B: I'm/I am
3. A: do you look;   B: we need
   are you thinking
4. A: You seem   B: I miss

- **Tip:** Before beginning exercise **9**, ask students what kind of TV shows they usually watch. In pairs, have them discuss their favorite shows.

9 pages 16–17   10 min.
1. like   9. 's/is
2. 's/is   10. sounds
3. love   11. seems
4. comes   12. doesn't resemble/
5. has   does not resemble
6. don't always agree/do 13. has
   not always agree   14. loves
7. 'm watching/am watching 15. own
8. are having   16. see

- **Tip:** Before beginning exercise **10**, have students look at the photo and read the caption to teach the word *chick* (a baby penguin). Ask, *Who is taking care of the chick?* (The father penguin).

10 page 17   10 min.
1. seem   6. 's/is
2. isn't/is not   7. weighs
3. resembles   8. doesn't need/does
4. doesn't have/does not   not need
   have   9. sees
5. has   10. knows

- **Expansion Tip:** After completing exercise **10**, write several comprehension questions on the board. Have students answer the questions with their books closed and check their answers in pairs.

Possible questions:
1. *Who keeps the penguin egg warm?* (*The father penguin.*)
2. *What does the penguin chick look like?* (*It looks like its parents, but it's smaller with gray feathers.*)
3. *How much does an average adult penguin weigh?* (*About 75 pounds.*)
4. *What does a penguin chick know how to do from birth?* (*Swim.*)

11 APPLY, page 17   15 min.

A *Answers will vary.*

- **Alternative Writing:** Have students write a short description of their favorite (or least favorite) TV show. If they do not watch TV, they can write about a movie or a book. Have them write about their favorite characters and their relationships to one another using at least five stative verbs.

B *Answers will vary.*

UNIT 1 LESSON 2 **13**

LESSON 3	**Simple Past and Past Progressive**
Student Learning Outcomes	• **Read** about scientific research on twins. • **Review** rules for the simple past and past progressive. • **Relate** two past actions using *when* and *while* in time clauses. • **Write** and **speak** about the history of a Peruvian family. • **Listen** to a story about a family secret. • **Find** and **edit** errors with the simple past and past progressive. • **Write** about a classmate's dream.
Lesson Vocabulary	(adv.) absolutely (adj.) identical (n.) performance (n.) recognition (n.) software (v.) emigrate (n.) imaging (n.) reaction (adj.) shocked (adj.) unusual

EXPLORE

1 READ, page 18   15 min.

- Before students read the article, have them look at the photos. Ask, *What do these people have in common?* Read the title of the article and the captions of the photos. Ask, *From these photos, what do you think happens at a Twins Days Festival?*

Be the Expert

- Twins Days Festival is a gathering of identical and fraternal twins of all ages. It is held around the world, but the largest festival is held annually in Twinsburg, Ohio. For more information about this event, do an Internet search using the term *Twins Days* or *Twins Festival*.

- Although researchers find it hard to tell identical twins apart by comparing their DNA, they can easily distinguish them from their fingerprints. Twins' DNA may be the same, but their fingerprints are very different.

2 CHECK, page 19   5 min.

Wording may vary, but answers should include the main ideas.

1. Over 2000 sets of twins were at the festival.
2. Some of the festival events were picnics, talent shows, parades, and contests.
3. Scientists and technicians were doing serious work at the festival.
4. It was hard to tell them apart because their beards covered half of their faces.

3 DISCOVER, page 19   5 min.

A 1. was walking; stopped
    2. were photographing; collecting; scanning
    3. looked; didn't see

B 1. simple past; past progressive
    2. simple past
    3. simple past

LEARN

Chart 1.5, page 20   15 min.

- **Note 3a:** It is common for students to overuse the simple past form, using it for all references to the past. Have students practice using the past progressive with specific times. Tell them that you saw them doing something impossible at a specific time last night. Students respond with what they were actually doing at that time.

   Teacher: *I saw you dancing in the street last night at 2:30 a.m.*

   Student: *That wasn't me. I was sleeping in my room at 2:30.*

14   PRESENT AND PAST: SIMPLE AND PROGRESSIVE

4 pages 20–21   10 min.

A
1. liked
2. preferred
3. had
4. practiced
5. played
6. woke up
7. knew
8. stayed
9. performed
10. found
11. didn't enjoy/did not enjoy
12. liked
13. was reading
14. was playing
15. threw
16. wasn't looking
17. hit
18. felt
19. was

B
1. did Carly stay
2. did Tori perform
3. was reading
4. happened
5. did Sam feel
6. did you prefer

- **Tip:** Before beginning exercise **C**, pair higher-level students together and lower-level students together. Have higher-level students take turns asking and answering the questions in exercise B. Then have the lower-level students take turns asking and answering the questions.

C *Answers may vary.*
1. Because she was ...
2. Because Carly was ...
3. Sam was.
4. He wasn't looking, so he missed the ball and it hit him on the arm.
5. Because his twin had been hit on his arm.

Chart 1.6, pages 21–22   10 min.

- **Note 1:** A main clause has a subject and a verb and forms a complete sentence. A time clause does not express a complete idea. It can't stand alone as a sentence.

- **Note 2:** To model correct punctuation, write the same sentence on the board using past time clauses with *when* and *while* in both first and second position. Ask, *Which sentence needs a comma? Where should I place the comma?*

- **Note 4:** To further illustrate the grammar point, have students look at the photo of the elephant on page 22. Then ask, *What were these elephants doing when the photographer took this photo?*

5 page 22   5 min.

1. saw
2. were driving
3. were drinking
4. When
5. lifted
6. was leading
7. when
8. was playing
9. fell
10. got
11. decided
12. when

- **Tip:** Before beginning exercise **6**, explain that because of poor economic conditions in Japan, Japanese immigrants, mainly farmers, began arriving Peru in 1899. For more information, do an Internet search using the search terms *Japanese-Peruvians* or *Japanese emigration to Peru*.

- **Tip:** Before beginning exercise **6**, have students look at the map of Peru. Elicit any information they know about the country. Then have them look at the time line at the top of the page. Make sure that they understand the term *emigration* (*leaving one's country to live in another*).

PRACTICE

6 WRITE & SPEAK, page 23   15 min.

B
1. When Julio't parents were living in Japan, they didn't know each other.
2. They each emigrated to Peru when they saved enough money.
3. Julio's grandparents were working on a sugar plantation when they met.
4. Julio's father, Jiro, was born while they lived/were living on the sugar plantation.
5. When Jiro turned six, the family moved to Lima, so he could go to school.
6. Jiro worked in the family store while he went/was going to high school.
7. When Jiro saw Susan at school, he introduced himself.
8. When Jiro and Susan were attending college in Lima, they got married.

C *Answers will vary.*

D *Answers will vary.*

- **Expansion Tip:** As a follow-up to exercise **D**, have students make a brief family tree. When their trees are completed, have them discuss their family histories in pairs or small groups.

7 LISTEN, page 24 — 10 min.

A
1. Bella's mother
2. Bella's mother
3. Marina
4. Maria and Marina
5. Maria
6. Marina

B
1. was cleaning
2. when
3. was looking
4. came
5. When
6. became
7. told
8. Maria
9. Marina
10. when
11. was packing
12. didn't want
13. did
14. looked
15. arrived
16. traveled
17. While
18. knew
19. were
20. found
21. was

8 EDIT, page 25 — 5 min.

A
Erica: Hello?
Mother: Hello, Erica? Were you asleep? ~~Was I waking~~ Did I wake you up?
Erica: Yeah. I ~~slept~~ was sleeping. I didn't sleep well last night, so I decided to take a nap.
Mother: Oh, I'm sorry. I just ~~was wanting~~ wanted to say hello.
Erica: Well, I ~~had~~ was having the strangest dream when the phone rang. I talked to Aunt Jelena. We were sitting in her living room. While we were talking, a bear suddenly ~~was appearing~~ appeared. It was terrifying! When the bear came toward us, we ~~were running~~ ran outside. That's when I heard the phone.
Mother: That sounds like a scary dream!
Erica: It was. It was a very strange dream. I'm glad I ~~was waking up~~ woke up.

B page 25

Erica's Dream	Notes
1. Where was Erica in her dream?	In Aunt Jelena's living room.
2. What was she doing?	They were catching up.
3. What happened?	A bear suddenly appeared.
4. What did they do when the bear came toward them?	She was scared.
5. How did she feel when she woke up?	She was glad when she woke up.

9 APPLY, page 25 — 10 min.

A Answers will vary.
B Answers will vary.

UNIT 1 Review the Grammar

1 page 26 5 min.

1. don't have
2. feel
3. don't know
4. believe
5. think
6. wasn't
7. went
8. played
9. was growing
10. gave
11. didn't get
12. are deciding
13. costs
14. are waiting/wait
15. have
16. don't plan

2 EDIT, page 26 5 min.

Hi Anna,

How ~~do things go~~ are things going? Everything is great with Emily, Max, and me. Max ~~grows~~ is growing day by day. He's four months old now. He is getting big! Emily is working part time now. She ~~was going~~ went back to work last month, so she's always really tired. It's too bad babies ~~aren't sleeping~~ don't sleep through the night. Max wakes up two or three times a night. I'm lucky. ~~I'm never waking up~~ I never wake up. Emily does.

I need my sleep. I'm working long hours these days. On top of that, my boss is always complaining about something. The other day, at 6:00 p.m., while I ~~walked~~ was walking out the door to go home, he said, "~~Do you leave already~~ Are you leaving already?" These comments upset me, so now I ~~think~~ I'm thinking about changing jobs. Anyway, enough about me. What ~~do you do~~ are you doing nowadays? Write soon!

Love,

Carlos

3 LISTEN, page 27 10 min.

A 1. F 2. T 3. F 4. F 5. T

B 1. love, don't   4. I'm not talking
2. know, know, knew   5. didn't fight
3. is   6. show, fight

4 SPEAK & WRITE 15 min.

A Answers will vary.

B Answers will vary.

UNIT 1 REVIEW THE GRAMMAR 17

Connect the Grammar to Writing

1 pages 28–29   15 min.

B

Verb Form	Example	Use
Present progressive	is increasing are living is affecting are taking	trend temporary situation trend trend
Simple present	is different cannot find they return home they want get too comfortable face economic challenges It seems	stative verb fact fact stative verb stative verb stative verb stative verb
Simple past	left home left his parents' house went to college he got a job never returned	past examples

2
BEFORE YOU WRITE, page 29   15 min.

A *Answers may vary.*

Why are people living longer?

B *Answers may vary.*

3 WRITE, page 29   20 min.

> **WRITING FOCUS, page 29**
>
> Providing examples to support an idea is a feature of good writing. Students will need to use commas correctly when they introduce examples at the beginning of a sentence or insert examples in the middle of a sentence.

- **Alternative Writing:** Have students write about another changing trend (e.g., in fashion, entertainment, education, etc.). Then have them describe their reactions and the reactions of their parents or older relatives to this trend. Tell them to use at least three examples. For example,

  Nowadays, more people are taking classes online.

UNIT 2 Passions

Present and Past: Perfect and Perfect Progressive

Unit Opener

Photo: Have students look at the photo and the caption. Ask, *What do you know about BASE jumping?* Explain that "BASE" stands for four categories of objects to jump from: a building, an antenna, a span (bridge), and earth (cliff).

Location: Yosemite National Park is in the U.S. state of California. It is famous for its mountains, cliffs, and spectacular scenery. It is popular among rock climbers and BASE jumpers.

Theme: This unit covers peoples' goals and ambitions. Have students look at the photo on page 48. Ask, *What is the man doing? Why?*

Page	Lesson	Grammar	Examples
32	1	Present Perfect	Tom **hasn't seen** the photos of your trip.
41	2	Present Perfect Progressive and Present Perfect	I**'ve been reading** this article for two hours. I**'ve read** the article. I finished it last night.
48	3	Past Perfect and Past Perfect Progressive	We **had finished** dinner, so we ordered dessert. She**'d been climbing** for an hour when she got a sudden pain in her leg.
58		**Review the Grammar**	
60		**Connect the Grammar to Writing**	

Unit Grammar Terms

past perfect: a verb form used to talk about an action that happened before another action or time in the past.
  ➤ *They **had met** in school, but then they didn't see each other again for many years.*

past perfect progressive: a verb form used for an action or event that was happening until or just before another action, event, or time.
  ➤ *He**'d been driving** for twelve hours when they ran out of gas.*

present perfect: a verb form that connects the past to the present.
  ➤ *Julia **has lived** in London for 10 years.*
  ➤ *Monika **has broken** the world record.*
  ➤ *Zack and Dan **have never been** to Germany.*

present perfect progressive: a verb form used for ongoing actions that began in the past and continue up to the present.
  ➤ *You**'ve been working** too hard.*

simple past: a verb form used to describe actions completed at a definite time in the past.
  ➤ *I **visited** my parents last weekend.*

19

LESSON 1 | Present Perfect

Student Learning Outcomes
- **Read** a book review about the adventures of an underwater photographer.
- **Identify** three uses of the present perfect verb forms.
- **Understand** the difference between the present perfect and simple past and **use** them correctly.
- **Listen** to and **practice** reduced forms of auxiliary *has/have*.
- **Speak** about hopes, dreams, and passions.
- **Find** and **edit** errors with the present perfect and simple past.
- **Write** an e-mail and **describe** your ideal job.

Lesson Vocabulary

(adj.) annual	(n.) behavior	(n.) expert	(v.) photograph	(v.) volunteer
(v.) approach	(n.) encounter	(v.) participate	(n.) technique	

EXPLORE

1 READ, page 32 — 15 min.

Have the students look at the photo and read the caption. Ask, *What is Paul Nicklen's profession?*

Be the Expert

- One of the most famous underwater photojournalists was Jacques Cousteau. He, along with French engineer Emile Gagnan, invented the Aqua-Lung—the first apparatus that allowed divers to stay underwater for long periods of time. Based on this model, SCUBA (Self-contained underwater breathing apparatus) was developed.
- Have students look at the photo at the top of page 33 and read the caption. Ask the students if any of them has ever gone diving. If someone has, ask what kind of sealife they encountered.

2 CHECK, page 33 — 5 min.
1. d   2. e   3. b   4. a   5. c

3 DISCOVER, page 33 — 5 min.

A 1. grew up; learned
   2. has loved
   3. has spent
   4. has followed; dived; studied
   5. approached; got

B 1. 1, 5
   2. 3, 4
   3. 2

- **Tip:** To prepare students for the chart 2.1, quickly review past participles of irregular verbs. Dictate the base form of several irregular verbs to students. Have students write the base forms and then the past participles of these verbs in their notebooks.

LEARN

Chart 2.1, page 34 — 15 min.

- **Note 1:** Some languages use the simple present form to describe actions that started in the past and continue to the present. Students whose native language uses the simple present in this way might use the simple present in contexts where the present perfect is correct.

- **Note 3:** Use *always* for an affirmative statement: *I've always tried to do the right thing.* Use *ever* in questions: *Have you ever been to France?* You can also use *ever* in statements to emphasize point: *It's the best movie I've ever seen.* Use *never* to form a negative statement: *I've never heard of him.*

4 page 35 — 5 min.

1. I've learned
2. Have you seen
3. I haven't
4. I've never heard
5. He has lived
6. worked
7. He has taken
8. Mr. Chin has just canceled
9. Has he rescheduled
10. Have you ever had

5 ANALYZE THE GRAMMAR, page 35 — 5 min.

1. 5, 6
2. 1, 2, 3, 4, 7, 10
3. 8, 9

20 PRESENT AND PAST: PERFECT AND PERFECT PROGRESSIVE

Chart 2.2, page 35   5 min.

- **Note 1c:** Explain that the present perfect verb form can never follow *since*. A subject and a simple past form or a time expression must come after *since*. Students also commonly get confused about when to use *for* and *since*. On the board, write, *I work at this school since six years.* Ask, *Is this sentence correct?* Ask for a volunteer to correct it. (I've worked at this school ~~since~~ for six years.)

6 page 36   5 min.
1. have enjoyed; for
2. has been; since
3. has had; for
4. have wanted; for
5. has not played /hasn't played; since
6. has not participated/ hasn't participated; for
7. has always jumped; since
8. have loved; since

Chart 2.3, page 36   10 min.

- **Notes 1 & 2:** On the board, write, *She lived in Japan for 16 years. She has lived in Japan for 16 years.* Ask, *Which sentence means that she still lives in Japan?* (The second one.) *Which sentence means that she doesn't live in Japan anymore?* (The first one.) Explain that both sentences are correct, but their meaning is different.

7 page 37   5 min.
1. a. has dreamed
   b. dreamed
2. a. have never photographed
   b. didn't photograph
3. a. went
   b. has gone
4. a. haven't seen
   b. didn't see

PRACT

[handwritten note: a. She lived in Japan for 16 years. She has lived in J]

8 page 37   5 min.
A
1. reduced
2. full
3. reduced
4. reduced
8. reduced

9 page 38   10 min.
A
1. have you been
2. I have had
3. did you become
4. I was
5. snakes have fascinated
6. I was
7. I did not read/I didn't read
8. I often volunteered
9. I majored
10. you spent
11. I really enjoyed
12. Have you ever experienced
13. I have worked
14. only one has bitten
15. I have paid more attention
16. I have been able

10 EDIT, page 39   10 min.

Dear Ms. Ramos,

I am writing to apply for the position of staff photographer that I ~~have seen~~ saw on your website. I believe that my experience has prepared me well for this job.

    Photography is my passion. I ~~loved~~ have loved photography ever since I was a child. That is when I ~~have gotten~~ got my first camera. The thrill of taking pictures has never gone away, but my interests have changed over the years. While I was growing up, I liked to photograph people; however, as an adult, I ~~have took~~ have taken more pictures of nature than people.

    I ~~lived~~ have lived in Hawaii since 2013, and I have traveled all over the islands to photograph rare birds and plants. I've learned a lot, and my technique has improved in the last few years. My photos ~~has never appeared~~ have never appeared in a magazine or book, but several have been on display at a local gallery ~~since~~ for several months. I would be happy to share my portfolio on request.

    I ~~heared~~ have heard, a lot about your magazine, and it would be a great pleasure to work for you. I look forward to talking to you about this opportunity.

Sincerely,

Katy Mills

11 WRITE & SPEAK, page 40   10 min.
A
1. What activities have you always loved to do?
2. What activities did you enjoy when you were younger?
3. Did you visit any interesting places when you were a child?
4. Have you visited any interesting places recently?
5. What dreams for the future did you have as a child?
6. What goals have you achieved in the last few years?

B Answers will vary.

12 APPLY, page 40   15 min.

A Answers will vary.

UNIT 2 LESSON 1   21

LESSON 2 — Present Perfect Progressive and Present Perfect

Student Learning Outcomes
- **Read** a magazine article about an adventurer's fulfillment of her lifelong goals.
- **Analyze** differences in usage between the present perfect and present perfect progressive.
- **Speak** about actions in your life that started in the past and continue up to the present.
- **Listen** to an interview.
- **Complete** a paragraph using the simple present and present progressive.
- **Write** a paragraph describing a goal and the actions needed to achieve it.

Lesson Vocabulary
(n.) companion	(v.) fulfill	(n.) lecture	(n.) nomad	(adj.) satisfying
(n.) custom	(adj.) intense	(adj.) lifelong	(n.) production	(n.) substitute

EXPLORE

1 READ, page 41 — 10 min.

Before students read the article, have them look at the photo. Ask, *What do you think the climate is like in the Gobi Desert?* (It can be extremely cold and extremely hot.) The detailed answers are in the "Be the Expert" box.

Be the Expert
- The Gobi Desert is the fifth largest desert in the world and covers an area of about 500,000 square miles (about 1,295,000 square kilometers). Temperatures in the Gobi Desert are very extreme and range from highs around 120 degrees F (49 degrees C) to lows of –40 degrees F (–40 degrees C).
- Use the information about the climate of the Gobi Desert to teach the phrase *harsh climate*.

- **Expansion Tip:** After completing the reading, have students name four places that Thayer has traveled to (the Gobi Desert, the Sahara Desert, the North Pole, and the Amazon rainforest). Ask, *What do these places have in common?* (They're all difficult to reach and difficult to cross.)

2 CHECK, page 42 — 5 min.

1. F   2. T   3. F   4. T   5. F

- **Tip:** Have students work in pairs and ask each other what three places they visited as a child that they enjoyed very much. Then have them ask each other what three places they haven't been to but want to visit someday.

3 DISCOVER, page 42 — 5 min.

A   1. b   2. a   3. a   4. b

LEARN

Chart 2.4, page 43 — 10 min.

- **Note 1:** Explain that we use *lately* with the present perfect progressive, not with other verb forms. (e.g., *What have you been doing lately? I haven't been doing much lately.*) Then describe some things that you've been doing lately (e.g., sports, hobbies, movies, books, etc.). Have pairs of students discuss what they've been doing lately.

- **Note 3:** Elicit examples of some verbs that usually don't appear in the present perfect progressive (e.g., *understand, belong, like, dislike, hate, love*). Write them on the board and then have students use three of these verbs in a true sentence about themselves.

4 pages 43–44 — 5 min.

1. have you been going
2. My husband has been hiking
3. Has it been getting
4. we have been working /we've been working
5. we have been causing /we've been causing
6. Have you been enjoying
7. We have been having/ We've been having
8. have you been doing
9. we have been visiting/ we've been visiting
10. taking

22 PRESENT AND PAST: PERFECT AND PERFECT PROGRESSIVE

Chart 2.5, page 44 — 15 min.

- **Note 1:** The present perfect progressive is sometimes used to complain about things. (e.g., *Who's been sleeping in my bed? You've been using my credit card without asking! You haven't been eating your vegetables.*) Tell students to imagine they are angry parents scolding a child. Go around the room asking them individually what they would say to the child. Continue calling on students until they run out of ideas.

5 page 44 — 5 min.

1. a. N
   b. Y
2. a. Y
   b. N
3. a. N
   b. Y
4. a. Y
   b. N

6 pages 44–45 — 10 min.

A
1. been taking
2. made
3. bought
4. owned
5. gotten
6. eaten
7. done
8. been watching

B Answers will vary.

PRACTICE

7 page 45 — 10 min.

1. Have you finished
2. Have you found
3. I have been looking for/I've been looking for
4. I have been working/I've been working
5. I have been chopping/I've been chopping
6. Have you heard
7. has Pat been studying; He has taken; learned/he has learned
8. Has Julio taken; he has been studying

8 LISTEN, WRITE & SPEAK, page 46 — 15 min.

A
1. F
2. T
3. T
4. F
5. F
6. F

B Answers will vary. Answers may include:

1. Barton Seaver has loved seafood his whole life.
2. Barton Seaver has worked as a chef in many restaurants.
3. Barton Seaver has owned restaurants.
4. Barton Seaver has developed a list of substitute fish for people to eat.
5. Barton Seaver has written a cookbook of seafood and vegetable recipes.
6. Barton Seaver has been giving lectures about the importance of the ocean.

C Answers will vary.

9 page 47 — 5 min.

A Hank

B
1. Both Hank and Jake have planned
2. Jake has not completed/Jake hasn't completed
3. Hank has already taken
4. he has been helping
5. Hank has already turned in
6. Jake has been working
7. he hasn't finished
8. Hank and Jake have been planning
9. They haven't served

10 APPLY, page 47 — 15 min.

A Answers will vary.

- **Tip:** To help students think of non-academic goals, on the board, write, *Health—Drink eight glasses of water a day. Get eight hours of sleep each night. Exercise for one hour every day.* Have students work in pairs for five minutes to brainstorm a list of goals related to other topics (other than *health*).

B Answers will vary.

UNIT 2 LESSON 2 23

LESSON 3 Past Perfect and Past Perfect Progressive

Student Learning Outcomes
- **Read** an article about how one man took a risk to fulfill his dream.
- **Express** past actions that happened before other past actions.
- **Write, ask,** and **answer** questions about childhood experiences.
- **Listen** to an interview.
- **Describe** a trip that presented problems and **explain** the reasons for the problems.

Lesson Vocabulary	(v.) abandon	(n.) confidence	(v.) occur	(n.) record	(n.) route
	(v.) adjust	(v.) hesitate	(adv.) potentially	(adj.) risky	(v.) sink

EXPLORE

1 READ, page 48   15 min.

- Have the students look at the photo and read the caption. Ask, What is free soloing? Use the photo to teach *risky, clinging,* and *vertical*.

Be the Expert

- Alexander J. Honnold is an American rock climber. He is known for making solo climbs on high cliffs at great speed. He has broken several speed records and has made the only known free solo climb of three important cliffs in Yosemite: Mount Watkins, The Nose, and the Northwest Face of the Half Dome.
- Tell the students to google "free solo" to see videos of some of the best free solo climbers.

2 CHECK, page 49   5 min.

1. rope   2. was   3. confidence   4. No

- **Tip:** After finishing exercise **2**, have students work in pairs and use the sentences from the exercise to summarize the story. Allow lower-level students to look at the page, but have higher-level students summarize with their books closed.

3 DISCOVER, page 49   5 min.

A 1. Honnold (2) <u>climbed</u> Half Dome without a rope. Others (1) <u>had climbed</u> it with a rope.

2. He (1) <u>had been</u> confident until he (2) <u>got near the top</u>.

3. This time (2) <u>was different</u> from the last time. The last time he (1) <u>had used a rope</u>.

4. He (2) <u>climbed the fastest</u>. Nobody (1) <u>had ever climbed so quickly</u>.

B first

LEARN

Chart 2.6, page 50   10 min.

- **Note:** All past perfect verbs begin with *had*. In speech, the auxiliary *had* is often reduced to /d/. For example, *She had already left*, is usually pronounced *She'd already left*. Be aware that when the auxiliary *would* is reduced, it sounds identical to reduced *had*; for example, *She'd go to the store every day* (*She would go to the store every day*). The context of the sentence makes the meaning clear.

4 pages 50–51   5 min.

- **Tip:** Before doing the exercise, ask students if they have ever heard of the Trans-Siberian Railway. Explain that the Trans-Siberian is one of the longest railways in the world. It extends from Moscow, through Mongolia and Korea to Vladivostok on the Eastern Sea (also called the Sea of Japan).

1. did you take
2. I'd always wanted
3. did the trip take
4. I'd traveled
5. Had you ever been
6. I'd ever taken
7. did you do
8. I'd made
9. had gone
10. I never met/I'd never met

Chart 2.7, page 51   10 min.

- **Note 1a:** The past perfect can be described as setting the background prior to an event. The past perfect progressive stresses an ongoing action (an action in progress) that either led up to or was interrupted by another action in the past.
- **Note 2:** Remind students not to use past perfect progressive with stative verbs such as *know, believe, become,* and *own*. The same rule applies for any progressive form.

PRESENT AND PAST: PERFECT AND PERFECT PROGRESSIVE

5 page 52 — 15 min.

A
1. had been hiking
2. had been following
3. had been preparing
4. had not been camping
5. had been staying
6. had been waiting
7. had been heading
8. hadn't been thinking/ had not been thinking

B
1. had; been hiking
2. had; been following
3. had; been preparing
4. had; been camping
5. had; been staying
6. had; been waiting
7. had; been heading
8. Had; been thinking

C Answers will vary.

PRACTICE

6 WRITE & SPEAK, page 53 — 10 min.

A
1. had you learned
2. did you learn
3. had you studied
4. did you learn
5. did you never do
6. had you never done
7. had your parents lived
8. did you live

B Answers will vary.

- **Expansion Tip:** After students have completed exercise **B**, have them write four additional questions similar to those in exercise **A**. Have them work in pairs to ask and answer their new questions.

7 SPEAK & WRITE, pages 53–54 — 15 min.

A Dan Osman's passion was cliff jumping.

B
1. hadn't been /had not been
2. hadn't climbed/had not climbed
3. had become
4. hadn't appeared/had not appeared
5. had met
6. hadn't finished /had not finished
7. had already jumped
8. had completed

C Answers will vary.

> **REAL ENGLISH, page 54**
> Read through the text and example sentence in the box. On the board, write several situations that might require excuses (e.g., *I missed the test, I didn't finish my homework, I got a parking ticket,* and *I didn't call*). Tell students to work in pairs and think of excuses for each situation: *I missed the test because my car had broken down.*

8 page 54 — 5 min.

1. hadn't gone/ had not gone
2. had wanted
3. had been planning
4. had slept
5. had been riding
6. hadn't eaten/ had not eaten
7. had noticed
8. hadn't rested/ had not rested

9 page 55 — 5 min.

A By the mid-nineteenth century, Europeans <u>had been trying</u> to find a quick way to travel to Asia for hundreds of years. They <u>had been looking</u> for a waterway through the icy Canadian Arctic since the sixteenth century; however, no one <u>had ever found</u> it. Then in 1845, Sir John Franklin <u>tried</u>. He <u>set out</u> on the risky journey with an expedition of 128 men. Two years <u>passed</u> by, but Franklin <u>did not return</u>. What <u>had happened</u> to him and his men? <u>Had</u> their ship <u>sunk</u>? <u>Had</u> they <u>gotten lost</u>? A rescue team <u>went</u> to find out.

B Answers may vary. Possible answers:
1. a quick way to travel to Asia
2. to get to Asia quickly
3. went on an expedition to find it
4. (up to students)

10 LISTEN, pages 55–56 — 15 min.

A 1. F 2. T 3. F 4. T 5. T

B Answers may vary. Possible answers:
1. No explorers had been through the Northwest Passage before Franklin.
3. The rescue team found a message that gave ~~all the~~ a few details about the challenges that Franklin's men were facing.

11 APPLY, pages 56–57 — 20 min.

A Answers may vary. Possible answers:

What Happened	Why It Happened
1. While kayaking, they got lost.	1. They hadn't been paying attention to their location.
2. They got sunburned.	2. They hadn't brought any sunblock.
3. They lost a paddle.	3. They were paddling through rapids.
4. Their kayaks overturned.	4. They had been walking around.
5. They got mosquito bites.	5. They hadn't brought any insect repellent.

B Answers will vary.

- **Tip:** Before having students share their answers in exercise **B**, remind them how to use *because* (to express a reason) and *so* (to express a result).

C Answers will vary.

- **Writing Expansion:** Have students write about a bad experience they had in the form of a diary or journal entry, using first-person narrative.

UNIT 2 LESSON 3

Review the Grammar | UNIT 2

1 page 58 — 5 min.

1. had
2. lost
3. had been
4. had won
5. took
6. did not/didn't think
7. told
8. suggested
9. had always wanted
10. had been training
11. listened
12. started
13. have been swimming
14. have won
15. have been training

2 EDIT, page 58 — 10 min.

It had always been our dream to travel to southern Africa, and we'd ~~make~~ made a lot of plans for our trip. I wanted to take a lot of wildlife photographs, so my friend ~~has~~ recommended that I bring two cameras. When I got to Namibia, I ~~had~~ panicked. One camera ~~had been~~ was missing. Luckily, I ~~was finding~~ found it later.

The next day, we ~~had~~ started out on our safari with a tour. By the end of our tour, we ~~saw~~ had seen some amazing things. One time, when we stopped to take pictures, we were only a few feet away from a cheetah. Amazing!

We ~~had~~ never bothered the animals at night. However, we heard their various calls and other noises outside our tent every night. At first, I ~~had been~~ was afraid of the sounds, but not by the end of the trip. It was really the most incredible trip I've ever ~~been taking~~ taken.

3 LISTEN & SPEAK, page 59 — 15 min.

A
1. has ever sent
2. trained; joined
3. has flown; has done
4. has also participated
5. has never experienced

B *Answers may vary. Possible answers:*

1. She has flown different types of aircraft, participated in military exercises, emergency rescues, and in disaster relief work. She has also gone into space.
2. No, she never imagined she would be an important part of her country's space program.
3. Her coworkers have described her as smart, calm, and very friendly.
4. She'd been in the Air Force for nine years before she began training to be an astronaut.

Connect the Grammar to Writing

1 pages 60–61   15 min.

A *Answers will vary.*

B *Answers will vary. Answers may include:*

    About a year ago, I was watching the Olympics, and I **decided** that I **wanted** to become a runner. I **knew** I should set an achievable goal, so I **decided** to train for a 5K race.

    My parents **were** surprised when I **told** them about my goal, because I had never been interested in running before. In fact, I had never run more than a mile, and I had always been very slow. My friends **thought** I was joking. Everyone **assumed** that I would quit after a week.

    Fortunately, I **proved** them all wrong. I **did** two things to achieve my goal. First, I **went** online and **researched** a good training plan. I **found** a website that helps you plan workouts. You start by walking, and then you gradually start running. After that, I **joined** a local running group. We **ran** in the park twice a week, and I **made** friends who had also decided to run a 5K.

    Three months later, I **achieved** my goal: I **ran** in my first race. I **didn't** win, but I **ran** the whole way, so I **was** proud of myself. Since then, I have run in several races. I have also started training for a longer run. My next goal is to run in a 10K race. My friends have stopped laughing at me, and a few of them have even asked me to help them start running!

C b, f, d, g, c, e, a

2 BEFORE YOU WRITE, page 61   15 min.

A *Answers will vary.*

B *Answers will vary.*

> **WRITING FOCUS, page 57**
>
> After reading through the Writing Focus box, elicit other adverbs of sequence (e.g., *next*, *then*, and *finally*) and write them on the board. Note that no comma is required after *then* when it begins a sentence.

3 WRITE, page 61   20 min.

- **Alternative Writing:** Have students write about how someone they admire achieved an important personal goal.

UNIT 3 A Look into the Future

The Future

Unit Opener

Photo: Have students look at the photo and ask, *What do you think these are?* Read the caption. Ask, *Why do you think they are called supertrees? What are some possible benefits of these supertrees?*

Location: Gardens by the Bay, Singapore.

Theme: This unit talks about developing technology that could have a big impact on our future. Have students look at the photos and captions on pages 71, 72, and 79. Ask, *What do these photos all have in common?*

Page	Lesson	Grammar	Examples
64	1	*Will*, *Be going to*, Present Progressive, and Simple Present	Patty **will be** a doctor someday. We **are going to see** that new movie this weekend. My parents **are leaving** Sunday. The plane **leaves** at 8:30 Monday night.
71	2	Future Time Clauses	**After we do** the dishes, I'll serve dessert. We'll call you **when we get home**.
78	3	Future: Progressive, Perfect, and Perfect progressive	I**'ll be teaching** all day tomorrow. By tomorrow, everyone **will have heard** about your job offer. When I finally turn the essay in, I **will have been working** on it for a month.
86	**Review the Grammar**		
88	**Connect the Grammar to Writing**		

Unit Grammar Terms

clause: a group of words with a subject and a verb.
  ➤ *We watched the game.* (one clause)
  ➤ *We watched the game after we ate dinner.* (two clauses)

future perfect: a verb form used to talk about an action or event that will happen before a certain time in the future.
  ➤ *I'll have finished the work by the time you return.*

future perfect progressive: a verb form used to describe actions or situations that will be in progress until a particular time in the future.
  ➤ *When I finally get home, I will have been traveling for 12 hours.*

future progressive: a verb form used to talk about actions that will be in progress at a certain time in the future. Sorry. The bubble is a mistake. I can't seem to get rid of it.
  ➤ *Car companies will be making cars that use clean fuel.*

  ➤ *I'm going to be sitting on a beach this time next week.*

main clause: (also called *an independent clause*) a clause that can stand alone as a sentence. It has a subject and a verb. (See independent clause.)
  ➤ *I heard the news when I was driving home.*

present progressive: a verb form used to talk about an action that is happening at the present moment or is happening over a current time period.
  ➤ *I'm eating dinner right now. I can't talk.*

simple present: a verb form used to talk about the general present or about usual actions or habits.
  ➤ *He likes fruits and vegetables.*

time clause: a clause that answers the question *When*. Time clauses are introduced by conjunctions such as *when, after, before, while,* and *since*.
  ➤ *I have lived here since I was a child.*

28

LESSON 1   *Will, Be Going to,* Present Progressive, and Simple Present

Student Learning Outcomes	• **Read** a conversation about new developments in robotics for the future. • **Review** differences in use between *will* and *be going to.* • **Express** actions or events in the future with *will* and *be going to,* present progressive and simple present. • **Listen** to conversations about the immediate future. • **Speak** about your future goals, plans, and predictions. • **Complete** a conversation about the future using present progressive and simple present verb forms.
Lesson Vocabulary	(n.) appointment (n.) connection (n.) engineering (n.) government (adj.) responsive (adj.) artificial (v.) create (n.) generation (n.) robotics (n.) task

EXPLORE

1 READ, page 64   10 min.

- Use the photo and caption on page 65 to teach *humanoid robot, actroid,* and *robotics.*

Be the Expert

- This reading is a conversation between students about an online lecture on robots.
- The Actroid in the photo is a type of humanoid robot with strong visual human-likeness. The first actroid was developed by Osaka University in 2003. It is manufactured by the Kokoro Company. Kokoro means "heart" in Japanese. Humanoid robots are now being developed in the United States, Canada, Germany, and the U.K. For more information, do an Internet search using the terms *Actroid, Android,* and *Humanoid Robot.*
- **Expansion:** Use the information to ask students about online learning and to review grammar from Unit 2. Ask, *Have you ever taken any online courses? Did you enjoy them? Why or why not?*

2 CHECK, page 65   5 min.

  1. T   2. F   3. T   4. F   5. T

3 DISCOVER, page 65   5 min.

A 1. are going to make   3. Are; going
   2. starts   4. 'll e-mail/will e-mail

B Answer: 3

- **Tip:** To prepare for the chart, have students return to the reading and find the future forms. Tell them to circle *will,* underline *be going to,* double underline the present progressive, and check the simple present, and then compare answers in pairs. Finally, have them read the conversation aloud.

LEARN

Chart 3.1, page 66   15 min.

- **Note 1:** Both *will* and *be going to* can be used to make predictions based on the present situations. Usually *be going to* is used when there is obvious outside evidence to support a prediction: *Look at those clouds. It looks like it's going to rain. Will* is preferred when the evidence is not obvious, or when someone is stating an opinion: *Kesha won't eat that. She's allergic to chocolate.* However, *will* and *be going to* are often both used for predictions in informal, spoken English with almost no change in meaning.
- **Note 4:** When making a refusal, *won't* is very strong and sounds impolite. *I won't come to your party on Friday. I've got other plans.* For polite personal refusals, tell students to use *can't* or *won't be able to. I can't/won't be able to come to your party on Friday. I've got other plans.*

4 pages 66–67   10 min.

A 1. robots will scare   8. I'm going to talk/I am going to talk
   2. I'm going to make   9. he won't do/ he will not do
   3. I'll make/I will make   10. Will robots be
   4. Are you going to explain   11. Will you help
   5. Will you explain   12. I'll help/I will help
   6. We'll talk/We will talk
   7. Will you remind

Chart 3.2, page 67   10 min.

- **Note 1:** Tell students that they may hear the present progressive or *be going to* to discuss plans in the near future: *I'm driving/going to drive back to New York tomorrow.* However, a mention of *when* the action is going to occur is usually used with the present progressive.

UNIT 3   LESSON 1   29

- **Note 3:** Note that this use of the simple present is different from the uses discussed in Unit 1. The simple present with a future meaning refers to events that occur regularly or at a fixed time, often related to a schedule. A simple present form that is used to express a general truth is not related to a time; it is generally a factual statement. *The sky is blue. The sun rises in the east.*

> **REAL ENGLISH, page 67**
> Tell students that when we use the present simple with these verbs, we almost always include a clock time, a day of the week, or a unit of time (e.g., in a hour, in two weeks).

5 pages 67–68 10 min.

1. are you doing
2. I'm going/I am going
3. my train leaves/ my train is leaving
4. Are you going
5. I'm going/I am going
6. are you coming/do you come
7. The train gets in/The train is getting in
8. My friends and I are sharing
9. Are you working/Do you work
10. Are you going to
11. It begins
12. I'm playing/I am playing
13. we're/we are meeting
14. Is everyone going
15. does it start
16. We're meeting/We are meeting

PRACTICE

6 page 68 10 min.

1. are you going
2. I'm playing
3. You'll have
4. is
5. will take
6. I'm going to borrow
7. I'll drive
8. is going to

- **Tip:** After completing exercise **B**, have students read the conversation in pairs to practice fluency. Then play the conversation and have them try to speak with the audio.

7 page 68

| 1. a | 3. b | 5. b | 7. c |
| 2. a | 4. c | 6. a | 8. a |

8 LISTEN, page 69 10 min.

A
1. b 4. a
2. b 5. b
3. a 6. a

9 LISTEN, page 69 15 min.

A
1. a 5. a
2. b 6. b
3. b 7. a
4. a 8. b

B Answers will vary. Possible answers:
1. Sasha is graduating from high school next year.
2. She wants to work in robotics.
3. Sasha is going to do some research on engineering programs.
4. She won't apply to schools until she finds a good one.
5. Sasha's robot will respond to human needs.
6. Other robots will take care of the elderly and physically challenged people.

10 LISTEN & WRITE, page 70 15 min.

A Sasha's immediate future

✓ Graduate from high school
✓ Do some research on engineering programs
✓ Plan to read about robot projects this year

Herb and other robots

✓ Be a help in people's home
✓ Take care of the elderly

Sasha's robot

✓ Respond to human needs
✓ Understand what people say
✓ Be amazing

B Answers will vary.

LESSON 2 Future Time Clauses

Student Learning Outcomes
- **Read** an article about clothing of the future.
- **Use** future time clauses to indicate when something will take place in the future.
- **Identify** and **use** correct punctuation in sentences with future time clauses.
- **Find** and **edit** errors with future time clauses.
- **Listen** to people discuss their fears about the future.
- **Write** a paragraph of encouragement to a discouraged friend.

Lesson Vocabulary

(n.) advance	(v.) collect	(n.) manufacturer	(n.) purpose	(v.) track
(adv.) automatically	(n.) industry	(v.) monitor	(n.) revolution	(n.) textiles

EXPLORE

1 READ, page 71 — 10 min.
- Use the photo at the bottom of the page to teach *textiles*.

Be the Expert
- Researchers at universities in South Korea, Japan, and the United States have independently created different types of computerized clothing. For more information on the topic, do an Internet search using the term *Smart Clothing*.
- This reading contains specific vocabulary related to clothing (*textiles, sleeves*, and *uniforms*) and health care (*monitor, heart rate, blood pressure, injury*) that may need to be pretaught.

2 CHECK, page 72 — 5 min.

Answers will vary. Possible answers:
1. We want our clothes to look good and protect us from the weather.
2. Two items of clever clothing that will have a health purpose are:
   - a jacket that has a sleeve that allows you to control your cell phone.
   - shirts that check our heart rate and blood pressure.
   - clothing for children with GPS tracking systems that allow parents to know their child's location at all times.
   - military clothing for soldiers that helps them to mend broken bones.
3. They are not comfortable.
4. We'll want our clothes to look good and work for us.

3 DISCOVER, page 72 — 10 min.

A
1. when
2. while
3. as soon as
4. until
5. When

B
1. when we push
2. while we are wearing them
3. as soon as they happen
4. until they are
5. when that happens

C Answer: present

LEARN

Chart 3.3, page 73 — 10 min.
- **Notes 2 & 3:** Students may become confused about the order of events in sentences that use *before* or *after* to connect clauses. Tell them that *before* precedes the second action (*I'll wash the dishes **before I go to the store**.*) and *after* precedes the first action (***After I wash the dishes**, I'll go to the store*). Write an example sentence and point out that *will* is not used in the clause that starts with *before*. Then rewrite the same sentence using *after* to connect the clauses. Point out that *will* is not used in the time clause.

4 page 73 — 5 min.

A
1. develop; won't wear/will not wear/aren't going to wear/are not going to wear
2. are going to purchase/will purchase; see
3. are going to warn/will warn; falls
4. will sell/are going to sell; offer
5. have; will use/are going to use
6. become; will want/is going to want

B *Answers will vary.*

UNIT 3 LESSON 2 **31**

Chart 3.4, page 74 15 min.

- **Tip:** On the board, write the following: *as soon as = once = when.* Explain that these words can all be used interchangeably. Note that *before* and *after* can't be used in place of the other time adverbs (e.g., *I'll call as soon as I hear from the doctor. I'll call before I hear from the doctor.*)

5 page 74 5 min.

1. (2) Rob will receive a bionic arm (1) as soon as it is ready.
2. (1) Ron isn't going to be able to hold anything (2) until he gets a bionic arm.
3. (2) Before he has the new arm, (1) he will learn as much as possible about bionics.
4. (1) As soon as Ron gets the arm, (2) he is going to try to use it.
5. (1) When Ron thinks about moving his fingers, (2) his brain will send messages to his hand.
6. (2) The fingers in his bionic arm will move (1) after they receive the messages from his brain.
7. (2) Until he gets his bionic arm, (1) Ron is going to need help with everyday tasks.
8. (2) He will be very happy (1) once he is able to do everyday tasks.

6 page 75 5 min.

1. b
2. a
3. b
4. a
5. b
6. a
7. b
8. a

PRACTICE

7 pages 75–76 10 min.

1. The car manufacturer is going to sell its new self-driving car after it tests it.
2. As soon as a car in front of you stops, your self-driving car will stop automatically. /Your self-driving car will stop automatically as soon as a car in front of you stops.
3. Before you make a wrong turn, your self-driving car will warn you. /Your self-driving car will warn you before you make a wrong turn.
4. Until engineers make sure that these cars are safe, people won't feel relaxed. /People won't feel relaxed until engineers make sure that these cars are safe.
5. Once you find a parking space, your car will park itself. /Your car will park itself once you find a parking space.
6. When people name their destination, their cars will start up and drive there./Their cars will start up and drive there when people name their destination.
7. As soon as engineers build more automated highways, people will take more trips./People will take more trips as soon as engineers build more automated highways.
8. People are not going to buy self-driving cars until they become affordable. Until self-driving cars become affordable, people are not going to buy them.

8 WRITE & SPEAK, page 76 10 min.

A Answers will vary.

9 EDIT, page 77 5 min.

When Ari graduates next month, he ~~starts~~ is going to start working as a designer for a car company. It's a great job, but he's a little worried about it. When he ~~will go~~ goes to work on the first day, everything about the job will be new. Also, as soon as he begins, his long summer vacations will be over. Ari will miss all that free time, but after he works for a couple of weeks, he ~~loves~~ will love his new job. He will learn a lot, and definitely ~~doesn't~~ won't complain when he ~~will get~~ gets his first paycheck.

10 LISTEN & WRITE, page 77 15 min.

A He's worried that he won't remember everyone's name; he's worried he will have trouble working in an open room; he's worried that the job will be too hard for him.

B Answers will vary. Possible answers:
1. You'll learn everyone's name.
2. When you get comfortable in the new work space,
3. after you work at this job for a while.
4. try to take notes so you can remember all the information.
5. When you get your first paycheck, you'll be happy about your job.

11 APPLY, page 77 10 min.

A Answers will vary. Possible answers:
Janet's fears:
Will I understand the teachers?
Who will I ask for help when I don't understand something?
I'm worried that I'm going to miss my friends and family.
How will I make friends when I don't speak the language fluently?
I'm worried I'll be lonely.

32 THE FUTURE

LESSON 3 — Future: Progressive, Perfect, and Perfect Progressive

Student Learning Outcomes
- **Read** the web article about jobs of the future.
- **Analyze** and **use** future progressive, future perfect, and future perfect progressive.
- **Express** polite requests with the future prefect progressive.
- **Listen** to a designer talk about workplaces of the future.
- **Write** about your plans for the near future and later in life.
- **Speak** about expected future changes in your life.

Lesson Vocabulary

| (n.) billion | (n.) community | (adj.) global | (n.) solution | (n.) variety |
| (n.) challenge | (adj.) floating | (n.) population | (v.) translate | (adj.) vertical |

EXPLORE

1 READ, page 78 — 10 min.
- Use the illustration and the caption to teach the meaning of *vertical*.

Be the Expert
- How can we undo the damage to the environment we have caused? Here are some predictions for jobs in the future that will clean up our mess.
- A "garbage designer": someone who designs ways to make the waste from manufacturing into materials that can be used for producing goods.
- A "rewilder": You can think of a rewilder as a "farmer" of the future. Instead of growing crops, a rewilder will fix damage to the environment caused by people, cars, manufacturing, etc.
- This reading describes several more jobs of the future designed to find solutions to environmental challenges today.
- To find more information on the topics in the reading, do an Internet search with the keywords: *floating cities, clean cars,* and *vertical farms/vertical gardens.*
- Ask, *What are some problems that the world may face in the future? What do you know about climate change?* Ask for examples.

2 CHECK, page 79 — 5 min.
1. a 2. b; c 3. b 4. c 5. a

3 DISCOVER, page 79 — 10 min.
A 1. will be facing   3. will be living
   2. will have reached   4. will have lost
B 1. will be facing; will be living
   2. will have reached; will have lost
C 1. 1   2. 2

LEARN

Chart 3.5, page 80 — 15 min.
- **Note 1:** The future progressive can also be used to describe a future action that will be occurring over a period of time. The time expression *for + period of time* is used to point out the duration of the action. *They'll will be discussing the issue of climate change for years to come.*
- **Tip:** To practice the use of the future progressive as an action that occurs at a specific time in the future, do a guided visualization with students. Have students close their eyes and imagine what their lives will be like ten years from now. Talk them through it step by step. Tell them to think about details (e.g., what city or country they will be living in, how long they'll have lived there, what job they'll be doing, what their house or apartment will look like, and so on). When they have finished, tell them to describe their lives to a partner.

Student 1: *In ten years, I'm going to be living in Paris in a beautiful apartment. I'll be working as an engineer at a tech company.*

4 pages 80–81 — 10 min.
1. we're going to be meeting
2. we will not be doing/we won't be doing
3. I'm going to be testing; you'll be driving/you will be driving
4. I'll be shopping/I will be shopping
5. will Julio and Ramon be doing
6. They're going to be working/They are going to be working
7. Will you be helping them
8. I'm going to be writing/I am going to be writing
9. will the plane be taking off
10. I'll be coming/I will be coming

UNIT 3 LESSON 3 33

Chart 3.6, page 81   10 min.

- **Note 2:** Tell students not to repeat *have/has been* between future perfect progressive verbs connected by *and*. *By next June, he will have been living and working in Japan for eight years.*
- **Note 3:** In informal English, *finish* and *do* can be replaced by *will + be* in the future perfect. *He will have finished by Friday.* = *He will be finished by Friday.*

5 page 82   5 min.

1. will have written
2. will have built
3. will have seen
4. will have taken
5. will have made
6. will have performed

- **Expansion Tip:** Working in groups, have students make predictions about what their classmates will have done in fifty years. *Serena will have had eight children.*

6 page 82   10 min.

1. will have been translating
2. will have been serving
3. will have been playing
4. will have been working
5. will have been watching
6. will have been riding

PRACTICE

7 WRITE & SPEAK, page 83   15 min.

A
1. will be attending
2. will be checking
3. will have recycled
4. will not have made/won't have made
5. will have been working
6. he will be taking/he'll be taking
7. will have bought
8. will have returned

B Answers will vary.

> **REAL ENGLISH,** page 84
>
> Tell students that in some situations, such as requests for favors or when you are speaking to your boss, a direct question can sound impolite. *Will I get an increase in salary? Will I be getting an increase in my salary?*

8 WRITE & SPEAK, page 84   5 min.

A
1. Who will be taking notes at the meeting?
2. Will you be picking up your car today?
3. Will you be returning the homework next week?
4. When will you be handing in your project?
5. Will you be stopping at the next bus stop?

B Answers will vary.

9 WRITE & LISTEN, pages 84–85   10 min.

A
1. Large numbers of people won't be working in offices in the years to come.
2. Fewer people will be using company office space.
3. Over the next few decades, more and more workers will be having video conferences.
4. Desktop computers and phones will have disappeared from offices by the middle of the century.
5. Almost everyone will have been communicating with mobile phones and wireless computers for years.
6. By 2050 many companies will have rethought office space.
7. Some offices will have replaced office walls with electronic walls by then.
8. People won't be sharing information in the same ways they do now.

B Answers will vary.

10 APPLY, page 85   15 min.

A Answers will vary.

UNIT 3 Review the Grammar

1 page 86   10 min.

1. are going to send
2. are going to wait
3. will take
4. While
5. will be worrying
6. Will I get in
7. are they going to reject
8. won't receive
9. go
10. will be
11. are going to miss
12. It's happening
13. begin
14. won't be sorry

2 SPEAK, WRITE & LISTEN, pages 86–87   15 min.

A *Answers may vary.*

B 1. Hiro won't have sent his application by the end of May.
2. Jamal will be doing an internship in August.
3. Alex will have finished his online classes by January.
4. Hiro will not be starting/won't be starting a job search later this year.
5. Alex will be working as an urban designer in two years.
6. Hiro won't have started his own company in ten years.

C Jamal

4 EDIT, page 87   5 min.

    I finally have a plan for the future. ~~It is going to have worked~~ It's going to work like this. Next week, ~~I'm starting~~ I will start/I'll start my application for graduate school. I'm ~~studying~~ going to study/am going to study urban planning. At the end of the month, I ~~will sending~~ will send/'ll send in the application. While ~~I'm going to wait~~ I wait/I am waiting for a response, I'm going to do an internship. That will be between June and December. Hopefully, I'll start classes in January. By the time I ~~will graduate~~ graduate in two years, ~~I'll take~~ I'll have taken/I will have taken a variety of courses. They will prepare me for the job market, and hopefully in ten years ~~I'll be working~~ I'll have been working/I will have been working as an urban engineer for several years. In fifteen years, I ~~will have been starting~~ will start/'ll start my own company. At least, that's the plan right now.

5 SPEAK, page 87   10 min.

Answers will vary.

Connect the Grammar to Writing

1 pages 88–89   15 min.

A *Answers will vary.*

B *Answers will vary.*

C **Thesis:** I strongly believe self-driving cars are going to help us greatly in the future.

   Reason 1: Safer
Self-driving cars will take bad drivers off the road.

   Reason 2: Productivity
We can read and study in traffic
Help us use our time more

2 BEFORE YOU WRITE, page 89   15 min.

> **WRITING FOCUS, page 89**
>
> Read through the text in the box. Point out that *strongly* cannot be used with *think*. Explain that we can have strong feelings or strong beliefs but not strong thoughts.

3 WRITE, page 89   20 min.

- **Alternative Writing Topic:** If students are not interested in technology, have them make predictions about an issue they feel strongly about, such as animal rights or their favorite sports team.

UNIT 4 Exploration

Negative *Yes/No* Questions; Statement and Tag Questions

Unit Opener

Photo: Have students look at the photo and ask, *Where is this person? What is he doing?*

Location: The person is in a tunnel inside a glacier.

Theme: This unit covers modern and ancient exploration of space, islands in the Pacific, and the North and South Poles. Have students look at the photo on page 94 and ask, *What is this? What is it used for?* Have them turn to the photo on page 96. Ask, *What do you think this is?* Ask, *What do these all have in common?*

Page	Lesson	Grammar	Examples
92	1	Negative *Yes/No* Questions and Statement Questions	Wasn't that a terrible movie? Yes. I hated it. Haven't you finished that book yet? No, not yet. That's the teacher? I think so. Your address is 22 Main Street? Yes, it is. You don't like the food? No, not really.
101	2	Tag Questions; Answers to Tag Questions	Vanessa **is** the teacher, **isn't** she? **Yes**, she is. Carla and Lucca **came** yesterday, **didn't** they? **No**, they didn't. The test **doesn't** start at 1:30, **does** it? **No**, it starts at 2:00. They **haven't arrived** yet, **have** they? **No**, they're not here yet.
109	**Review the Grammar**		
112	**Connect the Grammar to Writing**		

Unit Grammar Terms

negative question: a *Yes/No* question in which *n't* is added to the auxiliary verb to make it negative. They are used to ask someone for agreement or to confirm information. They are also used to express annoyance or surprise.
➢ *Wasn't the food horrible?*

statement question: a *Yes/No* question with statement word order. They are used to ask someone for agreement or to confirm information. They are also used to express annoyance or surprise. The intonation rises at the end of a statement question.
➢ *You don't like the food?*

tag: the auxiliary + pronoun that follow the statement in a tag question.
➢ *The Smiths are going home, **aren't they?***

tag question: a statement with a two-word tag (auxiliary verb + pronoun) at the end. They are used to ask someone for agreement or to confirm information.
➢ *The movie wasn't very good, **was it**?*

LESSON 1	**Negative *Yes/No* Questions and Statement Questions**

Student Learning Outcomes	• **Read** a blog about scientists preparing for space travel. • **Discover** different meanings of negative questions and statement questions. • **Write** negative questions about space travel and **answer** the questions. • **Complete** a conversation about a Pacific Ocean Expedition. • **Listen** to a conversation about early Polynesian explorers. • **Speak** about a famous place you have visited.
Lesson Vocabulary	(n.) condition (adj.) extended (n.) pressure (n.) remote (v.) trade (adj.) essential (adj.) physical (n.) privacy (v.) specialize

EXPLORE

1 READ, page 92 — 15 min.

- Have students look at the photo and ask, *What is this a photo of? Why is the state of Utah shown on the map?*

> **Be the Expert**
>
> - The Mars Desert Research Station is in Hanksville, Utah. It is operated by the Mars Society, a nonprofit organization dedicated to the exploration and settlement of Mars. The Mars Desert Research Station is designed to *simulate*, or look and feel like, Mars. Three other Mars simulation sites are planned: one in the Australian desert, one in Iceland, and another in the Canadian Arctic. Russia had a Mars simulation. Six crew members spent 520 days locked inside a windowless space capsule in Moscow.
> - The reading contains important words related to space and stress: *aerospace engineers, radiation, claustrophobia*. Pre-teach these words. For example: *Aerospace engineers design, test, and build spacecraft and aircraft; Radiation is a kind of energy, for example, visible light (light that you can see); Radio waves and X-rays are examples of radiation; Claustrophobia is fear of being in a small and enclosed space. For example, you might feel claustrophia in a tunnel.*

- **Expansion:** Ask, *What do you know about the planet Mars?* Tell students, *Its nickname is the red planet. Why?*

2 CHECK, page 93 — 5 min.

1. The Mars Desert Research Station is on Earth in a remote desert area in Utah.
2. A space psychologist helps the crew of astronauts.
3. Astronauts have to put on special suits before they go outside the research station.
4. Some of the challenges that astronauts have to deal with are claustrophobia, pressure to get work done, stress of working together every day, crowded living space, and no privacy.

3 DISCOVER, page 93 — 10 min.

A 1. So life on Mars can drive you crazy?
    2. Isn't another challenge the special suits they have to wear?
    3. Don't the astronauts start to feel claustrophoobic in the research station?
    4. I guess that's why they need a psychologist.

B 1. 1; 4   2. 2; 3

LEARN

Chart 4.1, page 94 — 15 min.

- **Note:** Negative *Yes/No* questions are frequent in informal conversation. They are not generally used in written English or formal conversation
- **Tip:** To practice checking information, write two statements about yourself on the board. One should be true; the other should be false. Students ask you negative questions to check this information and you respond. Then have students write five statements about themselves. Tell them to include some true statements and some false ones. After they have finished, have them work in pairs, taking turns asking and answering negative questions.

4 page 95 — 10 min.

A 1. was   5. is
    2. began   6. are
    3. stepped   7. seems
    4. have been 8. wants

38 NEGATIVE *YES/NO* QUESTIONS; STATEMENT AND TAG QUESTIONS

B 1. Wasn't the first person in space American?
   2. Didn't space travel begin in the 1960s?
   3. Didn't the first astronaut step on the moon in 1969?
   4. Haven't there been trips to Mars already?
   5. Isn't space travel expensive?
   6. Aren't all objects weightless in space?
   7. Doesn't life in a space station seem exciting?
   8. Doesn't everyone want to travel to the moon?

C 1. b   5. a
   2. b   6. a
   3. a   7. a
   4. b   8. b

Chart 4.2, page 95   10 min.

- **Note 3:** Statement questions are also used in informal writing such as informal emails, instant messaging, or blog posts: *You went out with Jason on Friday? So life on Mars can drive you crazy?* They are rarely used in formal spoken or written English.
- **Note 4:** When a speaker is expressing strong emotion, intonation rises higher than in cases where the speaker is checking for information or asking for confirmation.
- **Tip:** Explain that there is no noticeable change in intonation for confirming or checking information. Model the intonation and stress patterns for each use of statement questions. Tell the students to raise their hands when they think you are showing strong emotion.

5 LISTEN & SPEAK, page 96   10 min.

A 1. There's a Mars research station on Earth?
   2. The training at the station isn't for everyone.
   3. There are people who specialize in space psychology?
   4. Astronauts haven't gone to Mars yet?
   5. It will take years for humans to travel to Mars.
   6. It takes longer to travel to Mars than to the moon?
   7. We aren't going to read about other planets?
   8. We have to learn all this information about Mars?

B a. 6   d. 8
   b. 3   e. 7
   c. 1   f. 4

- **Tip:** After students have finished **5B**, have them work in pairs and take turns asking and answering the questions in **5A** with the appropriate intonation.

PRACTICE

6 page 97   10 min.

A 1. You weren't   5. Weren't you
   2. Didn't you train   6. You're planning
   3. Wasn't it   7. Aren't you
   4. It didn't get

7 pages 97–98   15 min.

- **Tip:** Before beginning **7A**, tell students they will begin a new topic: explorers from the past. Ask, *What do you know about the Polynesian people? What part of the world do they live in?*

A 1. Weren't the Polynesians skilled explorers?
   2. Didn't it take only a short time to travel from Tahiti to Hawaii?
   3. Didn't the Polynesians discover Hawaii and many other islands?
   4. Didn't the Polynesians trade with islanders thousands of miles away?
   5. Aren't today's researchers trying to find out how far the Polynesians traveled?

C The Pacific Ocean

D 1. Yes, they were. They sailed all over the South Pacific.
   2. No, it was an extremely long journey from Tahiti to Hawaii.
   3. No, the Polynesians discovered many other islands.
   4. Yes, the Polynesians traded with islanders thousands of miles away.
   5. No, researchers are trying to find out why the Polynesians were so successful.

8 LISTEN, page 99   10 min.

A 1. b   5. a
   2. a   6. b
   3. b   7. a
   4. a   8. a

9 APPLY, page 100   15 min.

A 1. b   2. a   3. c

B a. 3   d. 3
   b. 2   e. 1
   c. 3   f. 1

C Answers will vary.

UNIT 4   LESSON 1   39

LESSON 2	**Tag Questions; Answers to Tag Questions**

Student Learning Outcomes	• **Read** website information about the exploits of a modern polar explorer. • **Form tag questions** and understand their functions. • **Listen** to the intonation in tag questions. • **Speak** about a famous place you have visited. • **Write** negative questions and tag questions.
Lesson Vocabulary	(adj.) ancient (n.) compass (n.) expedition (v.) face (n.) symbol (n.) cave (n.) concern (adj.) extreme (n.) occupation (n.) tradition

EXPLORE

1 READ, page 101   15 min.

• Have students look at the photo and ask, *Where is this man, and what is he doing?*

> **Be the Expert**
>
> Norwegian Børge Ousland is a photographer, writer, and polar explorer. He has made two solo crossings of the South Pole, as well as a solo crossing of the North Pole. He was the first man to travel around the North Pole without an icebreaker. In 2012, he was married at the North Pole. For more information on him, do an Internet search using the search terms "Børge Ousland."

• **Expansion Tip:** After reading the website with the class, write the comprehension questions below on the board for students to answer. Allow lower-level students to look at their books, but have higher-level students answer the questions with their books closed.

1. *How many miles was Ousland's trip around the North Pole?*
2. *How did he travel?*
3. *How many days was the trip?*
4. *What were some problems that Ousland faced?*

2 CHECK, page 102   5 min.

1. F   2. T   3. F   4. T   5. T

• **Tip:** Have students correct the false statements to make them true. Then call on students to write true statements on the board.

3 DISCOVER, page 102   10 min.

A 1. 've seen; haven't you   3. 's; isn't he
      2. didn't show; did it   4. was; wasn't it

B 2, 3

LEARN

Chart 4.3, page 103   10 min.

• **Note 1:** Studies in corpus linguistics show that tag questions are about four times more common in British English than in American English.

4 page 103   5 min.

1. wasn't it   6. didn't they
2. isn't he   7. aren't there
3. hasn't he   8. don't they
4. isn't it   9. doesn't it
5. haven't they   10. do we

Chart 4.4, page 104   10 min.

• **Note 3:** Another common way of giving unexpected answers is by using the word *actually* at the beginning of a sentence. The word *actually* shows the questioner that the answer will be a surprise.
A: *You've been studying English for a long time, haven't you?*
B: *Actually, I started studying it two months ago.*
A: *You aren't Turkish, are you?*
B: *Actually, I am. I'm from Ankara.*
In pairs, have students ask each other tag questions and give answers using *actually*.

40   NEGATIVE *YES/NO* QUESTIONS; STATEMENT AND TAG QUESTIONS

5 page 104   5 min.

1. Yes
2. Yes
3. Yes
4. No
5. Yes
6. No
7. Yes
8. Yes
9. No
10. No

PRACTICE

6 page 105   10 min.

A
1. aren't you
2. isn't it
3. wasn't it
4. were you
5. do you
6. doesn't she
7. have you
8. weren't you
9. are you

7 page 106   10 min.

A
1. Confirmation
2. Confirmation
3. Expecting
4. Expecting
5. Expecting
6. Confirmation
7. Expecting
8. Expecting

B 7. a   4. b   6. c   1. d   8. e   2. f   5. g   3. h

8 LISTEN & SPEAK page 107–108   10 min.

A
1. A
2. A
3. C
4. A
5. C
6. C

> **REAL ENGLISH, page 107**
>
> After students have read the text in the box, ask if they know the term *small talk*. Ask, *What topics are acceptable for small talk with someone you don't know?* (e.g., the weather, sports, traffic.) Write on the board, *It sure is hot today, isn't it?* Then have students write tag questions on these topics as possible conversation starters (e.g., *The traffic is terrible, isn't it?*). Explain that conversation starters usually expect agreement.

9 pages 107–108   15 min.

1. Sandy: The weather's great today, isn't it?
   Jessica: It's beautiful. And there are a lot of people here, aren't there?
   Sandy: Yeah. I never knew so many people loved rock climbing.
   Jessica: We're going to see some great views today, aren't we?
   Sandy: I hope so.

2. Ray: Have we met before?
   Hamid: Right. We were in the same map and compass training course last month, weren't we?
   Ray: Oh yeah. I remember now. That was hard, wasn't it?
   Hamid: It really was. But I don't think I'll ever get lost again, do you?
   Ray: Me neither!

3. Gisela: This climb can't get any harder, can it?
   Luca: I hope not. We've walked through so many dangerous spots already, haven't we?
   Gisela: I know. I'll be glad when it's over.
   Luca: The next mile is going to be the last part, isn't it?
   Gisela: I think so. After that, the trail gets easier.

10 APPLY, page 108   20 min.

A *Answers will vary.*

B *Answers will vary.*

- **Tip:** Have students do **11A** as a role-play, standing and moving around the room. Tell them to imagine what they are wearing and what they are eating and drinking in order to make it more realistic.

Review the Grammar — UNIT 4

1 READ, WRITE & SPEAK, page 109   15 min.

A 1. Isn't Dr. Albert Lin a professor and the creator of the *Valley of the Khans* project?

   Dr. Albert Lin is a professor and the creator of the *Valley of the Khans* project, isn't he?

2. Doesn't he want to help the Mongolian people locate Genghis Khan's burial site?

   He wants to help the Mongolian people locate Genghis Khan's burial site, doesn't he?

3. Wasn't Genghis Khan the founder of the Mongol Empire?

   Genghis Khan was the founder of the Mongol Empire, wasn't he?

4. Didn't he live in the thirteenth century?

   He lived in the thirteenth century, didn't he?

5. Don't Mongolians know the exact location of Genghis Khan's burial site?

   Mongolians know the exact location of Genghis Khan's burial site, don't they?

6. Didn't Genghis Khan conquer many different parts of Asia?

   Genghis Khan conquered many different parts of Asia, didn't he?

7. Didn't he bring the parts under one government?

   He brought the parts under one government, didn't he?

8. Don't people from Mongolia honor the memory of Genghis Khan?

   People from Mongolia honor the memory of Genghis Khan, don't they?

2 LISTEN, SPEAK & WRITE page 110   10 min.

B 1. (T) You're working on Dr. Albert Lin's project, aren't you?

2. (T) The use of technology is extremely important in Mongolia, isn't it?

3. (S) So Lin's team of explorers never disturbs the ground?

4. (S) And you do this right from your home computers?

5. Isn't Mongolia enormous? (N)

B 1. Yes, that's right.   4. Yes, but we're not alone.
2. Yes, absolutely.   5. Yes, it's huge.
3. That's right.   6. Yes, definitely.

3 EDIT, page 111   5 min.

A: You're here for information about our University Explorers Club, ~~isn't it~~ aren't you?

B: Yes. By the way, I'm only 18. I'm not too young for the program, ~~do I~~ am I?

A: No, you're not too young. The program is for anyone between the ages of 18 and 25.

B: I don't need a college degree?

A: ~~Yes~~. No. A college degree is not necessary, but previous exploration experience is. You have some experience, ~~do you~~ don't you?

B: Yes. Here is a list of the projects I've worked on.

A: You can keep that. First, you need to complete the application online.

B: ~~Do not~~ Don't you want to see my list of projects?

A: No, I don't need to see anything. You're going to list your projects in your application.

B: There isn't a deadline, ~~is it~~ is there?

A: Yes. You can apply all year long.

B: And the application is online?

A: Yes, it is.

B: It isn't difficult to find, ~~was it~~ is it?

A: No. It's at the very top of the website. You can't miss it.

Connect the Grammar to Writing

4 WRITE & SPEAK, page 111   10 min.

1 READ & NOTICE THE GRAMMAR,
pages 112–113   20 min.

A *Answers will vary.*

B *Answers may vary. Possible answers:*

Aren't you happy to see me again? (expects disagreement)

You want to borrow something? (surprise)

You're not still upset about that, are you? (confirming information)

You're sorry? You expect me to believe that? (annoyance)

You know which book I'm talking about, don't you? (expects agreement)

You want to borrow my Mayan caves book? (surprise)

C *Answers will vary.*

> **WRITING FOCUS,** page 113
>
> While students read the text and the examples in the box, write the sentences below on the board without punctuation. Have students come to the board and add the correct punctuation to the sentences.
> 1. Ray asks Have we met before?
> 2. Hamid looks at him and says We did the training course together last month.
> 3. Oh yeah Ray says slowly Now I remember. It was hard but very useful.

2 BEFORE YOU WRITE, page 113   15 min.

3 WRITE, page 113   15 min.

- **Alternative Writing:** If writing a new scene is difficult for students, tell them to write an ending for The Great Mayan Cave Quest in exercise **1A**. They can use the same characters, but they must write about what happens when Pierre returns on the next day. Remind them that they need to write what Pierre and Rosa are saying and use the appropriate question types to convey their meaning.

UNIT 5 Stages of Life

Nouns, Articles, and Subject-Verb Agreement

Unit Opener

Photo: Have students look at the photo. Ask, *Who are these people? How do you think are they related?*

Location: Outside a hogan (traditional Navajo dwelling) on the Navajo Nation. The Navajo Nation is an American Indian reservation located in northeastern Arizona, southeastern Utah, and northwestern New Mexico.

Theme: This unit includes information about infancy, adolescence, and longevity. Have students look at the photos on pages 123, 129, and 131. Ask, *What does each photo show?*

Page	Lesson	Grammar	Examples
116	1	Count and Non-Count Nouns: Quantity Expressions	She has **two** gold **necklaces**. / She has beautiful **jewelry**. It's **a great deal of** work, and we haven't **much** time.
124	2	Articles	I just read **an** interesting **article** about teenagers. Do you know **the name** of that man?
131	3	Subject-Verb Agreement	**A family** that has ten children **is** unusual. **Love and attention are** important to him.
138	Review the Grammar		
140	Connect the Grammar to Writing		

Unit Grammar Terms

count noun: a noun that names something you can count. They are singular or plural.
➤ *I ate an **egg** for breakfast.*
➤ *I have **six apples** in my bag.*

definite article: the article *the*. It is used when you are referring to a specific person, place, or thing.
➤ *I found it on **the** Internet.*
➤ ***The** children are sleeping.*

indefinite article: *a* or *an,* articles used when you are not referring to a specific person, place, or thing. They are used before singular count nouns.
➤ *We have **a** test today.*
➤ *She's **an** engineer.*

non-count noun: a noun that names something that cannot be counted.
➤ *Carlos drinks a lot of **coffee**.*
➤ *I need some salt for the **recipe**.*

quantifier: a word used to describe the amount of a noun.
➤ *We need **some** potatoes for the recipe.*
➤ *I usually put **a little** milk in my coffee.*

subject-verb agreement: the main verb in a sentence must agree in number with the subject.
➤ ***The sofa looks** comfortable.*
➤ ***Love and attention are** important to him.*

LESSON 1   Count and Non-Count Nouns; Quantity Expressions

Student Learning Outcomes
- **Read** the web page about naming customs in different countries.
- **Speak** about naming customs in your culture.
- **Analyze** and **categorize** nouns as count or non-count.
- **Discover** how to use a variety of quantifying expressions.
- **Write** a paragraph that describes a celebration in your culture.
- **Find** and **edit** errors with count and non-count nouns or quantity expressions.

Lesson Vocabulary

| (n.) ability | (v.) demonstrate | (n.) gender | (n.) infant | (n.) stage |
| (adj.) customary | (v.) distinguish | (v.) indicate | (v.) refer | (adv.) typically |

EXPLORE

1 READ, page 116   10 min.

- Ask students to describe the terrain (physical features of the landscape) and the climate in the photo.

Be the Expert

- The island of Bali lies just east of Java. Unlike the rest of Indonesia, where most people are Muslim, about 85 percent of people in Java are Hindu. The Luo people live mainly in Kenya, northern Tanzania, and western Uganda. The Wikmungkan people live on the Cape York Peninsula in Queensland in the far northeast of Australia. It is one of the largest unspoiled wilderness areas in the world.
- The small photo shows a young Balinese boy. The larger photo shows a rice field in Bubud, Bali, Indonesia.

- **Expansion Tip:** After students have read the article, put them in pairs to discuss their names. Ask, *Do you know what your name means? Are you or any other children in your family named after anyone? Do you like your name? If you could have any name, what would it be?*

2 CHECK, page 117   5 min.
1. T   2. F   3. T   4. F   5. F

3 DISCOVER, page 117   5 min.

A 1. *(P)* names; *(P)* boys; *(P)* girls; *(S)* way
     2. *(NC)* weather; *(NC)* information; *(S)* day
     3. *(S)* word; *(NC)* rain

B 1. Non-Count Nouns
     2. Singular Count Nouns
     3. Plural Count Nouns

LEARN

- **Tip:** To prepare students for Chart 5.1, have them return to the reading. Tell them to look at all of the boldfaced words and determine if they are (1) nouns and (2) if they are countable or non-countable.

Chart 5.1, page 118   10 min.

- **Note 5:** Explain that many nouns can be countable or non-countable, but there is a change in meaning. Write these sentences on the board: *1. I always buy a coffee in the morning.* (Here *coffee* means a cup of coffee.) *2. Studies show that coffee may be good for your memory.* (Here *coffee* means the general drink or liquid beverage.) Help students to understand the context for a noun that can be either count or noncount by reminding them to consider if the noun is an abstract idea or something that can be seen.

- **Tip:** On the board, write *chicken, electricity, fish, iron, paper, pepper,* and *suitcase.* Ask, *Which of these words can be countable and non-countable?* (chicken, fish, iron, paper, pepper) *Which words are only countable?* (suitcase) *Which is only non-countable?* (electricity)

- **Expansion Tip:** On the board, write categories below of non-count nouns. Write an example next to each. Then have students brainstorm in groups to write more examples.
Abstract ideas or feelings: love; **Activities:** swimming; **Food:** bread; **Gases:** air; **Groups of Similar Items:** baggage; **Liquids:** gasoline; **Natural Events:** rain; **Materials:** wool; **Small Pieces of Things:** dirt

4 page 118   5 min.

1. girl**s**	7. time	13. Buddhist**s**
2. name**s**	8. birth	14. infant**s**
3. beauty	9. survival	15. mother
4. boy**s**	10. bab**ies**	16. rice
5. health	11. month**s**	17. time**s**
6. strength	12. life	

UNIT 5   LESSON 1   45

5 SPEAK, page 119 — 5 min.

- **Alternative Activity:** Explain that names often follow fashions. It's often possible to guess when someone was born by their name, (e.g., many girls born in the 1980s in the US were named Ashley, Heather, or Tiffany). In pairs, have students discuss popular male and female names of their generation, their parents' generation, and their grandparents' generation.

6 page 119 — 10 min.

A
1. a. a
   b. Ø
2. a. Ø
   b. an
3. a. Ø
   b. a
4. a. a
   b. Ø
5. a. a
   b. Ø

Chart 5.2, page 120 — 10 min.

- **Notes 1 & 2:** Some students make mistakes when using *each* and *every*. Because these words refer to one person or thing of a group, students assume that the noun following these quantifiers should be plural. Point out that these quantifiers always take a singular form. Have students compare these sentences: *Every picture tells a story. All pictures tell a story.*

- **Note 3:** Explain that *a few* means *a small number* and *few* means *almost none*. Similarly, *a little* means *a small amount* whereas *little* signifies *almost none*.

7 pages 120–121 — 10 min.

1. all
2. many
3. some
4. some
5. a lot of
6. any
7. both
8. more
9. little
10. no
11. some
12. no

- **Tip:** After completing the reading in exercise **7**, ask students comprehension questions that elicit quantifying expressions. *How many babies can recognize a lot of faces before they're nine months old?*

8 page 121 — 5 min.

1. little
2. few
3. a few
4. little
5. a few
6. few
7. little
8. a little

PRACTICE

9 pages 121–122 — 12 min.

A
1. has
2. little
3. any
4. some
5. a lot of
6. a great deal of
7. is
8. many
9. many
10. little
11. a lot of
12. A few

B **ANALYZE THE GRAMMAR** — 10 min.

Singular Count Nouns	Plural Count Nouns	Non-Count Nouns
daughter	years	time
child	children	knowledge
people	relationships	patience
life	teachers	imagination
adult	things	pleasure

10 WRITE, page 122 — 10 min.

Answers will vary.

11 EDIT, page 123 — 5 min.

Shichi-Go-San (Seven-Five-Three) is a Japanese celebration. People have ~~many~~ a lot of fun at this time of year. Shichi-Go-San takes place on November 15 each year and celebrates different stages of childhood. Parents celebrate their children's growth and pray for their children's good ~~healths~~ health. Every ~~children~~ child receives a bag of candy. Boys receive the bags when they turn three and five years of age. ~~Girl~~ Girls receive them when they turn three and seven. In Japan, people think these are important ages in a child's life. The candy looks like a stick. All the bags have a picture of a turtle and a crane on them. The candy, the crane, and the turtle are ~~symbol~~ symbols of long life.

12 APPLY, page 123 — 15 min.

A
- **Tip:** Before students write the paragraph in exercise **A**, ask them to bring in pictures of themselves at celebrations when they were children. If they do not have any pictures, tell them to draw a picture of themselves and the celebration or find a similar photo on the Internet. They can use these pictures to help them add detail to their paragraphs.

B
- **Alternative Activity:** Using the information in their paragraph from exercise **A** and any pictures students themselves have brought in, have them give presentations to the class or to groups.

LESSON 2 — Articles

Student Learning Outcomes
- **Read** an article about research on the teenage brain.
- **Understand** how to use definite, indefinite, and zero articles.
- **Listen** and **practice** two pronunciations of *the*.
- **Listen** to a news report about three young daredevils.
- **Discuss** and **write** about differences between being a child and being a teenager.

Lesson Vocabulary

| (adj.) adaptable | (n.) characteristic | (n.) consequence | (n.) independence | (n.) thrill |
| (n.) adolescence | (n.) ceremony | (n.) desire | (n.) responsibility | (n.) transition |

EXPLORE

1 READ, page 124 — 10 min.
- Use the photo and the caption to teach the meaning of *risky*.

Be the Expert
- Brain scans have shown that the brain develops from back to front. The parts of the brain that develop first are those that control physical coordination, emotion, and motivation. The prefrontal cortex, which controls judgment, isn't fully developed until about age twenty-five.
- For more information on this topic, do an Internet search using the terms, "teenage brains" and "risk-taking behavior."

2 CHECK, page 125 — 5 min.
1. Late-twentieth-century researchers said the teenage brain is not yet fully developed.
2. Teens from all cultures have a desire for thrills and excitement.
3. Teenagers take the most risks between the ages of 16 and 17.
4. The positive side of teenage risk-taking is that it gets them ready to face the challenges of the future.

3 DISCOVER, page 125 — 10 min.

A 1. (a) teenager
   2. (a) good explanation; (the) late twentieth century
   3. (the) brain scans; (the) brain; childhood; adolescence
   4. researchers; (the) brain; behavior; (a) way
   5. (the) search for excitement and risk; teens; (the) safety of their homes; (the) world

B 2; 3; 4; 6

LEARN

Chart 5.3, page 126 — 10 min.

- **Note 1:** Explain that we use *the* when the speaker and listener have the same specific item in mind. Write the following sentences on the board:

  1. Can you give me a phone?

  2. Can you give me the phone?

  3. Can you give me the phone in my red bag?

  Ask, *what is the difference in meaning?*

  (Sentence 1 refers to any phone, not a specific phone. For example, someone might ask for a phone as a present. Sentence 2 means that the speaker and the listener know exactly which phone they are talking about and where it is located. They share common knowledge and a specific object is referred to. There is only one phone. Sentence 3 also refers to a specific phone and the sentence describes its location to distinguish it from any other phone.

- **Tip:** Write on the board: *at, in, out of, to* in one column. Then write: *bed, home, work, school, church,* and *jail* in another column. Have students write ten sentences using the words from both columns.

REAL ENGLISH, page 126
After students read the box, ask, *What kind of television shows do you watch?* Some possible answers: *sports, news, reality shows, game shows, soap operas, sit coms, crime drama, and movies.* Write them on the board. Then ask, *What did you watch on TV last weekend?* (Possible answers: *I watched a baseball game, a crime drama, and a movie.*) Ask, *Were they any good?* (*The crime drama was, but the baseball game and the movie weren't very exciting.*) Tell the students to work in pairs to have short conversations like this. Then have them change partners.

4 pages 126–127　　　　　　　　　　5 min.

1. Some; the
2. an; the
3. The; Ø
4. Ø; the
5. a; the
6. The; the
7. a; the
8. an; the
9. The; Ø
10. Ø; Ø

Chart 5.4, page 127　　　　　　　　10 min.

- **Notes 1 & 2:** Explain that we make generalizations to talk about all members of a group in general. The most common way to make a generalization is to use a non-count noun or a plural count noun without an article. For example: *Milk is good for you. Dogs are loyal animals.* Point out that when we define a count noun or describe something typical about it, we generally use *a/an: A camera is a machine that takes photographs.*

- **Notes 1 & 3:** Explain that we do not use an article when the plural nouns refer to classes or groups. For example, *Monkeys are social.* Explain that we can use *the* with a singular noun when we make generalizations about machines, inventions, plants, or animal species. For example: *Steve Jobs invented the iPhone. The Great White Shark is an endangered species.*

- **Tip:** Write the following categories on the board with an example for each. Explain that we use *the* when we make a generalization about these topics. Then have students work in groups to generate more examples.
Musical instruments: the guitar
Plants and animal species: the lowland gorilla
inventions: the refrigerator
money: the euro   body parts: the brain

5 page 127　　　　　　　　　　　10 min.

1. Adolescence can be a difficult time in a person's life.
2. Many teens want excitement.
3. A mother worries about her child.
4. The young sometimes do risky things.
5. Teenagers like to spend time with their friends.
6. The elderly often don't understand teenage behavior.
7. Many teens enjoy dangerous activities.
8. It is good for teenagers to have a job.
9. A job teaches responsibility.
10. Money doesn't make people happy.

6 page 128　　　　　　　　　　　10 min.

A
1. Ø
2. the
3. Ø
4. Ø
5. Ø
6. Ø
7. Ø, Ø
8. the
9. the
10. a

B *Answers will vary.*

7 pages 128–129　　　　　　　　　5 min.

A

	/ðə/	/ði/		/ðə/	/ði/
1.	✓		5.	✓	
2.		✓	6.	✓	
3.		✓	7.		✓
4.	✓		8.		✓

B
1. the flowers
2. the annual
3. the other
4. the celebration
5. the most amazing
6. the holiday dinner
7. the address
8. the age

- **Tip:** Have students work in pairs to take turns saying the noun phrases in exercise **B**. Tell them that their partners will listen and say if they heard /ðə/ or /ði/.

8 page 129　　　　　　　　　　　10 min.

1. a
2. the
3. Ø
4. Ø
5. a
6. the
7. the
8. Ø
9. Ø
10. Ø
11. the
12. an
13. a
14. Ø
15. a
16. a
17. Ø
18. Ø

9 LISTEN, page 130　　　　　　　15 min.

A 3

B
1. a sailboat
2. the world
3. bad weather; problems with his boat
4. the difficult trip
5. the West Coast
6. after-school jobs
7. Government officials
8. a young person

48 NOUNS, ARTICLES, AND SUBJECT-VERB AGREEMENT

LESSON 3 | Subject-Verb Agreement

Student Learning Outcomes	• **Read** an article about research on longevity. • **Understand** and **use** correct subject-verb agreement. • **Listen** to a conversation between a participant and a researcher studying the later stages in a person's life. • **Find** and **edit** errors in subject-verb agreement. • **Write** about the results of a study on physical activity. • **Survey** classmates about their exercise habits and **discuss** the results.
Lesson Vocabulary	(n.) accuracy (n.) centenarian (n.) implication (v.) prevent (n.) proverb (adj.) balanced (v.) honor (n.) longevity (n.) process (n.) span

EXPLORE

1 READ, page 131   10 min.

• Use the photo and the caption to teach the meaning of *longevity*.

Be the Expert

• The United States has the largest number of centenarians in the world, followed by China. The country with the largest number of centenarians per person in the population is Japan, followed by France.
• Females make up roughly 80 percent of centenarians.
• The Albert Einstein College of Medicine in New York City, U.S.A., sponsors the Longevity Genes Project, a study on the genetic factors leading to exceptionally long life. For more information about the study and its findings, do an Internet search using the term *Longevity Genes Project*.

• **Expansion:** Some countries have traditions for honoring centenarians. For example, in some countries the president or prime minister calls people on their 100th birthday. Have students discuss how 100th birthdays are honored in their countries.

2 CHECK, page 132   5 min.

1. In a study of over 1000 ~~75-year-olds~~ centenarians, researchers have discovered a set of "long-life" genes.
2. Long-life genes may ~~cause~~ prevent the typical diseases of the elderly.
3. Lifestyle, the environment, and plain good luck have ~~little~~ a big effect on life span.
4. Scientists are learning how to ~~destroy~~ use genes to help predict and cure certain illnesses.
5. Dan Buettner believes that scientists may even learn how to ~~stop~~ slow the aging process.

3 DISCOVER, page 132   5 min.

A 1. The authors of the study (think) that long-life genes may affect aging.
2. Every person with long-life genes (is not going to) (live) to be a hundred.
3. A number of other important factors (greatly) (influence) life span.
4. For example, lifestyle, the environment, and plain good luck also (play a big role.)
5. In fact, 23 percent of the people in the study (were not individuals) with long-life genes.
6. Years of research (have taught) him several things.

B 1. b   4. a
    2. a   5. a
    3. b

LEARN

Chart 5.5, page 133   10 min.

• **Note 6:** *There* is usually followed by *is/are*. The actual subject follows the verb. A common native speaker error is to use *There is* incorrectly with a plural subject: **There's always a couple of dogs and a cat hanging around outside.* (incorrect)

4 page 133   5 min.

1. is   5. needs
2. are   6. live
3. contribute   7. helps
4. chooses   8. have

Chart 5.6, page 134   15 min.

- **Note 1:** Explain that we also use singular verbs when giving the results of arithmetic problems: *Four times four equals sixteen. The square root of nine is three.*
- **Note 2:** The names of some academic subjects and sports ending in *-ics* are of Greek origin. Although these words end in *-s*, they are not plural (e.g., *statistics, gymnastics, athletics, mathematics, politics,* and *linguistics*). Note that *arithmetic* is an exception. Some other singular nouns that end in *-s* include diseases (e.g., *diabetes, measles,* and *rabies*).
- **Note 6:** Depending on the noun that follows, *most of* can be followed by a singular or plural verb form: *Most/All of the news is bad. Most/All of the flood victims were taken to shelters.*

5 page 134   5 min.

1. is
2. is
3. is
4. are
5. is
6. is
7. are
8. is
9. are
10. are

PRACTICE

6 page 135   10 min.

A

- **Tip:** Before doing **6A**, read the quotations to the students. Tell them you will read some of the quotations with correct subject/verb agreement, but others with errors in subject/verb agreement. Ask them to raise their hands and say *Stop* when they hear a mistake. Call on a student who raised his or her hand, and ask the student to give the correct answer.

1. continues
2. is
3. is
4. is
5. have
6. is
7. seem
8. knows

- **Tip:** To make the listening easier for lower level students, write on the board: *family, friendship, computers, birthday, money, friendship, listen, patience, shy, health, career, education, love.* Have students copy the words. Tell them to listen and check the words they hear. (*family, friendship, birthday, friendship, listen, patience, shy, career, education*)

7 LISTEN, page 135   15 min.

A Answers will vary.

B communication; education; family

C
1. All; were
2. Some; lives
3. Her experiences; have taught
4. All; have been
5. education; is

8 EDIT, page 136   5 min.

Gene Guerro has been working at Briteroom for 60 years and nothing ~~have~~ has ever prevented him from going to work. Briteroom Electronics ~~are~~ is going to be honoring him next month for being the company's longest-working employee. When he first started college, Gene majored in economics. But economics just ~~weren't~~ wasn't very interesting to him, so he changed to physics. "There ~~was~~ were many exciting things to learn in every physics class. In fact, physics still excites me today," says Gene. "Everybody ~~tell~~ tells me, I should retire." And I say, "Why should I do that? Watching TV and fishing ~~isn't~~ aren't for me. Half of my friends do that, but they aren't happy. Every day ~~are~~ is exactly the same for them." As Lucy Guerro says about her father, "Work is my dad's hobby."

9 READ, SPEAK & WRITE, pages 136–137   10 min.

B
1. All of the respondents were over 45 years old.
2. A little less than 40 percent of the group are more active now than they were five years ago.
3. Almost three-quarters of the respondents are physically active now.
4. Nearly a third of the group are not physically active.
5. Almost nobody plans to start an exercise program in the next month.
6. 50 percent of the people prefer walking to other forms of exercise. 50 percent of the people prefer other forms of exercise to walking.
7. A little over half of the group does four or more hours of physical activity every week.
8. Almost two-thirds are not more active now than they were five years ago.

50   NOUNS, ARTICLES, AND SUBJECT-VERB AGREEMENT

UNIT 5 Review the Grammar

1 page 138 10 min.

A
1. is
2. Ø
3. people
4. Ø
5. a
6. are
7. the
8. The
9. the
10. were

B ANALYZE THE GRAMMAR

Answers will vary. Possible answers include:

Singular Count Nouns	Plural Count Nouns	Non-Count Nouns
tradition	stories	storytelling
writer	elders	history
group	generations	culture
grandmother	lessons	hunting
family	children	food
example	grandmothers	preparation
responsibility	storytellers	
society	tasks	
	mothers	

2 EDIT, pages 138–139 5 min.

Every culture and country have has stories to pass down to the younger generation generations, and the young learns learn a lot of things from the stories. The stories also bring joy to a great deal of children.

There are many different kinds of stories, but a number of themes is are common across cultures. For example, the importance of family relationships appear appears again and again. Hard work and honesty is are also an important theme themes in children's stories. What else do the children learn? Perhaps most importantly, they learn that all human beings are the same. There is a little difference between people. Everybody have has the same dreams, hopes, and fears.

3 LISTEN, SPEAK, & WRITE, page 139 20 min.

A
1. a
2. the
3. an
4. was
5. the
6. the
7. a
8. was
9. the
10. a

C
1. Mr. Turtle listened carefully to both sides.
2. The turtle said both sides were equally right.
3. He made this decision because it would not cause any bad feelings.
4. The people voted him as their judge.

Connect the Grammar to Writing

1 READ & NOTICE THE GRAMMAR
page 140   10 min.

B 1. Subject following *be* in sentences with *there*: *The stream had almost no water, and* **there were big sharp rocks** *in it; There was no way I was going to chicken out now.*

2. Subjects with *every-, some-, any-,* or *no-* take a singular verb: *To this day, whenever* **someone dares** *me . . . Everybody was cheering me as I rode top speed.*

3. Non-count nouns as subjects take singular verbs: *(No additional examples in this exercise.)*

> **WRITING FOCUS, page 141**
>
> Read the text in the box. Write another example on the board with a timeline showing the past perfect. For example: *We almost hit a car that had stopped in the road.*
>
> ```
> ×————————×————————▶
> car stopped   we almost hit car   now
> ```
>
> Then to help students use past verb forms correctly, ask them to draw a timeline. Have them list two events that happened to them on the timeline and write a sentence with the past perfect.

2 BEFORE YOU WRITE, page 141   15 min.

- **Tip:** If students have not had an experience similar to the example in exercise **2**, tell them they can write about someone they know who had such an experience.

3 WRITE, page 141   20 min.

- **Tip:** To help students use past verb forms correctly, have them practice with timelines. First, ask to draw two timelines like the one on page 41. Have them list two events that happened to them. Then have them place these events on the timeline.

- **Alternative Writing:** Have students describe the events of an especially memorable celebration from their childhood or adolescence, such as a birthday, a coming of age party, or a wedding.

UNIT 6 Wellness

Gerunds and Infinitives

Unit Opener

Photo: Have students look at the photo and read the caption. Ask: *Do you think these girls are healthy and happy? Why?*

Location: These girls are swinging in a playground in Kabul, the capital of Afghanistan. Playgrounds like these have been built in war-torn areas by a Canadian nonprofit organization. They offer a safe place to help children experience joy away from the horrors of war.

Theme: Explain that the theme of the unit is *wellness* (staying healthy in body and mind). Have students look at the photos on pages 144, 152, and 161. Ask: *How do you think these photos are related to wellness?*

Page	Lesson	Grammar	Examples
144	1	Gerunds: Review and Expand	**Hiking** is fun for all ages. **Not getting enough sleep** can be a problem. They enjoyed **hearing that song**.
152	2	Infinitives: Review and Expand	We have **decided to go** to Chile. I **want you to see** the doctor. They **promised not to be** late.
161	3	More about Gerunds and Infinitives	It takes time **to lose** weight. The hospital is **big enough to treat** everyone. We use this scale **to weigh** ourselves.
170	**Review the Grammar**		
172	**Connect the Grammar to Writing**		

Unit Grammar Terms

gerund: an *-ing* verb form that is used as a noun. It can be the subject of a sentence, or the object of a verb or preposition.
➢ **Surfing** is a popular sport.
➢ We enjoy **swimming**.
➢ The boy is interested in **running**.

gerund phrase: an *-ing* verb form + an object or a prepositional phrase. It can be the subject of a sentence, or the object of a verb or preposition.
➢ **Swimming in the ocean** is fun.
➢ I love **eating chocolate**.
➢ We are thinking about **watching the new TV show**.

infinitive: *to* + the base form of a verb.
➢ He wants **to see** the new movie.

infinitive of purpose: *to* + the base form of the verb used to express purpose or answer the question *Why*.
➢ Scientists studied the water **in order to learn** about the disease.
➢ We went to the store **to buy** milk.

LESSON 1 Gerunds: Review and Expand

Student Learning Outcomes
- **Read** an article about the restorative powers of sleep.
- **Talk** about techniques for falling asleep.
- **Complete** sentences with gerunds.
- **Listen** to tips on how to lose weight.
- **Write** about healthy habits that help you live longer.
- **Find** and **edit** errors with gerunds.

Lesson Vocabulary
(v.) benefit	(v.) differ	(v.) improve	(adj.) relevant
(n.) decade	(adj.) effective	(n.) insomnia	(n.) theory

EXPLORE

1 READ, page 144 — 10 min.
- Ask students what the theme of the unit is.
- Have them look at the photo, and ask them how the photo relates to the theme.

Be the Expert
- Recent studies have shown that taking a twenty-minute nap during the day has benefits for the heart. In a Greek study, heart-related deaths were reduced by 37 percent just from napping.
- According to the American Center for Disease Control, at least 10 percent of Americans have chronic insomnia. This means that they have difficulty falling asleep or staying asleep three or more times a week.

2 CHECK, page 145 — 5 min.
1. Researchers have different theories for the reasons we sleep: For example, sleeping may help protect us from infection.
2. One reason some people don't get enough sleep is that they work long hours and have stress.
3. Not getting enough sleep can cause traffic accidents and low productivity at work.
4. He thinks that TV networks should consider changing their schedules so that people can spend more time sleeping.

3 DISCOVER, page 145 — 10 min.

A 1. Sleeping   4. Not getting
   2. letting   5. changing; sleeping
   3. living

B 1. T   2. T   3. F

- **Tip:** While students are doing exercise **B**, write the following questions on the board. If some students finish earlier than others, have them write answers to the questions. *How many hours of sleep do most people need? How does sleep help the body? How many Americans have trouble sleeping?*

LEARN

Chart 6.1, page 146 — 10 min.
- **Note:** Gerunds can be very confusing for students. Not every *-ing* word is a gerund. Remind students that a gerund is the noun form of a verb with *-ing*.

4 page 146 — 8 min.

A 2. Taking a nap in the afternoon
   3. Not getting eight hours of sleep a night
   5. Meditating
   6. waking up early in the morning
   7. sleeping with the light on
   9. exercising

B **ANALYZE THE GRAMMAR,** page 147

   2. S   7. O
   3. S   8. S
   5. S   9. O
   6. O

- **Expansion Tip:** Have students work in pairs to write sentences about health by replacing the gerund phrases in exercise **A** with phrases of their own. Model the task for the students: *Eating a lot of fruits and vegetables is good for you. Not getting regular exercise is a problem for many adults.*

54 GERUNDS AND INFINITIVES

Chart 6.2, page 147 — 15 min.

- **Notes 1 & 2:** Even advanced students have problems with gerunds as objects of prepositions. It is difficult to know which preposition to use after the noun, verb, or adjective that precedes the gerund. On the board, write several nouns, verbs, and adjectives that can be followed by gerunds, and elicit the correct preposition. Then have students write sentences using these combinations.

5 page 147 — 5 min.

1. in thinking
2. of dreaming
3. for having
4. in understanding
5. of meeting
6. of staying
7. in analyzing
8. of trying

Chart 6.3, page 147 — 10 min.

- **Note 1:** Point out that these special expressions all take the verb *have* and do not use prepositions. Explain that *having difficulty/having a problem/having trouble* are similar in meaning, but *having difficulty* is more formal than the other expressions.

6 page 148 — 5 min.

A
1. A: trouble staying
   B: difficulty falling
2. A: time lying
   B: problems causing
3. A: trouble calming
   B: experience teaching
4. A: fun learning
   B: time practicing

B Answers will vary.

PRACTICE

7 pages 148–149 — 10 min.

1. Dreaming about
2. believe eating
3. enjoy dining
4. Cooking and eating
5. benefits of eating
6. have difficulty believing
7. suggest looking
8. problems eating
9. avoid eating
10. in trying
11. think about including

8 LISTEN WRITE & SPEAK, page 149 — 20 min.

A
1. food cut in pieces
2. in the afternoon
3. slowly

B
1. a. Cutting your food
   b. Eating several small pieces
2. a. scheduling
   b. consuming meals
3. a. Eating slowly
   b. Limiting; gaining weight

C Answers will vary.

9 WRITE & SPEAK, page 150 — 10 min.

A
1. Flossing your teeth could add three to five years to your life.
2. Not smoking could add six years to your life.
3. Lifting weights could add five to six years to your life.
4. Eating fruits and vegetables could add five years to your life.
5. Getting enough sleep may add three years to your life.
6. Walking every day could add over two years to your life.

B Answers will vary.

10 EDIT, page 151 — 10 min.

~~Use~~ Using technology is a big part of daily life. Today there are many products that can help us succeed in ~~reach~~ reaching our dietary and fitness goals. Is planning meals a problem for you? Are you tired of ~~spend~~ spending time ~~search~~ searching for healthy recipes? Downloading diet-related apps to your cell phone may be the answer. Apps can put the fun back into ~~eat~~ eating well.

Apps are also great for helping you get a good workout. If you are a runner, perhaps ~~improve~~ improving your speed is your goal. If so, a GPS watch is perfect for you. Do you need to be especially careful during your run? Take advantage of the heart monitor. It will prevent you from ~~overdo~~ overdoing your workout. If you swim, you may find that doing laps can get boring, especially when you are swimming long distances. But swimming is much more fun with a pair of waterproof headphones that play your favorite music.

Try these different products—you will have no excuse for ~~being not~~ not being able to stay fit.

11 APPLY, page 151 — 15 min.

A Answers will vary.

B Answers will vary.

UNIT 6 LESSON 1 55

LESSON 2	Infinitives: Review and Expand
Student Learning Outcomes	• **Read** an article about shamans helping researchers identify medicinal plants in the rainforest. • **Discover** which verbs can be used with infinitives and object + infinitive. • **Understand** meaning changes when verbs are followed by gerunds or infinitives. • **Find** and **edit** errors with infinitives. • **Write** about and **discuss** ways you treat health problems.
Lesson Vocabulary	(v.) admire (n.) avalanche (n.) deforestation (adj.) medicinal (adj.) spiritual (n.) altitude (v.) chant (adj.) fortunate (n.) root (n.) venom

EXPLORE

1 READ, page 152   10 min.

- Use the photo and caption to teach the word *shaman*.
- Have the students read the title of the article. Ask them to make predictions about who uses medical riches: shamans or medical doctors?

Be the Expert

The photo shows a traditional Cofán healer who lives and works in the rainforests of Ecuador. The Cofán people are among the oldest indigenous cultures in the Amazon region.

- **Expansion:** For more information on medicinal plants of the rainforest, do a search on YouTube. Use the search terms *Ava Katuete* for a video on Noceda, or for information on the plants, use the search term *The Medicine Hunter*.

2 CHECK, page 153   5 min.

1, 3, 5

- **Tip:** Have higher-level students correct the false statements to make them true.

Possible answers:

2. Researchers have studied ~~most~~ a fraction of the plants in the rainforest.
4. Gervasio Noceda learned about plants in ~~a medical library~~ the forest.

- **Expansion Tip:** Bring in photos of traditional healers (shamans, curanderos, sangomas) and have a brief discussion. *What are they called? Would you try a traditional healer?*

3 DISCOVER, page 153   10 min.

A 1. to find   3. to find   5. to work
     2. to show   4. to have

B 1. hope: verb   4. fortunate: adjective
     2. healers: noun   5. need: verb
     3. him: pronoun

LEARN

Chart 6.4, page 154   10 min.

- **Notes 2–4:** Infinitives can confuse students even more than gerunds because students can't remember which verbs can be used after a direct object. A common mistake is using an infinitive after a preposition: *I'm excited about ~~to go~~ shopping.*

- **Tip:** Write sentences on the board that use verb + object + infinitive. Some should be correct; others should have errors. Read the sentences and ask students to raise their hands for sentences that are correct. Then, have students edit the sentences with mistakes.

4 page 154   5 min.

1. not to continue   5. me to use
2. needs me   6. not to forget
3. to finish   7. me to return
4. to present   8. you to come

5 page 155   10 min.

1. We ask people to be patient
2. I would like my patients to follow
3. I advise everyone to stop smoking.
4. We encourage our patients to exercise
5. We advise them to avoid
6. Older people need to be careful
7. I urge our patients not to worry.
8. I remind people not to lose

56   GERUNDS AND INFINITIVES

Chart 6.5, page 155–156 — 8 min.

- **Note 2:** When using *prefer* to compare two activities, use the base form of the verb after *rather than*. Write on the board: *I prefer to eat fruit rather than ~~to eat~~ candy.* Explain that we do not use the infinitive verb phrase after *rather than*.

6 page 155 — 10 min.

A 1. I can't stand to stay in bed all day long when I'm sick.
2. I prefer to use medicinal plants rather than medicine.
3. I like to get phone calls from friends when I'm sick.
4. When I feel ill, I start to look up my symptoms on the Internet.
5. I begin worrying right away when I have symptoms.
6. I prefer waiting rather than going to the doctor immediately.
7. I don't bother telling anyone when I don't feel well.
8. I hate sitting in the waiting room at the doctor's office.

B *Answers will vary.*

Chart 6.6, page 156 — 10 min.

- **Tip:** Write on the board: *Bill forgot to go there. Bill forgot going there.* Ask, *In which sentence did Bill actually go there?* Then have students work in pairs and ask and answer questions. What sorts of things do they remember or forget doing when they were children? What kinds of things do they usually forget or remember to do now?

7 page 157 — 5 min.

1. enjoying   5. to admire
2. falling   6. moving
3. to put   7. to bring
4. to bring   8. feeling

PRACTICE

8 page 157–158 — 5 min.

1. to take vitamin C
2. to take a walk by the sea
3. drink hot milk rather than take medicine
4. to rub plant oil on his back
5. to drink coffee or soda
6. to make noodle soup that cures colds
7. to rest as long as possible
8. to add garlic to his soup

9 page 158 — 8 min.

A 1. decided to go   5. encouraged him to do
2. wanted to get   6. remembers suffering
3. started to feel   7. advise people not to go
4. seemed to disappear   8. stop working

10 EDIT, page 159 — 5 min.

Do you remember ~~to cut~~ cutting yourself when you were a child? Did you know how to take care of the cut, or did you ask someone to help you? Of course, it's not only children who cut themselves. That is why we urge everyone ~~having~~ to have a first-aid kit at home. We also want you to follow this advice.

- For minor cuts: After the cut stops ~~to bleed~~ bleeding, start rinsing the wound with clear water. Clean the area around the wound with soap and a washcloth. Avoid getting soap directly in the wound.
- For deep cuts: Put pressure on the cut to stop the bleeding. Continue to ~~putting~~ put pressure on the wound for 20 or 30 minutes.
- If the wound gets dirty, put a bandage on it and remember ~~changing~~ to change it every day.
- Remember! Teach your children about first aid, and remind them ~~to not~~ not to play with sharp objects.

11 page 159–160 — 10 min.

1. running every weekend
2. missing her runs
3. to see a foot specialist
4. to wear proper shoes
5. to ice her feet
6. to give her trouble/giving her trouble
7. to mountain bike/mountain biking
8. to see a sports injury specialist
9. to raise the seat of the bike
10. to do leg muscle exercises
11. to do the exercises every day
12. to go mountain biking again soon

12 APPLY, page 160 — 15 min.

A & B *Answers will vary.*

- **Alternative Writing:** Instead of writing about medical problems, have students write about healthy habits they have adopted or plan to adopt.

UNIT 6   LESSON 2   57

LESSON 3 More about Gerunds and Infinitives

Student Learning Outcomes
- **Read** an article about the work of a musician and clean water activist in Mozambique.
- **Understand** and **use** infinitives with *it*, *too*, and *enough*.
- **Discover** how to use infinitives to indicate purpose.
- **Discuss** and **write** about amazing new and affordable medical inventions.
- **Listen** to an interview about healthcare improvements in Thailand.
- **Talk** about world health problems and **suggest** possible solutions.

Lesson Vocabulary
| (v.) access | (n.) broadcast | (adj.) determined | (v.) focus | (n.) motivation |
| (adj.) basic | (v.) detect | (n.) development | (n.) hygiene | (adj.) rewarding |

EXPLORE

1 READ, page 161   10 min.
- Have the students look at the photo and read the caption. Then, have them read the glossed words and definitions at the bottom of the article. Ask them what changes dos Santos wants to make.
- Have students use the context to guess the meaning of new words (*remote, access, environmentally friendly*).

Be the Expert
- The province of Niassa, Mozambique, borders the neighboring country Malawi, which is also poor and lacks safe water. Life expectancy in Niassa is short: the average man in Niassa will live to be only forty-two. In addition, much of the population is illiterate—sixty-one percent of the population cannot read or write. Santos' musical messages about safe sanitation reach many more people than written information can because so few people are able read.
- In 2008, Feliciano dos Santos received the Goldman Environmental Prize for his efforts to improve sanitation and get people access to clean water.
- **Expansion Tip:** Search YouTube for *Niassa* by Massukos to hear and see Santos and his band.

2 CHECK, page 162   5 min.
1. Feliciano dos Santos uses a ~~piano~~ guitar to teach people about keeping clean.
2. Santos's band plays songs in ~~English~~ the local languages to communicate their message.
3. Santos does most of his work in ~~small cities~~ remote villages in Mozambique.
4. For Santos, the lack of ~~traditional music~~ clean water is a major problem in Niassa.

5. Other countries have ~~little~~ a lot to learn from Santos's sanitation projects.

3 DISCOVER, page 162   8 min.
A
1. to meet
2. to travel
3. to make
4. to provide

B
1. c   2. b
3. d   4. a.

LEARN

Chart 6.7, page 163   10 min.

- **Note 3:** Many languages don't use *it* as the subject in the following structure: *it + be + adj*. It is common for students of such languages to omit *it*.
- **Tip:** On the board write *It's* with the following adjectives: *challenging, difficult, easy, exciting, important, necessary,* and *rewarding*. Have students choose four of these adjectives and write true sentences about themselves. Then, have them share their sentences with a partner.

4 page 163   8 min.
1. It is rewarding for Feliciano dos Santos to help
2. It is possible to communicate
3. It is important for children to learn
4. It takes a lot of thought to educate people
5. It is necessary to wash your hands frequently
6. It takes time to get clean water

58   GERUNDS AND INFINITIVES

5 page 164 — 5 min.

1. are reluctant to try new health practices
2. must be willing to solve problems
3. are unwilling to make changes that citizens need
4. are determined to get good health care
5. are hesitant to talk about illness
6. are ready to make the world a healthier place

Chart 6.8, page 164 — 10 min.

- **Note 1:** Using *too* instead of *very* is a common mistake students make: *This cake is ~~too~~ very delicious.*
- **Tip:** To demonstrate points 2 and 3, write on the board: *This dress costs $100. I have $75. The dress is too expensive [for me] to buy. The dress isn't cheap enough [for me] to buy. I don't have enough money to buy the dress. That dress is $60. I have enough money to buy that dress.*

6 page 165 — 5 min.

1. enough information
2. too many
3. big enough
4. for them
5. enough
6. too much
7. too far
8. enough health clinics

Chart 6.9, page 166 — 8 min.

- **Note 3:** In some European languages, such as French and Italian, *purpose* is expressed by a preposition followed by an infinitive. Speakers of these languages often try to use the same pattern in English: *I'm taking this class ~~for~~ to learn English.*

7 page 165 — 5 min.

1. to help/in order to help
2. in order not to make
3. in order to bring
4. to develop/in order to develop
5. to inform/in order to inform
6. to learn/in order to learn
7. in order not to confuse
8. to try/in order to try
9. to pay/in order to pay
10. to raise/in order to raise

PRACTICE

8 page 166 — 8 min.

Dr. Hayat Sindi is a medical researcher from Saudi Arabia. (1) She has co-invented and developed a way **to** detect disease with a tiny piece of paper. (2) It appears **to** be an ordinary piece of paper, but it is not. (3) It took a lot of time for her **to** develop the device; (4) however, she was determined **to** find a simple, inexpensive way **to** monitor health. Sindi's organization, Diagnostics for All (DFA) brings affordable health diagnoses to the world's poorest people.

(5) There has never been a problem too great for Sindhi **to** solve. (6) When she moved to England **to** continue her studies, (7) her English was not good enough **to** attend university. But that did not stop her. She improved her English by watching news broadcasts, and (8) she studied up to 20 hours a day **to** prepare for college entrance exams. She was the first Saudi woman **to** study at Cambridge University in the field of biotechnology.

Sindi's accomplishments have made her a role model for women and girls around the world. (9) She feels it is important for women **to** know that they can transform society.

9 SPEAK & WRITE, page 167 — 10 min.

1. The paper doesn't cost too much to produce.
2. DFA produces the paper (in order) to provide inexpensive medical health care.
3. It's not difficult to detect an illness with DFA.
4. Parents use a cell phone (in order) to diagnose their children's ear infections.
5. The CellScope Oto™ is not hard for parents to use.
6. Parents do not have enough time to go to the doctor for every earache.
7. People are glad to have relief from headaches.
8. The device acts early enough (in order) to prevent a headache.
9. The device is too big to fit inside a person's mouth.

- **Tip:** Take a quick class poll about which device is the most useful. Write on the board: *Patterned Paper Technology; CellScope Oto™; Remote-controlled device.* Ask for a show of hands for each device.

Have students work in pairs to give reasons for their choices.

UNIT 6 LESSON 3 59

> **REAL ENGLISH, page 168**
>
> After students read the box, explain that this is a short answer that commonly occurs in informal spoken English, but not in written English. An infinitive phrase is not an independent clause, so it cannot be used as a sentence.

10 page 168 — 10 min.

Answers will vary. Possible answers could include:

1. to avoid problems with their teeth
2. to help improve our quality of life
3. to help scientists prevent and cure diseases
4. to be ready for emergencies
5. to help save lives

11 LISTEN & WRITE, page 168 — 10 min.

A 1, 3

B 1. **Problem**: People in rural areas *lived too far away* to get medical treatment in hospitals.

   Solution: The government of Thailand *decided to spend money on the countryside* in order to bring health care to the rural areas.

2. **Problem**: There wasn't *enough clean drinking water* to meet people's needs.

   Solution: The government gave more people safe *water to* drink.

3. **Problem**: People lived *too far from cities* to access health services.

   Solution: The government built highways *to connect* remote areas to the cities.

4. **Problem**: There *weren't enough* medical workers to give people medical care in remote areas.

   Solution: New medical graduates must serve in rural areas, so there will always be *enough doctors for* people who live outside cities.

12 APPLY, page 169 — 15 min.

A *Answers will vary.*

- **Tip:** To help generate ideas, do an Internet search using terms such as "ending world hunger and poverty." Alternatively, bring in some photos that show people who are in need or receiving help. Some possible ideas are pictures of slums or favelas, families receiving mosquito nets, children receiving medical care, families receiving animals such as goats, cows, and camels.

- **Alternative:** Have students discuss the problems that were caused by recent natural disasters. Then, discuss what was done to solve the problems.

60 GERUNDS AND INFINITIVES

UNIT 6 Review the Grammar

1 page 170   10 min.

A 1. to take; breathing
2. to buy; sneezing
3. to taste; eating
4. not to eat; ordering
5. visiting; to be
6. taking
7. to learn; eating
8. cleaning; to have

2 page 170

A LISTEN
1. sitting at a computer
2. too busy to go
3. the benefits of spending (time)
4. people to start
5. to join the Eco-Club
6. Connecting to nature
7. don't have enough opportunities to connect
8. of getting

3 EDIT, pages 171   10 min.

~~Deal~~ Dealing with stress is becoming more and more of a problem for young people. Many students say that they are having trouble falling asleep at night because of the pressures of school. They also say that they are constantly worried about ~~get~~ getting good grades.

Some schools are trying to do something about the problem. In one high school, five-year-old Maddy greets the students as they enter the building every morning. Maddy seems happy ~~being~~ to be there, and the students like to see her. They have fun greeting her, and they walk away with smiles on their faces. It doesn't cost much for the school to have Maddy there every day because Maddy is a dog.

The school considered ~~to set~~ setting up a special room where students could go to relax, but it was too expensive to do. In addition, some parents didn't want their children to take time out from classes in order to relax. They thought that it was important for their children to be in class as much as possible.

Experts disagree and warn parents not ~~putting~~ to put too much pressure on their children. Encouraging children to relax ~~are~~ is the best way for parents to help them.

4 SPEAK, page 171   10 min.

Answers will vary.

UNIT 6 REVIEW THE GRAMMAR **61**

Connect the Grammar to Writing

1 READ & NOTICE THE GRAMMAR,
page 172   15 min.

B *Answers will vary. Possible answers:*

Gerund—as the subject of the clause: Exercising becomes more fun. Knowing that it is measuring your steps . . . encourages you to get out of your chair more often.

Infinitive—after a verb + object: It challenges you to try to take . . . ; I convinced my brother to get a Zip . . . encourages you to get out of your chair more often. You will probably decide to walk or take the stairs. . .

Infinitive- after *it* + a verb + an adjective: it is easy to connect to your smart phone or computer. . .

C great colors; a little expensive; good for vacations

2 BEFORE YOU WRITE, page 173   15 min.

Answers will vary.

> **WRITING FOCUS, page 173**
>
> Write on the board: *1. A good thing about Zip is its small size, no one notices it. 2. A good thing about Zip is its small size. No one notices it. 3. A good thing about Zip is its small size; no one notices it. 4. A good thing about Zip is its small size, so no one notices it.* Say, *One of these sentences is incorrect. Which is it?* Explain that sentence 1 contains a comma splice. Have students read the text in the box. Go over the different ways to deal with comma splices. Quickly review the seven coordinating conjunctions: *for, and, nor, but, or, yet,* and *so*. Point out that the first letters spell *fan boys*, which is an easy way to remember them.

3 WRITE, page 173   25 min.

- **Alternative Writing:** Ask students to imagine their ideal living situation. Say, *Imagine you could live anywhere. Where do you want to live?* Have students make a list of places they might want to live based on what they enjoy doing, can't stand doing, and situations that are challenging or easy for them. Have students go online to find more information about the place they have chosen, and then write two paragraphs about it.

62 GERUNDS AND INFINITIVES

UNIT 7 Globe Trotting

Modals: Part 1

Unit Opener

Photo: Have students look at the photo and read the caption. Ask: *What do you see?* Ask them if this is what they imagined the terrain of Alaska would look like.

Location: Wrangell St. Elias National Park is the largest national park in the United States (13.2 million acres). The second tallest mountain in the United States and Canada, Mount St. Elias, is located there. Mt. Wrangell is an active volcano. The ocean is only ten miles away.

Theme: This unit is about travel around the world and includes information about scuba diving, unusual hotels, and working on a farm. Have students look at the photos and titles on pages 176, 184, and 191. Ask: *How do these photos relate to the theme?*

Page	Lesson	Grammar	Examples
176	1	Necessity, Prohibition, Obligation, and Expectation	We **don't have to get up** early tomorrow. You **must check** your luggage. You **were supposed to be** here an hour ago.
184	2	Ability	**Can** I **go** to the party tonight? I **could ski** when I was 12, but I **couldn't ski** when I was 8. I want **to be able to travel** by myself.
191	3	Advice, Regret, and Criticism	You **should get** your passport soon. You **ought to buy** your tickets online. You'**d better get** your ticket soon.
200	**Review the Grammar**		
204	**Connect the Grammar to Writing**		

Unit Grammar Terms

formal: language used in academic writing or speaking or in polite or official situations rather than in everyday speech or writing.
➤ **Please** do not take photographs inside the museum.
➤ **May** I leave early today?

gerund: an *-ing* verb form that is used as a noun. It can be the subject of a sentence or the object of a verb or preposition.
➤ **Surfing** is a popular sport.
➤ We enjoy **swimming**.
➤ The boy is interested in **running**.

infinitive: *to* + the base form of a verb.
➤ He wants **to see** the new movie.

infinitive of purpose: *to* + the base form of the verb used to express purpose or answer the question *why?* (also *in order to*)
➤ Scientists studied the water **in order to learn** about the disease.
➤ We went to the store **to buy** milk.

informal: language used in casual, everyday conversation and writing.
➤ **Who** are you talking to?
➤ **We'll be there at eight**.

modal: an auxiliary verb that adds a degree of certainty, possibility, or time to a verb. *May, might, can, could, will, would, should* are common modals.
➤ You **should** eat more vegetables.
➤ Julie **can** speak three languages.

LESSON 1	**Necessity, Prohibition, Obligation and Expectation**

Student Learning Outcomes	• **Read** a web page about scuba diving vacations. • **Complete** paragraphs with modals expressing necessities and prohibition. • **Understand** and **pronounce** reduced forms. • **Find** and **edit** errors with modal verbs and modal-like expressions. • **Listen** to a podcast. • **Write** about a ceremony or ritual.
Lesson Vocabulary	(n.) assessment (n.) expectation (VP.) hold your breath (n.) necessity (adj.) optional (n.) certification (adj.) exotic (adj.) intensive (n.) obligation (n.) prohibition

EXPLORE

1 READ, page 176   15 min.

- Use the photo to teach or elicit vocabulary such as *air tank, mask, oxygen,* and *exotic*.
- Have students use context to guess the meaning of new words (e.g., *hold your breath, surface, athlete, assessment*).

Be the Expert

- The word *SCUBA* is an acronym for "self-contained underwater breathing apparatus." The term was first used during World War II to refer to the equipment divers used to breathe. There are two ways that divers can get oxygen: through tanks they carry on their backs, and from air sent through hoses from a source on the surface, such as a boat. When divers need to go long distances, they use scuba tanks.
- Today diving is a popular sport. Some of the most sought after places to go scuba diving include Bali, Thailand, the Red Sea, Turks and Caicos, Hawaii, the Great Barrier Reef off Australia, Mexico, Fiji, and Costa Rica.
- While many people go diving as a sport, diving is also an occupation. Professional divers can work as commercial divers, e.g., for the fishing industry, scientific divers, media divers, or military divers.

2 CHECK, page 177   5 min.

1. long
2. athletes
3. healthy
4. quickly
5. heavy rain

- **Tip:** After completing exercise **2**, have students work in pairs. One student asks the questions from the web page while the other answers without looking at the book. Then they switch roles.

3 DISCOVER, page 177   5 min.

A 1. must   4. will have to
       2. had to   5. is supposed to be
       3. have to

B 1. c   2. b   3. a

- **Tip:** As you go over the answers to exercise **B**, discuss the meanings of the words *prohibition* and *necessity (something that is necessary)*.

LEARN

Chart 7.1, page 178   10 min.

- **Notes 1–3, and 5:** Explain that *must* is used to express necessity or prohibition in the present or future only, not in the past. Also, elicit or explain that modal-like expressions such as *have to* have meanings similar to modals but don't follow the same grammatical rules; for example, the auxiliary agrees with the subject (*I have to, he has to*). Write sentences on the board in past, present perfect, present, and future, but omit *must* and forms of *have to*. (e.g., *We _____ take a test before we can go to the next level. I _____ leave work early yesterday. She _____ work the evening shift since July. Tomorrow, you _____ go to court.*) Elicit the ways each sentence can be completed. Make sure students use the modal and modal-like expressions correctly with different subjects and tenses as needed.

- **Note 4:** Write examples on the board: *Students can take the test in the class or in the lab. Students ____ take the test in the classroom. Students are not allowed to use cell phones during a test. If they do, their tests will be taken away. Students ___ use cell phones during a test.* Elicit the correct completions.

64   MODALS: PART 1

4 page 178–179 5 min.

1. had to
2. Did you have to
3. didn't have to
4. had to
5. do people have to
6. must/has got to
7. must/have got to
8. don't have to
9. doesn't have to
10. have got to/have to

5 page 179 5 min.

- **Tip:** Have students look at the photo. Before students do exercise **5**, elicit possible dangers of diving.

1. have to/must
2. must not
3. have to/must
4. have to/must
5. has to/must
6. must not
7. has to/must
8. don't have to

- **Tip:** Ask students to close their books after they have completed exercise **5**. Put them in pairs and have them talk about what you must do to be safe if you are going to go diving.

Chart 7.2, page 180 5 min.

- **Note:** On the board, write sentences with expectations: *The restaurant expects customers to make reservations. My parents expect me to call when I am late. The teacher expects us to e-mail her if we are going to miss class.* To focus on form, write the example sentences on the board with blanks for the target structure and subjects. For example, _____ *call my teacher when I am late.* _____ *the teacher if we are going to miss class.* Have students complete the sentences either verbally or in writing.

6 page 180 5 min.

1. is supposed to
2. is supposed to
3. was supposed to
4. was supposed to
5. were supposed to
6. is supposed to

- **Tip:** Have students work in pairs to take turns retelling the story in exercise **6**.

PRACTICE

7 page 181 5 min.

1. don't have to; are supposed to
2. was supposed to; had to; didn't have to
3. were supposed to; had to
4. have got to; will have to

- **Tip:** Have students use the sentences in exercise **7** as a guide to write about a trip they have taken.

8 PRONUNCIATION, page 181 5 min.

- **Tip:** Before beginning exercise **8**, review the contractions of *have/has* used in conversation.

A
1. have to
2. has got to
3. have to
4. has to
5. have to
6. have got to

- **Alternative Speaking:** Have students talk in pairs about a trip or tour they took in the past. They should talk about what they had to do and what they were supposed to do.

9 READ, WRITE, & SPEAK page 182 5 min.

A
1. has to/has got to
2. was supposed to
3. is supposed to
4. was supposed to; has to
5. doesn't have to
6. had to; doesn't have to

B *Answers will vary.*
C *Answers will vary.*

10 EDIT, page 183 5 min.

I'm writing to tell you some exciting news. I'm suppose**d** to go to Ethiopia in May. I know you had a great time there last year, so I want to ask you a few questions. First of all, when you were there, ~~must you~~ did you stay in Addis Ababa, or were you able to find good accommodations outside the capital? I also want to go to Bale Mountain National Park. ~~Have I got to~~ Do I have to camp there, or is there a hotel? Either way, I ~~got to~~ have to/have got to make a reservation very soon, so let me know. How about food? According to my travel guide, visitors are suppose**d** to try *injera*, an interesting kind of bread. I also read that in Ethiopia you don't have to use a fork. It's not the custom. You're supposed to use *injera* as both the fork and the plate. Is that true?

I don't have a visa yet, but I know that I ~~got to~~ have to/have got to have one. What am I supposed to ~~doing~~ do to get one? Do I have to go to the Ethiopian embassy, or can I do the application online? I'm sorry about all these questions. I promise that you ~~must not~~ won't have to answer any more until my next e-mail!

11 LISTEN, page 183 10 min.

1. must
2. must not
3. are supposed to
4. is supposed to
5. aren't supposed to
6. don't have to

12 APPLY, page 183 10 min.

Answers will vary.

- **Alternative Writing/Speaking:** Have students write six sentences about what people have to do or are supposed to do before traveling to a country they know about. Alternatively, have them write sentences about what they should do before going to a place they have never visited. Have them talk about their ideas in pairs.

UNIT 7 LESSON 1 65

LESSON 2: Ability

Student Learning Outcomes
- **Read** a web page about unusual places to stay while traveling.
- **Recognize** and **correctly use** modals for present, past, and future ability.
- **Complete** sentences with modals expressing ability.
- **Complete** sentences about personal abilities.
- **Ask** and **answer** questions about abilities.

Lesson Vocabulary
(n.) accommodations (n.) capsule (n.) jungle (n.) paradise (n.) retreat
(adj.) archaeological (n.) coconut (n.) kayak (n.) perception (v.) support

EXPLORE

1 READ, page 184 — 15 min.

- Have students look at the photo. Elicit what they see. Use the photo to teach the meaning of *rainforest*, *jungle*, and *treetops*.
- Ask students if they would like to stay at any of these places. Why, or why not?

Be the Expert

- Capsule hotels are popular in Japan and are relatively inexpensive. They are often only 2 meters by 1 meter (about 6.5 feet by 3.3 feet). They usually have a TV and wifi. The first capsule hotel opened in Osaka, Japan, in 1979. A variation on the capsule hotel, known as a pod hotel, began appearing in Europe, first at airports and then in big cities. The pod hotel offers rooms that are slightly larger and often have a private bathroom.
- Another interesting hotel is Jules' Undersea Lodge. It was named after the writer, Jules Verne. (He is best known for his novel, *20,000 Leagues Under the Sea*.) Located in Key Largo at the bottom of Emerald Lagoon, it used to be the Chalupa Research station. To enter, guests must dive 21 feet to reach the undersea entrance.

2 CHECK, page 185 — 5 min.

1. b 2. a 3. c

- **Tip:** Have students work in pairs to ask and answer questions about other details in the reading.

3 DISCOVER, page 185 — 5 min.

A
1. couldn't
2. can't
3. have to be able to
4. can
5. will be able to
6. was even able to

B 1. T 2. F 3. F 4. T

LEARN

Chart 7.3, page 186 — 10 min.

- **Notes 1 & 2:** Write other sentences on the board using *can* or *be able to*. (e.g., *I can swim. Jordan is able to snowboard*.) Ask students to say them using the other expression.
- **Note 3:** Elicit all the forms of *be* that can be used in the modal expression *be able to*: (*am, is, are, was, were, has been, have been, will be, had been*). Have students write the expressions out on the board. *am able to, is able to,* etc.
- **Note 4:** Write sentences with errors in the use of *can* and *be able to* on the board, at least one of which uses *can will*. Have students correct the errors.
- **Expansion Tip:** Have students write five abilities they have. Then, have them compare their abilities with a partner. Call on students to tell the class about what their partner can and can't do.

4 page 186 — 5 min.

A
1. have been able to
2. can/are able to
3. have been able to
4. won't be able to
5. haven't been able to
6. are going to be able to/can
7. have been able to
8. can/will be able to

Chart 7.4, page 187 — 10 min.

- **Notes 3 & 4:** Point out that *one time in the past* means on one occasion or in one instance, not one period of time. (e.g., *I was able to climb the tower the first time I tried. I could climb the tower when I was in 8th grade.*) Write several sentences on the board with blanks: *We ___ get inside during the storm. She ___ swim in the summer of 1992. They ___ buy tickets to the concert an hour before it started. I ___ speak Spanish on our vacation in Mexico. He ___ remember everyone's names at the party.* Elicit all possible completions.

66 MODALS: PART 1

5 page 187 — 5 min.

- **Tip:** Have students look at the photo. Ask students where they think this place is. If no one knows, explain that Cerbère is a community in France on the border with Spain, in the Pyrenees.

1. couldn't/weren't able to
2. was able to
3. couldn't/wasn't able to
4. was able to
5. could/was able to
6. could
7. could/was able to
8. couldn't/wasn't able to

Chart 7.5, page 188 — 10 min.

- **Note:** Write sentence starters on the board: *Being able to _____ was very helpful to ____, I want to be able to _____, Students should be able to _____*. Have students complete the sentences with their own ideas and then share in pairs.

6 page 188 — 5 min.

1. to be able to; being able to
2. to be able to; Being able to
3. be able to; being able to; to be able to; to be able to
4. being able to; being able to

- **Expansion Tip:** Have students write their own description of an alternative travel idea using several forms of *be able to*. Call on students to share their ideas with the class.

PRACTICE

7 page 188 — 5 min.

- **Tip:** Before students do exercise 7, have them look at the photo on page 189. Ask them what people have to be able to do if they stay in the cave houses, and what they might be able to do.

1. were able to
2. was able to
3. were able to
4. being able to
5. weren't able to
6. be able to
7. will be able
8. to be able to

8 ANALYZE THE GRAMMAR, page 189 — 5 min.

1. Being able to ride in a hot-air balloon was the best part of my trip to Turkey. *(NC)*
2. You <u>are able to</u> see so many things when you go up in a hot-air balloon. *(can)*
3. I <u>was able to</u> see dozens of caves from the air, and they were beautiful. *(could)*
4. We <u>were able to</u> take a lot of great pictures from the balloon. *(could)*
5. My sister <u>wasn't able to</u> come with us on the balloon ride because she was sick. *(couldn't)*
6. If my sister visits Turkey again, she <u>will be able to</u> go up in a balloon. *(NC)*

9 page 190 — 10 min.

- **Tip:** Bring in a photo of "castellers," or the people who build human towers/castles. If you can't find a photo, draw stick figures in a human tower on the board. Teams of 100 to 500 people form the tower, which will have six to ten tiers of participants. When students have finished exercise 9, have them close their books and form pairs to practice asking and answering questions about the information.

1. have been able to
2. can/are able to
3. to be able to
4. can/are able to
5. be able to
6. can't/aren't able to
7. was able to
8. will be able to
9. Being able to
10. couldn't/weren't able to

10 APPLY, page 190 — 20 min.

Answers will vary.

UNIT 7 LESSON 2

LESSON 3	**Advice, Regret, and Criticism**
Student Learning Outcomes	• **Read** a web page about working on an organic farm as an adventure. • **Complete** sentences with modals of advice. • **Talk** about personal regrets. • **Listen** to a conversation. • **Find** and **edit** errors with *should*, *ought to*, and *had better*. • **Write** and **talk** about ways travel impacts the environment.
Lesson Vocabulary	(n.) criticism (phr. v.) pick up (n.) regret (idiom) rough it (adj.) sore (adj.) organic (adv.) rarely (n.) reservation (n.) seedling (n.) weed

EXPLORE

1 READ, page 191   15 min.

- Have students look at the photo. Ask them to describe what they see. Use the photo to teach the meaning of *planting* and *organic farm*. When students read, have them use context cues to figure out the meanings of *seedling*, *weed*, and *rough it*, and then check their ideas with the glossary at the end of the text.
- Ask students if they would like to try this experience. Why, or why not?

Be the Expert

- WWOOF is the acronym for *World Wide Opportunities on Organic Farms* or *Willing Workers on Organic Farms*. Most WWOOF visits are one to two weeks, but some can be just a couple days or as long as six months. Participants are usually expected to work four to six hours per day in exchange for meals and lodging. Some of the tasks they do include making compost, gardening, planting, cutting wood, weeding, harvesting, packing food in boxes, milking, and making cheese and bread. Anyone with a farm, garden, vineyard, or woodland that follows organic and sustainable practices can apply to host a WWOOFer.
- Sue Coppard, a British secretary, started the organization in the UK in 1971. Today more than 50 groups worldwide participate in a WWOOF federation.

2 CHECK, page 192   5 min.

- **Tip:** Before students complete exercise **2**, have them look at the photo and read the caption.

1. Through WWOOF, you can ~~work for money~~ volunteer at an organic farm.

2. Angie was not in great shape when she went to Greece.

3. Michio came from a ~~village~~ city in Japan to work on a farm in Argentina.

4. Marie ~~didn't get used~~ got used to her accommodations in Ireland.

3 DISCOVER, page 192   5 min.

A   1. b   2. a   3. a   4. b

B   1. a, c   2. b

LEARN

Chart 7.6, page 193   10 min.

- **Notes 1 & 2:** Write the sentences from the chart on the board. Call on students to say or write them with other modals in the chart. Then, have students identify which sentences express stronger advice.
- **Note 3:** Point out that we also do not use *had better* or *had better not* in questions. Have students rewrite the sentences in the chart in the negative and as questions, using modals or expressions with the same meaning. Remind students that they will not be able to use some of the expressions. For example, for the sentence, *You ought to buy your tickets online*, students can write *You shouldn't / I'd better not buy your tickets online*, and *Should you buy your tickets online?* Variations with *had better (not)* aren't possible. Have students write sentences on the board and correct any errors.
- **Note 4:** Elicit other examples of what students should and shouldn't be doing now. Encourage them to use all the modals of advice.

68   MODALS: PART 1

4 page 193   10 min.

A 1. should do/ought to do

2. Should we offer
3. should keep/ought to keep
4. shouldn't work
5. should get/ought to get
6. should tell/ought to tell
7. shouldn't pick
8. Should we ask

B ANALYZE THE GRAMMAR, page 194

3, 4, 5, 7

5 page 194   5 min.

- **Tip:** Before students complete exercise **5**, have them look at the photo. Ask them where they think this place is.

1. shouldn't be wearing
2. should be wearing
3. ought to be working
4. had better be feeding
5. should be having
6. should be getting
7. ought to be walking
8. shouldn't be taking

Chart 7.7, page 195   10 min.

- **Notes:** To focus on form, write the example sentences on the board with the words in scrambled order. With books closed, ask volunteers to come to the board and put them in the correct order. Then, focus on meaning by asking about what actually happened. (e.g., *Did the speaker buy the tickets online? Did the speaker stay up late last night?*)

6 page 195–196

A 1. should have taken; shouldn't have left

2. shouldn't have kept; should have put
3. shouldn't have drunk; should have bought
4. shouldn't have packed; should have taken
5. shouldn't have taken; should have gone

B 1. Should Carlos have left his bag on the seat?

2. What should Carlos have done with his bag?
3. Should Anna have kept the copy and the passport together?
4. Who should Anna have notified about the lost passport?
5. Should Jake have thrown away some of his belongings?
6. What should Jake have brought with him on his trip?
7. Should Ira and Gina have taken photos of the crowd?
8. Where should they have gone when they saw the crowd?

C SPEAK, page 196

Answers may vary. Possible answers:

1. No, he shouldn't have.
2. He should have taken it with him.
3. No, she shouldn't have.
4. She should have notified the embassy.
5. Yes, he should have.
6. He should have brought cash.
7. No, they shouldn't have.
8. They should have gone back to the hotel.

PRACTICE

7 page 196–197   5 min.

1. ought to try   6. shouldn't have spent
2. shouldn't expect   7. had better make
3. shouldn't miss   8. ought to practice
4. should have stayed   9. should have practiced
5. should have spent   10. shouldn't have folded

- **Expansion Tip:** After exercise **7**, have students work in pairs to take turns asking and answering questions about the conversation.

8 PRONUNCIATION, page 197   5 min.

A 1. shouldn't have   5. should have

2. should have   6. should have
3. shouldn't have   7. should have
4. shouldn't have   8. shouldn't have

B *Answers will vary.*

- **Alternative Speaking:** Have students work in pairs to talk about people in the news and the mistakes they made. Tell them to use *should have* and *shouldn't have* to give their opinion about what the person did.

UNIT 7 LESSON 3

9 WRITE & SPEAK, page 198 — 10 min.

- **Tip:** Have students look at the photo. Ask them to describe the scene. To recycle modals of advice, ask students to give advice about a visit to the *suq* (the market). (e.g., *You should dress modestly.*)

A 1. We shouldn't have left the suq

2. The snake charmer shouldn't have given
3. We shouldn't have taken pictures
4. I shouldn't have told him
5. We should have asked
6. We should have gotten
7. We shouldn't have walked around the walls
8. We should have stopped and listened

10 LISTEN, page 199 — 5 min.

1. √
2. X
3. X
4. X
5. √
6. X

11 EDIT, page 199 — 5 min.

The message of your recent blogs has been that we ~~have~~ had better limit our traveling because it is bad for the planet. Yes, travel has negative effects on the environment, but people should ~~be~~ know about the positive effects as well. You should have ~~spend~~ spent some time discussing the benefits of travel. People should ~~to~~ realize that the income from tourism helps local economies.

We had ~~not~~ better not forget that without foreign money it is hard for some countries to build airports, roads, bridges, schools, and hospitals. All these things are very important, so tourists had better ~~to~~ keep visiting these countries and bringing their money with them! I believe we should be thinking about the cultural benefits of tourism, too. When tourists are interested in another culture, it can encourage a sense of pride and identity in that culture. That's very important, so I think you ~~ought to~~ should have mentioned that as well.

12 APPLY, page 199 — 15 min.

Answers will vary.

- **Alternative Writing:** Have students write sentences about a recent travel experience that did not go well and use *should/shouldn't have* + past participle to describe the mistakes they made.

70 MODALS: PART 1

UNIT 7 Review the Grammar

1 page 200   5 min.

 1. was supposed to
 2. wasn't able to
 3. were supposed to
 4. should have booked
 5. had to walk
 6. was able to
 7. didn't have to pay
 8. was supposed to
 9. shouldn't have gone
 10. had to; shouldn't

2 page 200–203   20 min.

A
 1. shouldn't miss
 2. should visit/can visit
 3. have to buy
 4. can see
 5. haven't been able to get
 6. isn't supposed to open
 7. have to have
 8. have to go
 9. can see
 10. don't have to spend
 11. didn't have to wait

B *Answers will vary.*

C
 1. have to make/'re supposed to make/should make
 2. should have turned
 3. 'd better ask/should
 4. should have brought
 5. aren't supposed to eat
 6. should find

3 EDIT, page 203   5 min.

Friends are always telling me that I should ~~taking~~ take a trip abroad. "You can learn so much. You will be able to have new experiences," they say. "You had better ~~to~~ travel before you get married and have a family. When you have a family, you ~~can't~~ won't be able to afford to travel so easily." I'm sure it's wonderful to go abroad, but I think people are able to learn a lot and have new experiences right at home. When I'm on vacation, I enjoy ~~be~~ being able to see all the exciting things right in my hometown. I ~~should not~~ don't have to go abroad to visit a great museum. There's a great museum ten miles from my home. I went there yesterday. I ~~could go~~ was able to go for free. I had a wonderful time. I also don't have to go far to hear good music. I could enjoy the performances at our great concert hall. In fact, I ought to go there more often. No, traveling isn't for me. At the end of the day, I want to be able to sleep in my own bed. I think all of my friends should ~~had~~ have stayed in town for their last vacation like I did. I had a terrific time, and I ~~must not~~ didn't have to spend as much money as my friends did.

4 SPEAK, page 203   20 min.

Answers will vary.

Connect the Grammar to Writing

1 READ & NOTICE THE GRAMMAR,
page 204   20 min.

B *Answers will vary. Possible answers.*

1. are supposed to tip, are supposed to offer, are supposed to tip
2. don't have to tip
3. ought to hand, should probably offer

C Hotels

Rule: tip the concierge $10–$20

Bonus: leave something extra for cleaning staff; give people who carry your bags $1–$2 per bag

Taxis

Rule: tip 15–20 percent

Bonus: if driver helps you with your bags, offer him a few dollars extra

2 BEFORE YOU WRITE, page 205   15 min.

Answers will vary.

3 WRITE, page 205   15 min.

> **WRITING FOCUS, page 205**
>
> Ask students to look at the subsections on page 204. Elicit the pattern the writer uses (they are all nouns, places where people tip). Write three possible subsections on the board related to a social norm. For example, on the topic of arriving on time, you could write: *Social Events, Going to Work, When You Have an Appointment.* Ask students to make the subtopics on the board follow the same pattern. Then, have them look at their charts from exercise **1B** and correct the subtopic names if necessary.

- **Alternative Writing:** Have students write about social norms in one of these places or communities: a social media site, a gym, an airplane.

72 MODALS: PART 1

UNIT 8 Our Mysterious World

Modals: Part 2

Unit Opener

Photo: Have students look at the photo. Ask: *What do you see? Where is this? What do you think happened to the people who built these statues?*

Location: Mount Nemrut is a UNESCO World Heritage Site (a site that UNESCO has deemed to be of special cultural or physical interest) in southeastern Turkey. It is famous for the many large statues at the summit that are believed to surround a royal tomb. King Antiochus had the statues erected. They represent eagles, lions, and ancient Greek, Armenian, and Iranian gods. At some point, their heads were removed from the seated bodies and their faces deliberately damaged.

Theme: This unit is about mysterious and unusual things. It provides information on mysterious weather events, the Emperor's Terra Cotta Army in China, and a colony in the United States that disappeared.

Page	Lesson	Grammar	Examples
208	1	Possibility and Logical Conclusion: Present and Future	The exam **could last** two hours. I'm not sure. That **couldn't be** Bill over there. Bill is much shorter. She just got a promotion at work. She **must be** happy.
216	2	Possibility and Logical Conclusion: Past	Pam **might have been** sick. Alex **could not have stolen** the money. She **must have loved** art. She **couldn't have been lying**.
229	**Review the Grammar**		
232	**Connect the Grammar to Writing**		

Unit Grammar Terms

modal: an auxiliary verb that adds a degree of certainty, possibility, or time to a verb. *May, might, can, could, will, would, should* are common modals.
➤ It **might rain** tomorrow.
➤ He **must have stolen** the money.
➤ He **could be joking.**

73

LESSON 1	**Possibility and Logical Conclusion: Present and Future**
Student Learning Outcomes	• **Read** a conversation about mysterious weather events. • **Write** statements about possibilities and conclusions using modals. • **Identify** and **use** modals of possibility and logical conclusion. • **Listen** to sounds and make logical conclusions about them. • **Discuss** a photo.
Lesson Vocabulary	(n.) colony (v.) discourage (v.) forecast (adj.) logical (n.) scene (n.) confusion (phr. v.) figure out (n.) funding (n.) observation (n.) vibration

EXPLORE

1 READ, page 208   15 min.

- Elicit examples of strange or unusual weather events that students know about.
- Have students use context to guess the meaning of new words (e.g., *mysterious, scene, waterspout, theory, updraft*).

Be the Expert

- Pliny the Elder first recorded the phenomenon of raining frogs in the first century AD. Since 2000 AD, frogs have fallen from the sky in Hungary, Great Britain, and Serbia. They may have been picked up by waterspouts (tornados that form over water and travel over land) and dropped some distance away. Wind from a waterspout can reach up to 200 mph, so they have a lot of force. Other things have fallen from the sky, including fish, worms, and squid.
- Suggest to students to research and report their findings to the class about other mysterious weather events such as ball lightning, red sprites, blue jets, water devils, dust devils, St. Elmo's fire, and ice balls.

2 CHECK, page 209   5 min.

1. Many people said that they saw ~~lizards~~ **frogs** fall from the sky.
2. Some ~~biologists~~ **climate scientists** have tried to explain frog rain.
3. A ~~snowstorm~~ **waterspout** is a possible reason for frog rain.
4. Strong winds can transport frogs ~~short~~ **long** distances.
5. Scientists ~~agree~~ **disagree** about about the causes of frog rainfall.

3 DISCOVER, page 209   5 min.

A   1. (can't) be   4. (may) not be

2. (must) mean   5. (might) be

3. (could) be

B   **Very Certain:** can't

Not Certain: could, might, may not

Almost Certain: must

- **Tip:** As you go over the answers to exercise **B**, have students look at Note 1 of Chart 8.1.

LEARN

Chart 8.1, page 210   10 min.

- **Note 1:** Point out that *could, may, might, may not,* and *might not* all express a low level of certainty that something is possible. *Couldn't* and *can't* express high levels of certainty that something is NOT possible. Provide sentences using each modal. From the class, elicit follow-up sentences similar to the ones in the chart. *It might rain today. The sky looks pretty dark. That couldn't be Jack. He's in Paris this week.*

4 page 210–211   5 min.

1. might be/may be/could be
2. can't be/couldn't be
3. might snow/may snow/could snow
4. could see
5. may not have/might not have
6. could; be
7. couldn't be/can't be

- **Tip:** Have students write three original sentences similar to those in exercise **4**. Then, have them exchange papers with a partner and rewrite their partner's sentences using different modals of possibility.

74   MODALS: PART 2

Chart 8.2, page 211 — 5 min.

- **Tip:** Draw a line on the board. On one side, write: *Very certain it is true or will be true.* On the other side, write: *Very certain it is not true or will not be true.* Then, write these sentences along the continuum to show degrees of certainty. *She is sick . . . She isn't sick.* Provide pairs of sentences and elicit which is more sure, e.g., *She must be sick* and *She might be sick*.

5 page 211-212 — 5 min.

A
1. must
2. must
3. must not
4. must
5. must
6. must not
7. must not
8. must

- **Tip:** Have students look at the photo. Ask them to describe what they see. Provide this information: *In 2006, American and European beekeepers started noticing a strange and worrying trend—their bees were disappearing.*

B 1, 2, 5, 7, 8

> **REAL ENGLISH, page 212**
>
> Have students work in pairs to create a conversation in which they use *may*, *might*, and *could* to talk about the chances of something happening. Ask volunteers to present their conversations to the class. Have the class provide feedback on appropriate usage of modals.

6 ANALYZE THE GRAMMAR, page 212 — 10 min.

- **Tip:** Review modals of obligation and prohibition from Unit 7.

  1. O
  2. P
  3. LC
  4. O
  5. P
  6. LC
  7. LC
  8. LC

- **Expansion Tip:** Have students work in pairs to write sentences using *must/must not* for logical conclusion, obligation, and prohibition. Call on students to read their sentences aloud. Elicit how each is used.

Chart 8.3, page 213 — 10 min.

- **Notes:** Have students close their books and listen to you say sentences with modal + *be* + verb + *-ing*. Have them raise their right hands if they think the sentence is a guess or conclusion and their left hands if it is about a possible future plan. Read the sentences from the chart and notes, or use your own ideas.

7 page 213-214 — 5 min.

1. must be studying
2. may be describing
3. might be complaining
4. could be recording
5. must be keeping
6. must not be bothering
7. couldn't be counting
8. might not be driving

PRACTICE

8 page 214 — 5 min.

1. might be
2. can't
3. may
4. could
5. must
6. may not
7. could
8. could
9. may not

- **Expansion Tip:** Have students work individually to write comprehension questions about the information in exercise **8**, and then ask and answer the questions in pairs.

9 page 214-215 — 5 min.

- **Tip:** Before students look at exercise **9**, read the headlines aloud or write them on the board. Elicit students' reactions. Then, ask them to speculate or draw conclusions about each situation.

  1. must like; must not think
  2. must be joking
  3. can't be
  4. might be
  5. might explain
  6. must love

10 LISTEN & SPEAK, page 215 — 5 min.

Answers will vary.

- **Alternative Speaking:** Bring in photos or objects that might show something unfamiliar to students (e.g., tools, artifacts). Have them work in pairs to discuss what the things are used for.

11 APPLY, page 215 — 5 min.

A *Answers will vary.*

UNIT 8 LESSON 1 75

LESSON 2 — Possibility and Logical Conclusion: Past

Student Learning Outcomes
- **Read** an article about an interesting archaeological discovery.
- **Complete** conversations with past modals of possibility and logical conclusions.
- **Answer** questions using past progressive forms of modals.
- **Pronounce** reduced forms of past modals.
- **Listen** for specific information.
- **Talk** about the reasons for place names.

Lesson Vocabulary

| (v.) colonist | (n.) exhibit | (n.) finding | (n.) mural | (n.) tomb |
| (n.) craftsman | (n.) feature | (n.) mold | (n.) mass production | (n.) weapon |

EXPLORE

1 READ, page 216 — 15 min.
- Have students look at the photo. Elicit descriptions of the sculptures.
- Use the photo to teach the meaning of *terra cotta*, *unique*, and *individual*.

Be the Expert
- Ying Zheng took the throne in 246 BC at the age of 13. By 221 BC he had unified warring kingdoms and became the First Emperor of Qin. During his rule, Qin standardized coins, weights, and measures; linked the states with canals and roads, and built the first version of the Great Wall.
- More than 700,000 laborers worked on the mausoleum and terra cotta army. Students can find out more on the Internet by using search terms such as "terra cotta army."

- **Tip:** After students read the article, have them write three *why* questions to ask and answer with a partner. This will get them thinking about the grammar.

2 CHECK, page 217 — 5 min.

1. F   2. T   3. F   4. T   5. F

3 DISCOVER, page 217 — 5 min.

A
1. must have wanted
2. must have been
3. could; have produced
4. may have used
5. must have added
6. might have wanted

B 1. 1, 2, 5   2. 3, 4, 6

- **Tip:** Go over the information in Chart 8.4 when you answer 1 in exercise **B**.

LEARN

Chart 8.4, page 218 — 10 min.
- **Notes 1 & 2:** After going over the notes, have students look at the sentences in the chart. Elicit other modals that can be used without changing the meaning.

4 page 218–219 — 5 min.

A
1. could the ancient artists have created
2. they could have asked
3. the artist couldn't have done
4. Could the artist have been
5. The artist could have painted
6. could people not have known
7. No one could have noticed
8. the emperor could have wanted

B ANALYZE THE GRAMMAR, page 219

In the negative statements and/or questions (items 1, 3, 4, 6), you can't replace *could* with *may* or *might*.

5 page 219–220 — 5 min.

1. couldn't have made
2. might not have heard
3. might not have liked
4. couldn't have left; might not have left
5. couldn't have seen

Chart 8.5, page 220 — 10 min.
- **Note:** After going over the chart, write sentences with *may/might/could have* + past participle and *must have/had to have* + past participle on the board. Put them in random order. Have students identify how confident the speaker/writer is in each sentence. For example, *I must have left my phone on.* (Quite confident.)

76   MODALS: PART 2

6 page 220–221 10 min.

1. must have studied
2. must have left
3. must not have prepared
4. must not have spent
5. must have made
6. must have completed
7. must have been
8. must not have discovered
9. must not have drunk
10. must have decided

7 page 221 10 min.

1. Your job must have been
2. Did you have to go
3. I didn't have to have
4. Did you have to work
5. it must have been
6. I must have spent
7. I had to analyze
8. work must have been

Chart 8.6, page 222 10 min.

- **Tip:** Write each part of the verb structure in a different color on the board. Point out that each has four to five parts.

8 page 222–223 10 min.

1. Yes, no one could have been touring the site after 5:00.
2. They must have been watching the site for several days.
3. He might not have been paying attention.
4. They could have been planning the theft for months.
5. They might have been planning to return for more things later.
6. They must have been having trouble finding the site.
7. The looters may have been hiding in a secret cave.
8. They must have been waiting all night for the looters to come out.

- **Tip:** Have students identify which sentences can be written with other modals and practice saying them in another way.

PRACTICE

9 page 223–224 5 min.

A Vasari

B
1. may/might/could have destroyed
2. couldn't have removed
3. may/might/could have painted
4. must have wanted
5. may/might/could have built
6. could not have stolen
7. must have
8. must not have wanted

10 PRONUNCIATION, page 224 15 min.

A LISTEN

1. may have
2. might have
3. could have
4. must have
5. may have
6. may not have
7. might not have
8. couldn't have

B SPEAK

Answers will vary.

11 page 225 15 min.

It was a strange crime. One night, a man climbed into a 5000-gallon fish tank. He must have ~~be~~ been crazy! The fish were halibut, and he wanted to steal them. He must not have ~~know~~ known how to catch fish properly because he attacked them with a heavy piece of metal. The tank became a mess. The man must not have cleaned up the area because he left a trail of evidence that led the police to his house. The police were looking for the most important fish that was stolen—a 50-pound halibut. She ~~may~~ must have been a well-loved fish because everyone called her "Big Mamma." Unfortunately, the police never found Big Mamma because she had been eaten at a dinner party at the man's house. The people at the party were shocked. They could not have ~~know~~ known that they were eating Big Mamma at the time. Those guests must have been very angry because they spoke against the man at his court trial. The court gave the man a sentence of four years in prison. He offered to catch a new halibut to replace Big Mamma. He was a diver and surfer, so it's possible he could have had caught another big fish. The court said thanks, but no thanks.

12 SPEAK & WRITE, page 226 5 min.

- **Tip:** John White was a colonist, artist and mapmaker. He made drawings of the land and the Native Americans.

A Answers will vary.
B Answers will vary.

13 LISTEN, page 227 15 min.

14 APPLY, page 228 10 min.

1. b
2. b
3. b
4. a
5. a

Answers will vary.

- **Alternate Speaking:** Elicit examples of common mysterious past events, such as *the building of the pyramids, Stonehenge, the Nazca Lines, Atlantis, the Bermuda Triangle*. Put students in groups to share their ideas about the mysteries.

UNIT 8 LESSON 2 77

Review the Grammar UNIT 8

1 page 229   5 min.

  1. must be
  2. might fall/may fall/could fall
  3. must have bothered
  4. must have been
  5. couldn't have done
  6. couldn't have succeeded

2 page 230   5 min.

  1. must be
  2. may have gotten/might have gotten/could have gotten
  3. must be
  4. could she have failed
  5. might not have heard/may not have heard
  6. couldn't have stolen

3 LISTEN, page 230   20 min.

  A *Answers will vary.*
  B 1. F   4. T
     2. T   5. F
     3. T   6. T

4 EDIT, page 231   10 min.

People sometimes believe in strange things. Some people believed that the Maya predicted the end of the world in 2012. They must ~~be~~ have been surprised when the world did not end. In fact, the Maya never made such a prediction. Other people used to believe in the existence of the Loch Ness Monster. They may have ~~saw~~ seen a photo of an odd creature in the water. The picture taken many years ago, looked real, so they thought the monster must have existed. But there ~~must not~~ could be another explanation. In fact, the Scottish doctor who took a famous photo of the creature said that it wasn't a monster. It was just an animal he didn't recognize. Now some people have a new theory: the Loch Ness Monster may have died because of global warming!

Some people also believe in crop circles. They think the circles may contain messages from aliens. The circles first appeared in England in the 1970s. In 1991, two Englishmen announced that they had made some of the circles. However, that announcement didn't stop people from believing that aliens had made them. The believers say that the men ~~maybe~~ may have made the crop circles in England, but they could not have made all the other circles in Europe, Australia, North America, and Japan.

So, the mystery is not why strange events happen. The mystery is really why people believe that such events happen, even when there is evidence that they didn't.

6 SPEAK, page 231   15 min.

Answers will vary.

78 MODALS: PART 2

Connect the Grammar to Writing

1 READ & NOTICE THE GRAMMAR,
page 232   20 min

B *Answers may vary. Possible examples:*

I <u>must have been</u> about ten years old.

I <u>must have forgotten</u> to tell my grandmother.

. . .<u>couldn't have been</u>

Something <u>could have happened</u> to you.

You <u>must have</u> some of my great-uncle's blood. He couldn't have been much older than I am now. . .

. . .he may have gone on ten different expeditions..

He might have seen tribes. . .

Bruno had to have been one of the most adventurous people in Brazil. . .

C

What the author knows for sure	What the author guesses
He has a distant relative who was an explorer.	Bruno must have been very brave.
The author went on an expedition.	The author must have forgotten to tell his grandmother.
His grandmother was worried.	The author couldn't have been away for more than three hours.
Bruno knew Candido Rondon and went on an expedition to Mato Grasso with him. They ran out of supplies and nearly died on the expedition.	Something could have happened to the author.
	The author must have some of his great-uncle's blood in him.
Bruno never married and died young.	Bruno couldn't have been very old when he went on his first expedition.
The author is proud that Bruno was part of his family.	Bruno may have gone on ten different expeditions.
	Bruno might have seen tribes that had never met outsiders before.
	Bruno had to have been very adventurous.

2 BEFORE YOU WRITE, page 233   15 min.

Answers will vary.

3 WRITE, page 233   15 min.

> **WRITING FOCUS, page 233**
>
> Write sentences on the board about the relative you talked about in exercise **1A** or someone fictional. For example:
>   *Katniss Everdeen knows how to hunt.*
>   *The people in her district are poor.*
>   *The capital is not poor.*
> Have students work in pairs to write follow-up sentences that begin with the phrase *in fact*.
> (In fact, she is an expert with a bow. In fact, they don't have enough food to eat. In fact, the people in the capital eat wonderful food and wear fancy costumes.)

- **Alternative Writing:** Have students write about a topic in the news, such as a famous crime, a natural disaster, or a new discovery. Have them explain what they already know about the topic and what may or must have happened in that situation.

UNIT 8 CONNECT THE GRAMMAR TO WRITING 79

UNIT 9 The Natural World

The Passive

Unit Opener

Photo: Have students look at the photo. Ask, *What do you see? What kind of animal is this? Where is it?*

Location: The divers are exploring sealife in Great Lameshur Bay, Saint John, U.S. Virgin Islands. The first nationally sponsored underwater research program was launched here. In 1969, four aquanauts lived for 58 days in Tektite, a capsule at the bottom of Great Lameshure Bay.

Theme: This unit is about the natural world. It includes information about an oceanographer, night gardens, and hurricane hunters. Have students look at the photos and titles on pages 236, 246, and 254. Ask: *How do these photos relate to the theme?*

Page	Lesson	Grammar	Examples
236	1	The Passive; Passive with Modals	Everyone's picture **was taken**. The dog **should be walked**.
246	2	Using the Passive	The problem **was solved**. The damage **was caused** by high winds.
254	3	Passive Gerunds and Infinitives; *Get* Passives	I don't like **being given** extra work. I'm worried about **getting fired**. I tried **not to be caught** in the storm. He **got punished** for staying out too late. Have you ever **gotten stung** by a bee?
261	Review the Grammar		
264	Connect the Grammar to Writing		

Unit Grammar Terms

active voice: a sentence in which the subject performs the action of the verb. See *passive voice*.
➤ *Michael **ate** the hamburger.*

gerund: an *-ing* verb form that is used as a noun. It can be the subject of a sentence or the object of a verb or preposition.
➤ ***Surfing** is a popular sport.*
➤ *We enjoy **swimming**.*

infinitive: *to* + the base form of a verb.
➤ *He wants **to see** the new movie.*

modal: an auxiliary verb that adds a degree of certainty, possibility, or time to a verb. *May, might, can, could, will, would, should* are common modals.
➤ *You **should** eat more vegetables.*
➤ *Julie **can** speak three languages.*

passive voice: a verb form that expresses who or what receives the action of the verb, not who or what performs the action.
➤ *My wallet **has been stolen**.*

80

LESSON 1	The Passive; Passive with Modals
Student Learning Outcomes	• **Read** an article about an oceanographer. • **Complete** sentences with passive and passive forms of modals. • **Write** sentences using the passive. • **Find** and **edit** errors with passives. • **Listen** to a tour guide talk about a cruise. • **Speak** about environmental problems.
Lesson Vocabulary	(n.) commitment (n.) cycle (n.) food chain (n.) nature preserve (v.) regulate (v.) conserve (adj.) delicate (v.) generate (n.) organism (adj.) rapid

EXPLORE

1 READ, page 236   15 min.

- Use the photo to review vocabulary such as *air tank*, *mask*, and *oxygen*.
- Have students use context to guess the meaning of new words (e.g., *fascinated, oceanographer, ecosystems, cycles, regulate, food chains, organisms, dump*).

Be the Expert

- Oceanographers study a wide variety of topics related to the ocean, including ocean circulation, the geology of the sea bottom, marine life and ecosystems, and the chemical and physical properties of the ocean.
- Sylvia Earle focuses on the part of oceanography that deals with marine life and ecosystems. She was the first female chief scientist at the U.S. National Oceanic and Atmospheric Administration. She is often called in to consult on oil spill disasters.

2 CHECK, page 237   5 min.

1. F   2. T   3. F   4. T   5. F

- **Tip:** Have students identify where they found the answers to the exercise.

3 DISCOVER, page 237–238   5 min.

A
1. was
2. are
3. are
4. could be
5. are being
6. must be

B

Simple Present Passive	Simple Past Passive	Present Progressive Passive	Passive with Modal
2	1	5	4
3			6

LEARN

Chart 9.1, page 238   10 min.

- **Tip:** Write the sentences from the top chart on the board. Use one color for the subject, one for the verb, and one for the object in the active sentence. Use the same color for the object in the active sentence as you do for the subject in the passive sentence. The use of colors will highlight the relationship of the nouns to the verb (agent/performer vs. receiver). Circle *eat* and *are* to show that both verbs are in simple present.

4 pages 238–239   5 min.

  __P__ 1. During the expedition, Sylvia Earle's instructions were followed by the team.

  __P__ 2. Most of our oxygen on Earth is generated by the ocean.

  __A__ 3. The changes in the ocean ecosystem affect all of us.

  __A__ 4. Nearly half of the world's coral reefs have disappeared.

  __P__ 5. The sea around the Galápagos Islands is being polluted by boats.

  __P__ 6. In the last 50 years, more than 90 percent of the big fish in the sea have been eaten.

  __A__ 7. Many sea creatures have been dying from water pollution.

  __P__ 8. Action is being taken to protect the California and Oregon coasts.

__P__ 9. An area of Antarctica is protected by scientists and international governments.

__A__ 10. The efforts of researchers have increased public awareness of our ecosystem.

5 page 239   5 min.

1. We protect about 12 percent of the land on Earth in some way.

    About 12 percent of the land of the Earth is protected in some way.

2. Local officials are considering new guidelines for beach preservation.

    New guidelines are being considered for beach preservation.

3. The mayor has created a nature preserve near the river.

    A nature preserve has been created near the river.

4. Were guides giving tours yesterday at the nature preserve?

    Tours were being given at the nature preserve.

5. Villagers have cut down all the trees in that forest.

    Have all the trees been cut down in that forest?

6. Did swimmers see dolphins near the beach?

    Were dolphins seen near the beach?

7. Is the Parks Department protecting the birds on the island?

    Are the birds being protected on the island?

8. Volunteers cleaned up the trash on the riverbank.

    Did the volunteers clean up the trash?

9. Fishermen catch tens of thousands of fish everyday.

    Tens of thousands of fish are caught everyday.

10. Has anyone reported the environmental problems to governmental officials?

    Have the environmental problems been reported to the government officials?

Chart 9.2, page 240   5 min.

6 page 240   5 min.

1. must not be disturbed
2. should be followed
3. can be found
4. are going to be posted
5. will be turned on
6. should only be taken
7. might be understood
8. will be saved

PRACTICE

7 page 241   5 min.

1. has been shaped
2. is drying up
3. is used
4. are using
5. can be seen
6. have not survived
7. is also harming
8. may be reduced
9. could be done
10. should be conserved

8 pages 241–242   5 min.

- **Tip:** Have students look at the photo before doing exercise **A**. Elicit what they know about sharks.

A
1. are killed
2. are attacked
3. was the megamouth shark discovered
4. are threatened
5. is sold
6. is shark-fin soup eaten
7. is shark-fin soup served
8. can sharks be protected

B page 243

1. Researchers say that at least 60 million sharks are killed each year. Many estimate that the number is much higher, possibly well over 200 million sharks per year.
2. Fewer than 100 people are attacked by sharks each year.
3. The megamouth shark was discovered in 1976.
4. More than 100 shark species are threatened by human activity.
5. The fins are sold for food.
6. Shark-fin soup is most popular in Asia.
7. Shark-fin soup is often served at weddings.
8. Sharks can be protected if people stop hunting them.

- **Alternative Speaking:** Have students talk in pairs about a food or product they know well using the passive. Write these questions on the board to prompt students: *Where is it grown/made? What is it used for? When is it eaten/used? How can it be prepared? What can be done to improve it?*

9 page 242–243   5 min.

A baobabs, lemurs, chameleons, ground rollers (birds), Harlequin mantella frogs

B
1. Madagascar is located off the coast of Africa.
2. Baobab trees and lemurs are found in Madagascar.
3. A few areas of Madagascar are protected by the government.
4. Most of the island is not protected.
5. Many of Madagascar's plants and animals live in small, unprotected areas.
6. Many of these plants and animals are endangered.
7. A lot of the rainforest areas in Madagascar are being destroyed./ A lot of the rainforest areas in Madagascar have been destroyed.
8. Some rainforest areas are being preserved. / Some rainforest areas have been preserved.
9. Every year, more and more trees are being cut down./Every year, more and more trees are cut down.
10. The rainforest in Madagascar should be protected to save endangered species.

- **Expansion Tip:** Have students use the sentences about Madagascar as models to write at least five sentences about endangered species in a place they know well.

10 LISTEN, page 244   10 min.

1. b	4. b	7. a
2. b	5. b	8. b
3. a	6. b	

11 EDIT, page 245   5 min.

Construction on the Three Gorges Dam on the Yangtze River began in 1994. It was completed in 2012. The dam is considered a great success because it has had some positive effects on the environment. In the past, a lot of coal is was used for energy. Now the dam generates water power, and the need for coal has been reduced by the dam. This means that there is less carbon dioxide in the air. Unfortunately, there have also been some negative effects. Many places were flooded because of the dam. Over a million people had to being be moved. Also, the dam is located in a region with many plants and animals. Many plant species in this region have being been harmed by the dam. More could be harmed in the future. The dam has also caused changes to the temperature and increased the amount of pollution in the water. This has been threatened the freshwater fish in the area. Changes should been made should be made to improve the environmental situation soon. Authorities have promised to make these changes.

12 APPLY, page 245   20 min.

A Answers will vary.
B Answers will vary.
C Answers will vary.

- **Expansion Tip:** Have students make presentations on an environmental problem, its causes, and possible solutions.

UNIT 9 LESSON 1 83

LESSON 2	**Using the Passive**
Student Learning Outcomes	• **Read** an article about night gardens. • **Rewrite** sentences in the passive. • **Complete** sentences using the active and passive. • **Listen** to a conversation and identify its topic. • **Write** an imaginary news report using passive and active.
Lesson Vocabulary	(n.) ban (n.) cape (n.) fine (v.) pollinate (x.) scent (v.) bloom (n.) captivity (v.) glow (v.) propose (n.) tranquilizer

EXPLORE

1 READ, page 246 15 min.

- Have students look at the photo. Ask students to describe what they see. Use the photo to teach the meaning of *bloom* and *glow*.
- Have students use context clues as they read to guess the meaning of *transform*, *pollinate*, *nocturnal* and *fragrant*.

Be the Expert

- Most night-blooming flowers, including the moonflower, moon vine, and angel's trumpet have white or pale yellow flowers that are easy to see at night. Some of the cereus cacti only bloom for one night. There is a famous hedge of night-blooming cereus surrounding the Punahou School in Honolulu.
- Pollinators such as bees, birds, moths, and bats move the pollen from the male part of the plant to the female part of the plant. This allows the plant to reproduce.

- **Expansion Tip:** Have students work in pairs to write sentences using any unfamiliar words in the article. Call on students to read sentences aloud.

2 CHECK, page 247 5 min.

1. Flowers look ~~the same~~ different at night and during the day.
2. The colors of flowers change in ~~sunlight~~ moonlight.
3. ~~Bees~~ Bats and moths pollinate night bloomers.
4. Pollinators locate flowers that ~~are hard to see~~ glow in the dark.
5. Science ~~can~~ can't explain the effect that night gardens have on us.

3 DISCOVER, page 247 5 min.

A 1. At night, the colors of flowers <u>are transformed</u>.
2. They <u>are lit</u> by moonlight.
3. Night-bloomers <u>are pollinated</u> by bats and moths.
4. Their pollinators <u>are attracted</u> by scent as well as color.

B 1. X 2. A 3. A 4. A

C by

- **Tip:** To lead into Chart 9.3, ask: *In which questions is the agent important? Why is the agent not mentioned in sentence 1?*

LEARN

Chart 9.3, page 248 10 min.

- **Tip:** After you go over the notes, write other sentences on the board (e.g., *The Eiffel Tower is located in Paris. Corn is grown in Mexico. The mail is delivered at 3 p.m. His house was built in 1690. Mistakes were made.*). Elicit reasons why the passive was used and the agent omitted.

4 pages 248–249 5 min.

- **Tip:** Before students do the exercise, have them look at the photo of the goat on page 249. Ask: *What do you see? What is the goat wearing? Why do you think he is at the courthouse? Who is in the background?*

1. Flowers are loved for their beauty and scent.
2. In Australia, the golden wattle was chosen as national flower.
3. Wax flowers can be seen in Western Australia.
4. An unusual story was reported from Sydney, Australia.
5. A destroyed flowerbed was discovered outside a museum.
6. The museum's flowerbed had been eaten.

84 THE PASSIVE

7. Gary's owner was ordered to pay a fine.

8. Gary was brought to the courthouse for his trial.

Chart 9.4, page 249   10 min.

- **Notes:** Point out that it is also common to use a *by*-phrase when the agent is not human: *Forty people were killed by the tornado.*

- **Tip:** Ask students to look at the sentences in exercise **4**. Have them identify the sentences in which the agent is important *(6)*, is very general *(1, 2, 3)*, can be guessed from context *(4, 5, 7, 8)*.

5 page 249–250   10 min.

1. was written by Jack London
2. are picked
3. was released
4. is visited by millions of tourists
5. was stolen
6. will be given by the president of South Africa/is being given by the president of South Africa.
7. are eaten by birds
8. was destroyed by a forest fire

PRACTICE

6 page 250   5 min.

- **Tip:** Before students do exercise **6**, have them look at the photo at the bottom of the spread. Elicit what they know about South Africa, including any plants or animals that are native to it.

1. are threatened
2. was started
3. are posted
4. is endangered
5. has to be protected
6. has been reduced by terrible disease/is being reduced by terrible disease
7. has been damaged by deforestation/is being damaged by deforestation
8. are caught by wild-parrot traders/are being caught by wild-parrot traders
9. are sold

7 page 251   5 min.

1. is considered
2. is located
3. has been placed/ was placed
4. is called
5. is visited by
6. proposed
7. was completed
8. have taken
9. is also known
10. are named/ were named

8 page 252   10 min.

1. shouldn't be missed by tourists
2. have to turn
3. was discovered
4. was called
5. was renamed
6. bought
7. was built by
8. were told
9. can be found
10. can be seen

- **Expansion Tip:** Have students research another interesting place to visit. Suggest that they use these questions to guide their research: *Who discovered it or settled it first? What is important about this place? What is it known for? What products or crops are made and grown there? What sights do tourists visit there?* After the research is completed, have students write a paragraph using both active and passive verbs. Then have students exchange paragraphs with a partner to edit as necessary.

9 page 253   10 min.

1. is proposed/was proposed /has been proposed/is being proposed
2. was found/has been found
3. were observed
4. is being raised by a Brazilian family
5. are killed by cats
6. were caught/have been caught
7. was discovered by a repairman

- **Expansion Tip:** Bring in headlines or have students bring in headlines from newspapers or online news sources. Write the headlines on the board and have students write them in complete sentences using the passive.

10 APPLY, page 253   20 min.

A 7

B
1. was found
2. was not bitten by
3. was contacted
4. was chased
5. was caught
6. was released
7. was given

C Answers will vary.

- **Alternative Speaking:** After students write their news reports, have them give the reports in small groups. Have listeners take notes on the sentences that use the passive.

UNIT 9   LESSON 2   **85**

LESSON 3 Passive Gerunds and Infinitives; *Get* Passive

Student Learning Outcomes
- **Read** an article about hurricane hunters.
- **Complete** conversations with *get* passives.
- **Ask** and **answer** questions using the passive.
- **Understand** when to use passive gerunds, passive infinitives, and *get* passives.
- **Listen** to a conversation about a camping trip.
- **Find** and **edit** errors with passives.
- **Write** and **speak** about a photo using passives.

Lesson Vocabulary
| (n.) birdwatching | (v.) determine | (n.) exception | (n.) hurricane | (n.) limb |
| (n.) data | (v.) evacuate | (n.) humidity | (v.) issue | (n.) wetland |

EXPLORE

1 READ, page 254 15 min.

- Have students look at the photo. Ask them to describe what they see. Use the photo to teach the meaning of *hurricane*. Explain that the circular clouds show the eye of the hurricane. When students read, have them use context clues to figure out the meanings of *device, humidity, forecasters, evacuate,* and *considerable*.
- Ask students what kind of person they think might like to be a hurricane hunter.

Be the Expert

- Before satellites provided information about weather patterns, military airplanes would gather data about hurricanes. Although satellites can now tell us that hurricanes are forming, they cannot give information about barometric pressure (also called atmospheric or air pressure, which is the weight of the air pressing down on Earth) and wind speeds, so hurricane hunters are still needed. In the U.S., some hurricane hunters are military pilots, and others work for the National Oceanographic and Atmospheric Administration (NOAA).
- Hurricanes are rated by their wind speeds. There are five categories: 1. 74–95 mph (119–153 kph); 2. 96–110 mph (154–177 kph); 3. 111–129 mph (178–208 kph); 4. 130–156 mph (209–251 kph); and 5. ≥157 mph (≥252 kph). The highest recorded wind speed was over 200 mph (320 kph).

2 CHECK, page 254 5 min.

1. Hurricane hunters collect information when they fly through the calm eye of the storm.
2. A dropsonde checks humidity, temperature, and wind speed.
3. They want to find out the strength of a hurricane and where it is heading.
4. Weather forecasters consider the data and then issue warnings.

- **Tip:** Have students take turns asking and answering the questions in exercise **2** with a partner.

3 DISCOVER, page 255 5 min.

A 1. Being caught   3. getting caught
   2. to be affected   4. being asked

B 1. F   2. T   3. T

- **Tip:** Have students identify the passive gerunds and infinitives in exercise **B**.

LEARN

Chart 9.5, page 256 10 min.

- **Notes 1 & 3:** Students often have difficulty with word order of negative gerunds and infinitives. To practice this, write several affirmative sentences using passive gerunds and passive infinitives and have students rewrite them in the negative.
- **Tip:** After going over the chart, write these sentences on the board: *I dislike _____ (give) presents. I'm interested in _____ (tell) about volunteer opportunities. I was angry about _____ (not, invite). I'm determined _____ (promote) at work. They're lucky _____ (choose) for the team. They hope _____ (elect) to office.* Elicit completions and ask students to identify which note on the chart provides the information.

86 THE PASSIVE

4 page 256 — 10 min.

1. to be sent
2. being injured
3. being expected
4. being damaged
5. to be evacuated
6. to be told
7. being allowed
8. to be given

Chart 9.6, page 257 — 10 min.

- **Note 1:** *Get* passives can also be used to talk about something with a benefit. (e.g., *He got paid.*)
- **Tip:** Write sentences on the board in the active voice that address the items in the notes. (e.g., *A car hit the tree in his front yard. The teacher yelled at Kate for being late. Vandals damaged the school building. The storm delayed Lisa's plane. The company offered Victor a new position.*) Have students rewrite the sentences using *get* passives.
- **Tip:** Have students complete these sentence starters with their own ideas: *I'm worried about . . .* and *I don't expect . . . .*

5 page 257 — 5 min.

1. got hit
2. got broken
3. got hurt
4. got flooded
5. got hit
6. get damaged
7. got ruined
8. will get delivered

- **Expansion Tip:** Have students work in pairs to write conversations that include at least three *get* passives. Call on students to perform their conversations for the class.

PRACTICE

6 page 258 — 5 min.

- **Tip:** Have students look at the photo. Ask: *What is the bull doing? How are animals affected by wildfires?*

1. being harmed/ getting harmed
2. get damaged
3. get filled/are filled
4. get blown/are blown
5. Being removed
6. are killed/get killed
7. was reduced
8. are not affected/do not get affected
9. to be rescued
10. was found

- **Expansion Tip:** Have students research a major wildfire in the news. Write these questions on the board as prompts: *When was the fire? How did it get started? What towns or buildings got damaged? How many animals got killed or hurt?* Have students share their research in pairs or small groups.

7 page 259 — 5 min.

A
1. gotten caught
2. getting burned
3. gotten rescued
4. gotten injured
5. get stung
6. gotten bitten

B SPEAK

Answers will vary.

- **Alternative Speaking:** Have students form new pairs and tell about their first partner's experience.

8 LISTEN, page 259 — 5 min.

1. F   2. F   3. T   4. T   5. F   6. T

9 EDIT, page 259 — 5 min.

When I was a child, I remember being show shown a bird nest in a tree in our yard. It was a robin's nest, and it was amazing. There were four blue eggs in the nest. The bird didn't seem to mind be being watched, and I was careful not to get too close. I was very young, maybe four, but I never needed telling to be told not to touch the nest. Somehow I knew that without being reminded. One day, I looked and saw baby robins in the nest. I don't think they liked be being/to be left alone by their mother, but sometimes she had to fly away to get food. When she came back, the babies made a lot of noise while they were waiting to being to be fed!

Since that time I have always loved birds, and I love to go on birdwatching trips. In recent years, I have traveled all over the world to observe birds. I sometimes get invite invited to speak at birdwatching conferences. Be Being asked to share my knowledge of birds with others gives me a lot of pleasure. Fortunately, birdwatching is a very safe hobby. I've never gotten get injured while doing my favorite thing.

10 APPLY, page 260 — 15 min.

Answers will vary.

- **Alternative Writing:** Bring in photos of an event that had a big impact on the surroundings, or suggest that students find a photo to write about. Have students write at least five sentences using *get* passives, passive gerunds, and passive infinitives.

UNIT 9 LESSON 3

Review the Grammar — UNIT 9

1 page 261 — 5 min.
1. disappeared
2. was never seen
3. noticed
4. must have taken
5. were caught
6. got sent
7. to get punished
8. are being saved
9. have been released
10. have learned

2 page 261 — 5 min.
1. Bats are found throughout most of the world.
2. Bats can be seen all over the world.
3. [passive not possible]
4. The destruction of bat habitats should be stopped.
5. More than 5.7 million bats have been killed by a deadly disease.
6. The spread of the disease is being investigated.
7. [passive not possible]
8. These endangered animals should have been protected from this disease.

3 page 262 — 5 min.
1. being caught/getting caught; to be evacuated; to be left
2. got hurt; to be picked up; to be fed
3. Being trapped/Getting trapped; being burned/getting burned; was started; got rescued/were rescued; got promoted/was promoted

4 EDIT, page 262 — 5 min.

Good news for the gray seal population has been announced. Seal populations are ~~being~~ growing off the north Atlantic coast of the United States. For many years, seals were killed for their skins, oil, and meat. However, since 1972, they have ~~be~~ been protected by U.S. law, and they cannot be killed. Many people worry, however, that the seal population is getting out of control, and that nothing will ~~been~~ be done to manage it. Fishermen are complaining because large amounts of fish are being ~~eating~~ eaten by the seals. In addition, there is the shark problem. Sharks like to eat seals, so when seals move into an area, sharks usually follow. In fact, many more sharks can be seen in the areas where seal populations have increased. Naturally, swimmers are concerned about ~~to be~~ being attacked by sharks. Swimmer Jon Turner says, "It's great that the gray seal population has come back, but now I have to be careful not to get ~~bite~~ bitten by a shark!"

5 LISTEN & SPEAK, page 263 — 15 min.

A 1. d 2. d 3. b 4. c 5. d

B
1. They are being harmed.
2. Rainfall patterns and polar ice have been affected by increasing temperatures.
3. Activities such as golf and mountain climbing increase your risk of being hit by lightning.
4. Fish and shellfish are being pulled out of the ocean by fishermen.
5. The biggest wave was caused by a hurricane.

Connect the Grammar to Writing

1 READ & NOTICE THE GRAMMAR, page 264 — 20 min.

B *Answers may vary. Possible answers:*

can be found/no agent

get stuck/no agent

is being sold/no agent

do not get punished/no agent

are endangered/no agent

C

Endangered Species: African Manatee	
Threat	**Specific examples**
Habitat is being destroyed	1. Building of dams 2. Pollution from boats on the river 3. Clearing of wetlands
Hunting	1. Meat is sold in markets 2. Bones are used to make walking sticks 3. Illegal hunters do not get punished

2 BEFORE YOU WRITE, page 265 — 15 min.

3 WRITE, page 265 — 15 min.

> **WRITING FOCUS,** page 265
>
> Have students look at the Explore texts (also page 257 and 258) in this unit to see if they can find other examples of *especially*.

- **Alternative Writing:** Have students write an informative essay about another topic suggested in the unit: threats to the ocean, the effect of dams, the effect of tourists on Antarctica, the threats posed by hurricanes, and other powerful storms.

UNIT 10 Beauty and Appearance
Causative Verb Patterns and Phrasal Verbs

Unit Opener

Photo: Have students look at the photo. Ask: *What do you see? What is it doing?*

Location: This is a photo of an io moth, whose habitat is deciduous forests, thorn scrub, and suburban areas. The moth in this picture is a beautiful, female moth, in Little Orleans, Maryland.

Theme: This unit is about beauty and appearance. It includes information about a camel beauty contest, beauty products in ancient Greece, and a researcher interested in protecting "uncute" animals. Have students look at the photos and titles on pages 268, 275, and 282. Ask: *How do they relate to the theme?*

Page	Lesson	Grammar	Examples
268	1	*Have, Let, Make, Get,* and *Help*	The teacher **has her students** do a lot of homework. I **get my friend** to exercise with me after work.
275	2	Passive Causative	I **had my watch repaired** last week. Why have you **gotten the locks changed**?
282	3	Phrasal Verbs	He **looked over** the contract carefully. He **looked** the contract **over** before signing it. We can't **get over** the changes.
290	**Review the Grammar**		
292	**Connect the Grammar to Writing**		

Unit Grammar Terms

direct object: a noun or pronoun that receives the action of the verb.
➢ Aldo asked a **question**.
➢ Karen helped **me**.

inseparable phrasal verb: a phrasal verb that cannot have a noun or pronoun between its two parts (verb + particle). The verb and the particle always stay together.
➢ I **ran into** a friend in the library.
➢ We **waited for** her in front of the library.

intransitive verb: a verb that can't be followed by an object.
➢ We didn't **agree**.
➢ The students **smiled** and **laughed**.

phrasal verb: a two-word or three-word verb. The phrasal verb means something different from the two or three words separately.
➢ **Turn off** the light when you leave.
➢ She's **come up with** an interesting idea.

separable phrasal verb: a phrasal verb that can have a noun or pronoun between its two parts.
➢ **Turn** the light **off**.
➢ **Turn** it **off**.

transitive verb: a verb that is followed by an object.
➢ We **took an umbrella**.

90

LESSON 1	**Have, Let, Make, Get, and Help**

Student Learning Outcomes	• **Read** an article about a popular contest in Abu Dhabi. • **Complete** an interview with a beauty contest participant. • **Write** questions with *have, let, make, get,* and *help.* • **Ask** and **answer** questions with *have, let, make, get,* and *help.* • **Listen** to a conversation about a man who loves beautiful plants.
Lesson Vocabulary	(v.) evaluate (adj.) lively (v.) massage (n.) permission (v.) respect (n.) judge (v.) loosen (n.) participant (n.) prestige (n.) scholarship

EXPLORE

1 READ, page 268   15 min.

- Use the photo to teach vocabulary such as *floppy, eyelashes,* and *hump.*
- Have students use context to guess the meaning of new words (e.g., *flutter, remote, shine, loosen, massage, decorate, evaluate, prestige*).

Be the Expert

- The largest camel beauty contest is held in Madinat Zayed, Emirate of Abu Dhabi, a city in the desert, and takes place in December. Camels are bought and sold for an incredible amount of money. A top camel is worth as much as $1 million.
- The Bedouin, an ethnic group originally from the Sahara Desert, value the camel very highly as it represents transportation, food, and wealth. Even today, urbanised Bedouins maintain traditional activities such as camel riding.
- Camels are particularly well-suited to the desert—their eyelashes keep out sand, their hump stores fat for energy, and their lips help them drink water very quickly.

2 CHECK, page 269   5 min.

1. The beauty contest is for camels from all over the ~~Abu Dhabi~~ Arabian Peninsula.
2. Camel owners get help from their ~~trainers~~ family members before the contest.
3. A camel's hair shines after it is ~~washed~~ massaged.
4. The ~~trainers~~ judges evaluate the camels at the contest.
5. On the last day, the judges choose the most ~~skillful~~ beautiful camel.

- **Tip:** Have students identify where in the article they found the answers to exercise **2**.

3 DISCOVER, page 269   5 min.

A 1. help owners to make
    2. makes their hair shine
    3. get the camels to loosen up
    4. have the camels walk
    5. lets this community celebrate

B

Verb	Object + Base Form of Verb	Object + Infinitive (*to*+verb)
1. help		✓
2. make	✓	
3. get		✓
4. have	✓	
5. let	✓	

LEARN

Chart 10.1, page 270   10 min.

- **Note:** Students may want to have the main verb agree with the object that follows, resulting in errors (e.g., *The teacher has the student takes the test*) or use the infinitive (e.g., *The teacher has the student to take the test*). Write incorrect sentences such as these on the board and have students correct them.

4 page 270   5 min.

1. make	4. make	7. let	10. make
2. have	5. let	8. make	
3. lets	6. make	9. make	

UNIT 10   LESSON 1   **91**

Chart 10.2, page 271   5 min.

- **Note 1:** *Get* is the only causative verb that must use the infinitive after the object. Read each example sentence from Chart 10.1. (e.g., *Did you have anyone read your essay?*) Elicit the sentence using *get*. (e.g., *Did you get anyone to read your essay?*) After each sentence, have a student say the sentence using *get*.

5 page 271   5 min.

1. got them to agree
2. got me to promise
3. helped us prepare/helped us to prepare
4. got me to practice
5. helped each other do/helped each other to do
6. get the judges to respect
7. helped my family pay/helped my family to pay
8. help you get/help you to get
9. help people solve/help people to solve

PRACTICE

6 page 272   5 min.

A 1. gotten you to change your appearance
2. get to cut your hair
3. make people worry about their appearance
4. make you wear certain clothes
5. let anyone borrow your clothes
6. help you shop for new clothes

- **Alternative Writing & Speaking:** Ask students to write sentences about someone who has made a dramatic change in his or her appearance. It could be someone they know, someone on TV, or someone they make up. Then have them share their sentences in pairs.

B SPEAK

Answers will vary.

7 page 272   5 min.

1. make	4. made	7. get
2. help	5. make	8. let
3. make	6. help/get	9. get

8 page 273   5 min.

1. let Pam borrow
2. have the painters
3. help Jen decorate/help Jen to decorate
4. made Kyle take
5. got a salesperson to choose
6. let children participate/let their children participate
7. have Jorge mow/ask Jorge to mow
8. make Rachel feel

9 LISTEN, page 274   10 min.

A 1. T   4. F
2. T   5. F
3. T

- **Tip:** Have students correct the false statements in exercise **9**, and then check their ideas with a partner.

10 APPLY, page 274   15 min.

A *Answers may vary. Possible answers:*

1. Why do flowers make people feel happy?
2. How do team sports make people act?
3. How does travel help people see things differently?
4. What kind of music gets people to relax?
5. What do teachers let students do in the classroom?
6. What things help people to fall asleep?

B *Answers will vary.*

- **Expansion Tip:** Have students choose one of the questions to research online. Then have them prepare a one-minute presentation to give to the class or a small group.

LESSON 2	**Passive Causative**				
Student Learning Outcomes	• **Read** an article about ancient Egyptians. • **Complete** sentences using passive causative. • **Listen** to a conversation and identify who completed the tasks. • **Find** and **edit** errors with passive causatives. • **Speak** and **write** about things others do for you.				
Lesson Vocabulary	(v.) beautify (n.) concern	(n.) cosmetics (v.) install	(adj.) internal (n.) organ	(n.) possession (v.) shave	(v.) style

EXPLORE

1 READ, page 275   15 min.

- Have students look at the photo and read the caption. Ask them if they think Nefertiti was beautiful. If they think so, ask them what characteristics make her beautiful.
- Use the photo to teach the meaning of *cosmetics*.

Be the Expert

- Cleopatra, the last active pharaoh in Egypt, was famous for her beauty. She came from a line of royalty called the Ptolemys, who were originally from Greece. Although most of her forebears only spoke Greek, Cleopatra learned to speak Egyptian. Her relationships with Julius Caesar and then Mark Antony are well known and a subject of one of Shakespeare's plays. After Mark Antony committed suicide, Cleopatra did the same, as this was the custom.
- Nefertiti was the wife of a pharaoh who ruled more than a thousand years before Cleopatra. She and her husband were responsible for a religious revolution in Egypt in which people began to worship only one god instead of many. The photo in the text is a famous bust of Nefertiti, which is exhibited in the Neues Museum in Berlin.
- Elicit examples of other members of royalty or heads of state that are known for their beauty.

2 CHECK, page 276   5 min.

   1. F   2. T   3. T   4. F   5. F

3 DISCOVER, page 276   5 min.

A 1. had her hair dyed and styled
   2. had her nails polished
   3. had large images of her painted
   4. had their hair; had their heads shaved

B 3

LEARN

Chart 10.3, page 277   10 min.

- **Notes 1 & 2:** The subject of a passive causative can be a pronoun. However, the pronoun *it* is rarely the subject because things that are not human cannot ask someone to do something.

4 page 277   5 min.

   1. had many things done
   2. had their portraits painted
   3. had their images put
   4. had large tombs built
   5. had their heads shaved
   6. had the wigs dyed
   7. had their bodies preserved
   8. had their belongings placed
   9. had special words written
   10. had their pets buried

- **Tip:** With their books closed, have students retell the information in this exercise to a partner.

Chart 10.4, page 278   10 min.

- **Note 2:** Have students choose one of the sentences in the Chart 10.4 and then write it using all of the forms in the note.

REAL ENGLISH, page 278

Review the reasons agents are omitted in the passive voice (page 248). Elicit examples of passive causative sentences where the agent is fairly obvious (e.g., getting hair done by a hair stylist, getting a car fixed by a mechanic). Then, explain that if the agent is important, speakers would probably mention it. Have students write three sentences in which they name the agent because it is important or surprising.

UNIT 10 LESSON 2 **93**

5 page 278　　　　　　　　　　　　10 min.

1. got it cut
2. got my eyes checked
3. get them shortened
4. am getting it serviced
5. get it delivered
6. get the application signed
7. got it washed
8. get my prescriptions filled

PRACTICE

6 page 279　　　　　　　　　　　　10 min.

- **Tip:** Before students do exercise **6**, have them look at the calendar. Ask questions: *What does the director have to get done by April 1? By April 9? By the end of April?*

1. had the catalog printed
2. had the audio tour recorded
3. had the gallery painted
4. will have lighting installed/is going to have lighting installed/is having the lighting installed
5. he will have the artworks unpacked/he's going to have the artworks unpacked/he's having the artworks unpacked
6. will have the artworks arranged/is going to have the artworks arranged/is having the artworks arranged
7. will have photographs taken of the exhibit/is going to have photographs taken of the exhibit/is having photographs taken of the exhibit
8. will have the tickets designed and printed/is going to have the tickets designed and printed/is having the tickets designed and printed

7 LISTEN & WRITE, page 280　　　　5 min.

- **Tip:** Before students do exercise **A**, have them read the tasks in the chart. Ask them to predict which tasks someone else did.

A

Task	The director did this	Somebody else did this
1. painting the gallery		✓
2. installing the lights		✓
3. unpacking the artworks	✓	
4. arranging the artworks	✓	
5. preparing the labels		✓
6. labeling the artworks		✓
7. photographing the exhibit		✓
8. designing and printing the tickets	✓	

- **Alternative Speaking:** Have students ask and answer questions in pairs about the information in the conversation. (e.g., *Did the director paint the gallery? No, he had it painted by his assistants.*)

8 EDIT, page 280　　　　　　　　　　10 min.

- **Tip:** Before doing exercise **8**, have students look at the map on page 280 and the photo on page 281. Ask them what they know about the Maya people.

　　Thousands of years ago, the Maya often had things ~~do~~ done to themselves to improve their looks. This is shown in the Maya art that archaeologists have found. We can see from the art that Maya kings and nobles got holes ~~to make~~ made in their teeth. Then they had pretty stones put in the holes. Ordinary Maya probably couldn't afford to have pretty stones put in their teeth. Pictures show them with sharp, pointed teeth. They probably had their teeth ~~make~~ made sharp to decorate themselves. Upper-class people had fancy tattoos on their bodies. Researchers believe that they didn't create the tattoos themselves. They must have had ~~decorated their bodies~~ their bodies decorated with these designs. Today, some people do similar things to their bodies. For example, it is common for people to have their ears pierce**d**. Other people get ~~dyed their hair~~ their hair dyed or their nails painted. They do these things to look good. Will people still be getting these things done hundreds of years from now, or will they think that people in the twenty-first century had some very strange habits?

9 APPLY, page 281　　　　　　　　　20 min.

A *Answers will vary.*
B *Answers will vary.*
C *Answers will vary.*

LESSON 3 Phrasal Verbs

Student Learning Outcomes
- **Read** an article about an animal researcher.
- **Complete** conversations with phrasal verbs.
- **Say** sentences with phrasal verbs.
- **Find** and **edit** errors with phrasal verbs.
- **Write** responses to questions using phrasal verbs.

Lesson Vocabulary

| (v.) adapt | (v.) digest | (n.) metabolism | (n.) request | (idiom) take advantage of s.t./s.b |
| (v.) deserve | (adj.) humorous | (n.) predator | (n.) sanctuary | (n.) zoologist |

EXPLORE

1 READ, page 282 — 15 min.
- **Tip:** Have students look at the photo. Ask them to describe what they see. Use the photo to teach the meaning of *sloth* and *funny-looking*. Ask students what they know about sloths.
- **Tip:** Have students use context, including the fun facts, to guess the meaning of *adapt, oddness, metabolism, predator,* and *humorous*.

Be the Expert
- There are two families of sloths: two-toed sloths and three-toed sloths. Most sloths primarily eat leaves, which are hard to digest. For this reason, sloths have complicated digestive systems. Leaves provide relatively little fuel for activity, so sloths have evolved with slow metabolisms and low body temperatures. Some two-toed sloths also eat insects and small birds.
- Lucy Cooke has written a lot about sloths, including two books, *The Little Book of Sloths* and *The Power of Sloth*. Her blog and some videos of sloths can be found online. Have students search "Lucy Cooke sloths" and they will find both.
- **Expansion Tip:** Ask students to watch several videos on Lucy Cooke's blog and report on what they learned and what they found humorous.

2 CHECK, page 283 — 5 min.

Answers may vary. Possible answers:
1. The most interesting animals to Lucy Cooke are the less attractive ones.
2. The sloth's slowness helps it survive in its environment.
3. The problem with attractive animals is that they get all of the attention.
4. Cooke communicates her message to the world through funny online videos.

3 DISCOVER, page 283 — 5 min.

A
1. off
2. out
3. out
4. out
5. across
6. up

B T

LEARN

Chart 10.5, page 284 — 15 min.
- **Note 1:** Write pairs of sentences on the board: *I looked up in the air. I looked up the definition in the dictionary. He turned into a monster. He turned into the driveway. They came up with some good ideas. They came up the stairs after dinner.* Elicit which sentences have a phrasal verb (different meaning) and which have a verb + a preposition.
- **Note 5:** Write formal words on the board: *indicate, communicate, select, admire, discover, encounter, return.* Have students work in pairs to write phrasal verbs that mean the same thing.

4 page 284 — 10 min.

A
1. point out
2. ended up
3. look after
4. dying out
5. help out
6. come up with
7. found out
8. keep up with

B ANALYZE THE GRAMMAR
1. point out a website
3. look after the sloths
5. help out the sloth rescue group
6. come up with many great ways
7. found out how to join
8. keep up with the society's activities

Chart 10.6, page 285 — 10 min.

- **Notes 1 & 2:** Have students refer to the article on page 282 to find examples of phrasal verbs that have a noun or a pronoun between the verb and preposition.

5 page 285 — 5 min.

1. looked it up
2. check it out; turn me off
3. ran into him; get together with him
4. fell for her; go out with him; get over it
5. pick it out
6. come across this/it

- **Expansion Tip:** Put students in pairs to create conversations using at least one separable and one inseparable phrasal verb. Ask volunteers to read their conversations to the class.

PRACTICE

6 page 286 — 5 min.

1. came across
2. looking up
3. pointed out
4. go along with
5. turn off
6. give up
7. cheers them up
8. figure it out
9. came up with
10. ended up

7 page 287 — 5 min.

1. c
2. j
3. a
4. b
5. g
6. h
7. f
8. i
9. e
10. d

- **Alternative Speaking:** Working in pairs, have students take turns saying the sentences in another way, using the definitions on the right if possible (e.g., *They returned their paintbrushes to their usual place after art class*).

8 WRITE & SPEAK, pages 287–288 — 15 min.

A *Answers will vary. Possible answers: give away money/give money away, give back my laptop/give my laptop back, put their paintbrushes away/put away their paintbrushes, put on a shirt/put a shirt on, turn down a request, turn into a frog, and turn off the lights/turn the lights off/turn off a person/turn a person off.*

B *Answers will vary.*

C *Answers will vary.*

9 EDIT, page 288 — 5 min.

A: The other day I came ~~over~~ across an interesting article. It was about a beautiful bird called the Gouldian finch.

B: What was so interesting about it?

A: Well, when a male finch chooses a mate, he uses his right eye to ~~pick out her~~ pick her out. For some reason, his right eye helps him choose a better mate.

B: That's strange. How did they figure that ~~up~~ out?

A: They covered the finch's right eye. They noticed that with its left eye, the finch chose any bird as a mate.

B: Wow. It's amazing how animals and plants choose mates in different ways.

A: Well, choosing a mate is really important. If animals and plants choose the wrong mates, their species could die ~~over~~ out.

B: What does that say about the way that people choose mates?

A: The article points out that human beings also choose mates to keep their species alive.

B: So when people go ~~over~~ out with each other for a while and then break up, are they really trying to stay alive?

A: You could look at it that way.

B: Or maybe they just can't put up with each other anymore!

A: That's possible, too.

10 APPLY, page 289 — 15 min.

A *Answers will vary. Phrasal verbs to be used are as follows:*

1. get across
2. fall for
3. figured out
4. run into
5. look up to
6. stand out

B *Answer will vary.*

- **Alternative Writing:** Have students write a paragraph on one of these topics: a person you look up to, ways to stand out in a job interview, the advantages of figuring out solutions to your own problems, when you should not go along with the crowd.

UNIT 10 Review the Grammar

1 page 290 5 min.

1. make
2. them
3. point
4. out
5. to
6. across

2 page 290 5 min.

1. made
2. to make
3. design
4. designed
5. decorated
6. to decorate
7. created
8. create

3 LISTEN, page 291 5 min.

1. lets
2. has
3. lets
4. makes
5. help
6. had

4 EDIT, page 291 5 min.

Wearing masks lets people ~~to~~ hide their identity from others. This can help to create a feeling of mystery at a masquerade ball, a dance where people wear costumes. In a normal situation, you might be able to come up with some ideas about people's qualities because you can see their faces and expressions. You think about whether they are good-looking and how often they smile. Their appearance gets you **to** form certain opinions about them. It may help you to decide if you want to talk to them.

Some masks stand ~~up~~ **out** from all the rest because they are so fancy. People may pay a lot of money to have ~~made~~ these masks **made**. Do such amazing masks make you ~~to~~ want to meet the people who are wearing them? Once a friend of mine fell **for** her husband ~~for~~ at a costume party before she ever saw his face. She loved his voice and personality, and didn't think about his appearance at all. Sometimes a masquerade ball can turn ~~it~~ out to be a very special day.

5 page 291 10 min.

Answers will vary.

UNIT 10 REVIEW THE GRAMMAR **97**

Connect the Grammar to Writing

1 READ & NOTICE THE GRAMMAR,
pages 292–293   20 min.

A *Answers will vary.*

B help her get ready, got her hair done, let me do her makeup, to make her eyes stand out, have beautiful patterns painted, had a professional henna artist paint her nails, helped her put, helped her get dressed, let my sister borrow, had gotten his hair cut, made his brother lend

C *Answers may vary. Possible answers:*

got hair done at salon

let me do her makeup

had a henna artist paint her hands

he had gotten his hair cut

he made his brother lend him

2 BEFORE YOU WRITE, page 293   15 min.

A *Answers will vary.*

B . . . to help her get ready
My sister got her hair done . . .
. . . she had a professional henna artist paint her hands.
My mother let my sister borrow some fancy gold jewelry.
. . . he had gotten his hair cut . . .
He made his brother lend it to him . . .

3 WRITE, page 293   15 min.

> **WRITING FOCUS, page 293**
>
> Have students look through the unit to find examples of words that mean *attractive* and sort them into three categories: women, men, both. Then, have them compare ideas with a partner.

- **Alternative Writing:** Have students write about the topic they diagrammed in exercise **2B**. For example, they might write about how brides and grooms prepare for a wedding in their culture, or how job applicants usually get ready for an interview.

98 CAUSATIVE VERB PATTERNS AND PHRASAL VERBS

UNIT 11 The Power of Images

Relative Clauses

Unit Opener

Photo: Have students look at the photo and read the caption. Ask, *What do you see?*

Location: The Geghard Monastery in Armenia is partially carved out of a mountain located at the head of the Azat Valley. It is listed as a UNESCO World Heritage Site.

Theme: This unit is about the power of images. It includes information about a photography website, a wilderness photographer, and films in India. Have students look at the photos and titles on pages 296, 308, and 318. Ask, *How do they relate to the theme?*

Page	Lesson	Grammar	Examples
296	1	Subject Relative Clauses	The people **that took these pictures** are my friends. Cy went to Peru, **which is a beautiful place to visit.** I know the woman **whose son won the award.**
308	2	Object Relative Clauses	The photo **that he posted on the Internet** tells a story. The movie **I saw** won an Academy Award.
318	3	Relative Clauses: Reduced, with *Where* and *When*	The woman **starring in the movie** has a beautiful voice. We visited the region **where the film was made.**
327	**Review the Grammar**		
330	**Connect the Grammar to Writing**		

Unit Grammar Terms

clause: a group of words with a subject and a verb. (See *dependent clause* and *main clause*.)
- We watched the game. (one clause)
- We watched the game after we ate dinner. (two clauses)

dependent clause: a clause that cannot stand alone as a sentence. It must be used with a main clause.
- I bought a new car **although I couldn't afford it**.

identifying relative clause: a relative clause that gives information about the noun it is describing. The information is necessary to understand who or what the noun refers to. (Also called a restrictive relative clause.)
- Minnesoata is a state **that is known** for its cold winters.

main clause: a clause that can stand alone as a sentence. It has a subject and a verb.
- **I heard the news** when I was driving home.

non-identifying relative clause: a relative clause that gives extra information about the noun it is describing. The information is not necessary to understand who or what the noun refers to. (Also called a non-restrictive relative clause.)
- Nelson Mandela, **who was a great leader,** died in 2013.

relative clause: a clause that follows a noun and gives extra information about the noun. (Also called an adjective clause.)
- The thief **who stole the woman's purse** was caught.

relative pronoun: a pronoun that begins a relative clause. *Who, that, which, whom, when,* and *where* can all be relative pronouns.
- The town **where** I grew up has a population of 45,000.

99

LESSON 1 | Subject Relative Clauses

Student Learning Outcomes
- **Read** an article about a photography site.
- **Complete** sentences giving advice.
- **Combine** sentences using relative clauses.
- **Pronounce** relative clauses.
- **Listen** to a discussion about photographs.
- **Discuss** and **write** about photographs.

Lesson Vocabulary
(n.) composition	(n.) element	(n.) mood	(v.) peek	(n.) reflection
(n.) contrast	(n.) exposure	(v.) oppress	(n.) perspective	(adj.) varied

EXPLORE

1 READ, page 296   15 min.
- Use the photo to teach vocabulary such as *dangle* and *flood*.
- Have students use context to guess the meaning of new words (e.g., *devastating*, *crops*, and *untouched*).

Be the Expert

The Sundarbans is a large mangrove forest on the Bay of Bengal. It is also a UNESCO World Heritage site. It shows a variety of ecological processes because it is on the delta of the Ganges, Brahmaputra, and Meghna rivers, and it is intersected by tidal waterways and small islands. The area is known for animals such as the Bengal tiger, the Indian python, the estuarine crocodile, and hundreds of species of birds.

2 CHECK, page 297   5 min.
1. The photo was taken in the Sundarbans of West Bengal, India.
2. The area is known for its mangrove forest and royal Bengal tigers.
3. The region experienced a devastating storm.
4. The storm flooded the fields and destroyed crops.

3 DISCOVER, page 297   5 min.

A 1. In this photo, the farmers <u>who live in the area</u> had recently experienced a devastating storm that flooded the fields and destroyed crops.

2. Maybe that's because the boy, <u>whose feet dangle over the water</u>, seems untouched by the flood.

3. I like the way it captures the child, <u>who seems to be living in the moment</u>.

4. This photo, <u>which shows the highs and lows of life in the Sundarbans</u>, sends a powerful message.

- **Tip:** To help students focus on the ways in which relative clauses are similar to and different from adjectives, ask, *What kind of words are used to describe nouns? Do they usually come before or after the noun?*

B 1. who, that
2. that, which
3. whose

LEARN

Chart 11.1, page 298   10 min.
- **Note 1:** Relative clauses are also sometimes called adjective clauses because they behave like adjectives, i.e., they describe or modify nouns.
- **Note 3:** *Who* is used more commonly than *that* in describing people. *That* is used more frequently for things in identifying relative clauses (clauses that are necessary to identify the noun).

4 page 298   5 min.

Today anyone <u>who has a digital camera</u> can produce a clear photo. However, that is not enough to make it a great photo. Photographers <u>who want to take powerful shots</u> have to make sure that the photo has good composition. In photography, composition is the way <u>that things or people in a picture are placed, or positioned</u>. Look at some photos of your friends or family, and you'll

100   RELATIVE CLAUSES

see what I mean. Where are the people in the photo? Are they standing in the center with a lot of empty space in the background? If so, the picture probably isn't very interesting. Photographs are more striking when they show someone or something <u>that is</u> on the right or left, or off-center. In addition, a picture <u>that does not have too many details</u> will not have a clear focus. So think carefully about how you take your photos. Photos <u>that have good composition</u> will be the most successful.

5 page 299 — 5 min.

A 1. When you're just starting out, don't buy equipment <u>which costs</u> a lot.
2. People <u>who keep</u> their camera with them at all times will get better photos.
3. Places <u>which don't seem</u> unusual might still make great photos.
4. Look at photography magazines and websites <u>which can offer</u> you a range of information on technique.
5. Look closely at a photo <u>which demonstrates</u> strong composition and lighting.
6. Take a workshop from a photographer <u>who does</u> interesting work.
7. Copy the style of someone <u>who takes</u> pictures that you admire.
8. Avoid subjects <u>which might be</u> extremely difficult to photograph.

B SPEAK

Answers will vary.

6 page 299 — 5 min.

1. was playing; was
2. shows; is
3. is sitting; has been taking
4. appear; are from
5. are facing; live
6. is drifting; has never injured
7. work; have been collecting
8. have bloomed; come out

Chart 11.2, page 300 — 5 min.

- **Note 1:** As in English, the relative clause follows the noun it is modifying in most European languages. However, in languages such as Chinese, Japanese, and Korean, the relative clause precedes the noun. Speakers of these languages may have some difficulty when learning this structure.

7 page 300 — 5 min.

1. Photo sharing, <u>which</u> is now extremely popular, has changed over time.
2. Websites such as Flikr, <u>which</u> became available in 2010, offered lots of space.
3. Facebook, <u>which</u> started in 2004, allowed people to share messages and later photos.
4. College students, <u>who</u> were the first users of Facebook, were later followed by users of all ages.
5. I just bought the latest smartphone, <u>which</u> has a powerful built-in camera.
6. Kevin Systrom and Mike Kreiger, <u>who</u> wanted a way to edit photos, started Instagram in 2010.
7. Instagram, <u>which</u> was originally an application for iPhones, is now available for Android devices.
8. Have you ever met Dr. Jones, <u>who</u> teaches Photography 101?
9. Amsterdam, <u>which</u> is the capital of the Netherlands, is a wonderful city to photograph.
10. The photography exhibition was created by my friend Laura, <u>who</u> is a professional artist.

8 page 301 — 15 min.

A 1. Photography, which can be very creative, is a highly competitive profession.
2. My friend Erin, who has just started his own business, is a great photographer.
3. Online photography classes, which are often free, can be a great way to learn the basics.
4. Disposable cameras, which are usually good for one use only, are popular with tourists.
5. Digital storytelling is popular with Professor Wong, who has experience telling stories with photos.
6. Displays on cameras, which can be difficult to use, give you valuable information.
7. Camera reviews, which are easy to find online, can help you choose a good camera.
8. Digital photographs, which are inexpensive, are extremely popular.

B *Answers will vary.*

Chart 11.3, page 302 — 5 min.

- **Note:** Point out that *whose* is the pronoun used to show possession and can replace any noun that can possess something else, or that something else belongs to. Remind students that *whose* sounds like *who's* (*who* + is), but means something very different.

UNIT 11 LESSON 1 **101**

9 page 302   5 min.

1. The statues, whose faces are difficult to see, show a king and gods. (pages 206–207)
2. Does the frog, whose face peeks out from the mushroom, feel the rain? (pages 234–235)
3. Jimbo Bazoobi is an Australian citizen whose goat Gary has become famous. (page 249)
4. An insect whose wings display beautiful colors is a hawk moth. (pages 266–267)
5. The sloth, whose eyes are closed, sleeps peacefully. (page 282)
6. The starry night picture was taken in Armenia, whose sky shows a meteor. (pages 294–295)
7. The photographer, whose image captures star trails, used time exposure. (pages 294–295)

10 pages 302–303   15 min.

A
1. The woman in the photo, whose name is unknown, is from the Maori tribe.
2. The Maori woman in the photo, whose eyes are deep brown, has a mysterious expression.
3. New Zealand, whose population is mostly European, is 14.6 percent Maori.
4. The Maori, whose ancestors came to New Zealand around 1250–1300 CE, still live there today.
5. The Maori, whose native language is close to Polynesian, mainly speak English.
6. New Zealand, whose terrain is mountainous, is a beautiful country.
7. The Maori, whose culture has changed, have lost some of their traditions.
8. We should try to respect people whose cultures are different from ours.

B Answers will vary.

PRACTICE

11 page 304   5 min.

A
1. viewpoint that comes
2. The people who/that appear
3. whose expressions show
4. People who/that influence
5. people who/that are powerful
6. Groups of people who/that stand together
7. Individuals who/that are
8. whose eyes meet
9. Red and orange, which are
10. Green and blue, which are

B 9, 10

12 pages 304–305   5 min.

1. Photography can capture moments that/which will be remembered forever.
2. Photography is an activity that/which will always hold your interest.
3. A photograph can communicate ideas that/which are hard to express in words.
4. Photos of loved ones who/that are far away are important possessions.
5. With photography, we speak to people whose language is different from ours.
6. Sharing photos allows you to connect to people who/that are important to you.
7. Photography is an art whose origins go back to the mid-1820s.
8. The first surviving photograph, which was taken in 1825 or 1826, shows a landscape.

13 PRONUNCIATION, page 305   10 min.

A
1. The contest, which is held once a year, has a $5000 cash prize.
2. Many people who have won the prize have gone on to be successful photographers.
3. The judges, who are professional photographers, consider the creativity and quality of each photo.
4. The judges, who do not always agree, have a difficult task.
5. The contestant whose photo gets the highest score is the winner.
6. The photo which won last year's prize was taken by a 15-year-old.

B Answers will vary.

14 LISTEN, pages 306–307   10 min.

A 2

B
1. a   4. b
2. b   5. b
3. b   6. b

C
1. that shows the buildings and the sea
2. , which is the capital of the Republic of Maldives,
3. that was taken
4. that is holding something
5. that captures

15 APPLY, page 307   15 min.

Answers will vary.

102 RELATIVE CLAUSES

LESSON 2 — Object Relative Clauses

Student Learning Outcomes	• **Read** an article about a photojournalist. • **Combine** sentences using object relative clauses. • **Listen** to a professor and students talk about a photographer. • **Find** and **edit** errors with relative clauses. • **Write** about photojournalism.
Lesson Vocabulary	(n.) client (n.) conservationist (adj.) extraordinary (adj.) key (n.) portrait (adj.) compelling (n.) determination (v.) initiate (n.) photojournalist (adj.) unpredictable

EXPLORE

1 READ, page 308   15 min.

- Have students look at the photo. Ask them to describe what they see. Use the photo to teach the meaning of *habitat*.
- Have students use context clues to guess the meaning of new words (e.g., *endangered, threatened, extraordinary,* and *critical*).

Be the Expert

- Nick Nichols has been a staff photographer for National Geographic since 1996. Before that, he belonged to a photography cooperative started by Henri Cartier-Bresson and Robert Capa. He uses interesting techniques and equipment to process his photos, including infrared, robots, and mini-helicopters.
- Michael Fay is a lifelong conservationist. The 2000-mile walk across Central Africa was a project called Mega-Transect.

- **Expansion Tip:** Have students work in pairs to list some difficulties Nichols might have in photographing lions, elephants, and gorillas. For each difficulty, ask them to suggest a possible solution. Encourage them to use their imaginations.

2 CHECK, page 309   5 min.

1. Michael "Nick" Nichols is concerned about the future of ~~zoo~~ wild animals.
2. Fay walked a total of ~~500~~ 2000 miles through Africa's wilderness.
3. Nichols thinks it is most important for his photos to ~~look cool~~ be natural.
4. The subjects of Nichols's photographs are usually ~~easy~~ difficult to manage.
5. Nichols works in some of the most ~~populated~~ remote parts of the world.

- **Expansion Tip:** Have students work in pairs to write true or false statements using new words from the text. Then have them read their sentences in pairs.

3 DISCOVER, page 309   5 min.

A
1. His passion has always been to photograph the things *that he cares about*.
2. The president of Congo made the 13 endangered areas *that Fay and Nichols had identified* into national parks.
3. People won't believe the stories *that the images tell*.
4. "I can't stand a photograph *that I've made*, no matter how cool it is, if I set it up," he says.
5. Nichols has a special ability to work in environments *that others find too difficult*.

B object

LEARN

Chart 11.4, page 310   10 min.

- **Notes 3–5:** After going over the notes, have students identify the sentences in the chart from which the relative pronouns can be omitted.
- **Expansion Tip:** Write example sentences containing the errors discussed in Notes 3–5 on the board. Have students correct the errors.

REAL ENGLISH, page 310

Find examples of *whom* in texts or online presentations and bring them to class. Provide the context and ask students why they think the speaker or writer used *whom*.

UNIT 11   LESSON 2   103

4 pages 310–311   10 min.

A
1. that
2. that/which
3. that/which
4. that/which
5. that/which
6. whom

B It is possible to cross out the relative pronouns in item numbers 1, 2, 3, 4, and 5.

5 pages 311–312   5 min.

1. Forests have low light, which people have a difficult time photographing.
2. Redwood National Park, which Mario loves, attracts many campers each year.
3. Lance had a tent that/which he preferred.
4. Emin ate the dinner that/which he had cooked over an open fire.
5. Nancy asked Joe, who was very knowledgeable, for directions.
6. The redwood trees that/which the campers saw were beautiful.

Chart 11.5, page 312   10 min.

- **Note:** Object relative clauses with prepositions can be written in two ways. To illustrate this, write every object relative clause in the chart and notes in both ways (e.g., *who/whom I spoke to, to whom I spoke; that I met with, with whom I met; that we were talking about, about which we were talking*). If appropriate, elicit the more formal options from students.

6 pages 312–313   10 min.

1. that/which
2. about
3. whom
4. for
5. with
6. which
7. in
8. whom/who/that
9. that/which
10. whom

7 page 313   10 min.

1. Take photos of areas that endangered animals are found in./Take photos of areas in which endangered animals are found.
2. Look up information on the animals that/which you take pictures of./Look up information about the animals of which you take pictures.
3. Volunteer for a citizen science project that/which you care about./Volunteer for a citizen science project about which you care.
4. Take photos for environmental groups that/which you want to contribute to./Take photos for environmental groups to which you want to contribute.
5. Take photos of environmental projects that/which you have volunteered for./Take photos of environmental projects for which you have volunteered.
6. Write information about the scientists who/that you work with./Write information about the scientists with whom you work.
7. Be respectful of natural areas that/which you work in./Be respectful of natural areas in which you work.
8. Collect stories of the subjects that/who/whom you take pictures of./Collect stories of the subjects of whom you take pictures.
9. Know the issues that/which people often argue about./Know the issues about which people argue.
10. Start a blog about current topics that/which people will be interested in./Start a blog about current topics in which people will be interested.

PRACTICE

8 pages 314–315   10 min.

- **Tip:** Before students do exercise **8**, have them look at the photo and read the caption. Ask students to describe the photo using relative clauses.

1. a, c, d
2. a, c, d
3. a, b, c
4. a, b, c
5. b, c, d
6. a, c, d
7. a, c
8. a, c, d

9 page 315   5 min.

1. that/which/ø I like the most
2. that/which/ø I eat when I am on assignment
3. who/whom/that/ø I usually take with me
4. who/whom/that/ø I work with
5. that/which/ approached me OR that/which I was approached by
6. that/which/ø I most enjoy taking pictures of
7. that/which/ø the average hasn't heard of
8. who/whom/that/ø I observe

- **Alternative Speaking:** Have students work in pairs to write questions to ask classmates. Suggest that they use the Frequently Asked Questions as models to elicit answers that use relative clauses. (e.g., *What part of being a student do you like the best? What do you eat when you are studying for exams?*) Then, have students find new partners to take turns asking and answering the questions.

104 RELATIVE CLAUSES

10 LISTEN, page 316　　　10 min.

A
1. that/which/ø he has photographed
2. that/which/ø he has traveled all over the world for
3. , which Sartore is deeply committed to,
4. that/which/ø they may never see
5. that/which/ø he has

B *Answers will vary.*

11 EDIT, page 317　　　10 min.

　　　JR is a French street artist ~~who~~ whose public photography exhibits have appeared in over 100 countries. His project, which JR calls ~~it~~ *Inside Out*, requires the general public to interact with his pictures. The idea is for people to share photos of themselves in public spaces to support ideas ~~about~~ that they care about. Here is how it works: special photo booths in which people can take their own photos are set up. The self-portraits are then printed and made into huge posters, which are displayed on the street. These photos attract attention to the causes, such as human rights.

　　　JR, for ~~who~~ whom *Inside Out* is a way to make the world a better place, believes in the power of ordinary people. He is convinced that they can create positive change in the world. In JR's words, "Together, we'll turn the world inside out."

- **Culture Tip:** Street art became popular during the growth of graffiti in the 1970s and 1980s. It is visual art in public spaces, often on buildings, sidewalks, and other structures in the city. Common forms of street art include painting, photography, stencils, posters, and stickers. One of the most famous street artists lives in the UK and is known as Banksy.

- **Alternative Writing:** Have students research a street artist and write a paragraph about him or her using at least five relative clauses. Working in pairs, have students exchange papers and edit the paragraphs.

12 APPLY, page 317　　　20 min.

A
1. c
2. b
3. a

B *Answers will vary.*

C *Answers will vary.*

UNIT 11　LESSON 2　**105**

LESSON 3	**Relative Clauses: Reduced, with *Where* and *When***
Student Learning Outcomes	• **Read** website information about films in India. • **Combine** sentences with *when* and *where*. • **Complete** a conversation between production assistants. • **Find** and **edit** errors with relative clauses. • **Write** a description of a movie. • **Ask** and **answer** questions about a movie.
Lesson Vocabulary	(n.) diaspora (adj.) memorable (n.) pattern (n.) sketch (n.) storyboard (adj.) flexible (adj.) musical (n.) satellite (n.) spices (n.) visualize

EXPLORE

1 READ, page 318 — 15 min.

- Have students look at the photo. Ask, *What kind of movie do you think this is?* Ask students what they know about Bollywood films.
- Have students use context to guess the meaning of new words (e.g., *diaspora, elements, spices,* and *values*).

Be the Expert

- The first Hindi film was made in 1913, and by the 1930s, India was making several hundred films per year. Hindi films are influenced by ancient epics, Sanskrit drama, folktales, and Hollywood conventions. Some of the most famous actors are Imran Khan, Aamir Khan, Salman Khan, Kareena Kapoor Khan, and Aishwarya Rai Bachchan.
- The Indian diaspora includes all parts of the world, with more than a million Indians in eleven other countries including Malaysia, Saudi Arabia, South Africa, Canada, the UAE, the UK, and the United States.

- **Expansion Tip:** Put students in pairs to discuss these questions: *From what countries do many people migrate? Where do they tend to go? Why do you think Indians have moved to countries such as the UK, Malaysia, and the United States?*

2 CHECK, page 319 — 5 min.

1. F 2. F 3. F 4. T 5. T

3 DISCOVER, page 319 — 5 min.

A 1. nicknamed Bollywood
  2. mixing
  3. living

B (Bollywood) where mostly Hindi language films are made
  (the late 1990s) when new technology was developing

- **Tip:** Ask students to describe how the pairs of sentences in exercise **A** are different and have them try to write a rule.

LEARN

Chart 11.6, page 320 — 15 min.

- **Tip:** Before students read the notes, write the pairs of sentences from the chart on the board. Have students work in pairs to write the rules. Then, have them check their ideas against the notes on page 320.
- **Note:** The *–ing* form of the verb is sometimes called the present participle. In relative phrases that use *be* + participle, either past or present, we omit the pronoun and *be* and simply use the participle.

4 pages 320–321 — 10 min.

A 1. named after Bollywood
  2. mostly made in English
  3. a neighborhood in Nairobi, Kenya
  4. set in Nairobi
  5. known as Eastleighwood
  6. interested in world politics

B 1. having a lot of singing and dancing
  2. featuring beautiful scenery
  3. promoting social awareness
  4. starring my favorite actors
  5. showing at midnight
  6. showing life in Mumbai

106 RELATIVE CLAUSES

5 page 321 — 10 min.

A
✓ 1. Bollywood, <u>which was named after Hollywood</u>, makes different kinds of films.
✓ 2. Bollywood, <u>which is also referred to as Hindi cinema</u>, is one of the largest film producers in India.
  3. Bollywood films, <u>which many people enjoy</u>, do not pretend to show reality.
✓ 4. Bollywood, <u>which inspired many cinema movements</u>, was followed by Nollywood.
  5. Bollywood's production studio, <u>which the government built</u>, is called Film City.
✓ 6. The actors <u>who appear in Bollywood movies</u> come from all over India.

B
1. Bollywood, named after Hollywood, makes different kinds of films.
2. Bollywood, also referred to as Hindi cinema, is one of the largest film producers in India.
4. Bollywood, inspiring many cinema movements, was followed by Nollywood.
6. The actors appearing in Bollywood come from all over India.

Chart 11.7, page 322 — 10 min.

- **Note:** Point out that statement word order rather than question word order is used after *where* and *when* in relative clauses.
- **Expansion Tip:** Have students work in pairs to rewrite the sentences in the chart or notes that can be changed from *where* or *when* to a relative clause using a preposition and *which*, and vice versa. For example, students can rewrite the first sentence in the chart as: *I remember the day on which I first saw a lion in the wild.*

6 pages 322–323 — 5 min.

1. The history of film starts in the late nineteenth century when movies had no sound.
2. People wanted to go to a relaxing place where they could escape from their troubles.
3. Moviegoers saw silent movies in theaters where there were usually pianos or organs.
4. The age of silent movies ended in the late 1920s, when talking movies became popular.
5. *The Artist* takes place during the last years of silent films, when people were losing interest.
6. Today, there are a few silent film festivals where people show modern silent movies.

PRACTICE

7 page 323 — 5 min.

1. where
2. meaning
3. which
4. where
5. when
6. showing

- **Alternative Writing/Speaking:** Have students work individually to write a blog in which they give tips on how to do something they know well. When students finish, have them present their tips in pairs. Have their partners ask questions to get more information.

8 page 324 — 10 min.

1. when filming begins
2. where the bus scene happens
3. where Tom, Richard, and Marge meet
4. when we need
5. when we stop
6. where Marge's house is
7. where the director wants
8. when Tom is
9. when Tom gives
10. where the film takes

9 page 325 — 5 min.

1. wanting to be an extra in a movie
2. posted on websites
3. listed on movie studio websites
4. requested
5. required for scenes
6. requiring long hours
7. talking while filming

- **Expansion Tip:** Have students write job descriptions for one of the occupations discussed in the unit (photographer, production assistant, movie extra, etc.) using relative clauses and relative phrases.

UNIT 11 LESSON 3 **107**

10 EDIT, page 325 — 5 min.

I will never forget how I felt the night ~~where~~ when I saw the movie *The Birds*. I was watching it on TV with my family in the house where I grew up. The movie, ~~is~~ directed by Alfred Hitchcock, was made many years ago, but to this day just thinking about it scares me to death. I'll never forget the moment ~~in~~ when the woman was locked in a room with all the birds attacking her. My oldest brother, ~~who~~ wanting to be funny, started making loud bird noises and moving his arms like wings. The shadows created by his moving arms frightened me even more. Since then I have never been able to look at a lot of birds ~~are~~ sitting on a telephone wire or on tree branches without getting scared. I will never forgive Alfred Hitchcock, or my brother, for that.

11 APPLY, page 326 — 15 min.

A This is a horror movie directed by Alfred Hitchcock. The film, released in 1963, is based on a short story written by British author Daphne du Maurier. It takes place in a northern California town where birds start attacking people for no obvious reason. The main characters are Melanie and Mitch. Melanie Daniels, played by actress Tippi Hedren, is a rich young woman who follows a San Francisco lawyer named Mitch Brenner to the coastal town of Bodega Bay, where his mother and sister live. Strangely, on the day when Melanie arrives to town, birds start attacking people. At the end of the movie, Melanie hears noises coming from the attic of the Brenner home. Hundreds of birds rush at her as she opens the attic door. It's a terrifying movie!

B *Answers will vary.*

UNIT 11 Review the Grammar

1 page 327   5 min.

1. who
2. where
3. whose
4. which
5. where
6. whom, who

2 page 327   5 min.

1. In classrooms *where presentations are done well*, images can be a powerful teaching tool.
2. In the past, *when professors used fewer images*, students had to rely on listening skills.
3. Most people remember things *that/which they see* better than things *that/which they listen to*.
4. The images *that/which hold an audience's attention* are the most successful.
5. During class presentations, *which are done in all kinds of classes*, presenters use images in different ways.
6. There are many presentations *that/which use still or moving images* to illustrate a difficult concept.
7. Other presentations use images *that/which encourage discussion and debate*.
8. Sometimes a presenter's goal is to surprise students with an image *that/which gets them to look at an issue* in a new way.

3 EDIT, page 328   5 min.

　　Images communicate meanings *that/which* can't always be expressed as quickly in words. That's why images are so important in advertising. We see ads everywhere, and they affect us in ways *which* we don't realize. For example, we might see an ad for a candy bar in a movie *that/which* is shown at the local theater. Maybe a few days later, we're in the supermarket and we buy the same candy bar, ~~that~~ *which* we didn't plan to buy. When we put it into the shopping cart, we probably aren't thinking about the candy that we saw ~~it~~ in the movie.

Some people think they're not influenced by advertising because they don't buy products from ads ~~whom~~ *that/which/ø* they see right away. They don't realize that ads don't usually lead us to act immediately. This is the way ads work, though—they put ideas in our heads which we act on later.

　　Consider this photo of someone selling flowers and other products in Thailand, *where* floating markets are common. What kinds of thoughts do you associate with the image? Do you think this is a better advertising image for a travel company or for a company that sells products made in Thailand?

4 LISTEN, page 329   5 min.

A coconuts

B
1. that can provide you with iron and other minerals
2. which humans have been using for about half a million years
3. people needing refreshment
4. where you'll see coconut palm trees everywhere you look
5. which ships about 3000 of these postcards a year
6. who will feel grateful

5 WRITE & SPEAK, page 328   10 min.

Answers will vary.

UNIT 11 REVIEW THE GRAMMAR 109

Connect the Grammar to Writing

1 READ & NOTICE THE GRAMMAR,
pages 330–331   20 min.

A *Answers will vary.*

B *Answers will vary. Answers may include:*

Identifying subject relative clause:
In an instant, he changes from an ordinary person to a man who must make a heroic effort to survive.

Reduced relative clause:
Scenes from the real life event, shown at the end of the film, add to the emotional impact.

Object relative clause:
The Deep reminds us of the simple, and at times dangerous, lives that many people must live and the incredible choices that they sometimes have to face.

Relative clause with a preposition:
The gray colors and tough, weather-beaten look of everything really give viewers a taste of a different world; it is one in which people must work hard and take great risks.

Relative clause with *where*:
The whole movie does not take place only in the icy waters where Gulli floats and tries to swim (although these are certainly the most dramatic parts).

We also see many scenes of the town where he lives, both before and after the accident.

Relative clause with *whose*:
It is based on the true story of a fisherman whose boat sank at sea in 1984.

C *The Deep*
2012
Baltasar Kormakur
Gulli (Olafur Darri Olafsson)
icy waters, town where Gulli lives
Answers will vary.

2 BEFORE YOU WRITE, page 331   15 min.
Answers will vary.

3 WRITE, page 331   15 min.

> **WRITING FOCUS, page 331**
>
> Have students look at the description of *The Birds* on page 326 to notice the tense used. Then, have them rewrite the review on page 326 in the simple past. Ask them how using the present tense affects the way they read the review.

- **Alternative Writing:** Have students write about a recent television program. They do not need to include the director, but have them include information on how the episode fits in with the show as a whole.

110   RELATIVE CLAUSES

UNIT 12 The Rise of the City

Adverb Clauses

Unit Opener

Photo: Have students look at the photo. Ask, *What do you see?* Have students read the caption. Ask, *What is a financial district?*

Location: This is an aerial photo of skyscrapers in New York City's Financial District.

Theme: This unit is about cities. It includes information about why people still want to live in cities. It also describes cycling in Amsterdam. Have students look at the photos and titles on pages 334 and 345. Ask, *How do the photos relate to the theme?*

Page	Lesson	Grammar	Examples
334	1	Adverb Clauses	It started to snow **just as we were leaving the theater**. **Although I've studied a lot**, I'm still nervous about the exam.
345	2	Reduced Adverb Clauses	I saw the accident **while walking down the street**. **Being tired**, he went to bed early.
352	Review the Grammar		
354	Connect the Grammar to Writing		

Unit Grammar Terms

adverb clause: a kind of dependent clause. Like single adverbs, they can show time, reason, purpose, and condition.
➢ **When the party was over**, everyone left.

dependent clause: a clause that cannot stand alone as a sentence. It must be used with a main clause.
➢ I just bought a new car **although I couldn't afford it**.

main clause: a clause that can stand alone as a sentence. It has a subject and a verb.
➢ **I heard the news** when I was driving home.

time clause: a clause that tells when an action or event happened or will happen. Time clauses are introduced by conjunctions such as *when, after, before, while,* and *since*.
➢ I have lived here **since I was a child**.
➢ **While I was walking home**, it began to rain.

111

LESSON 1	**Adverb Clauses**

Student Learning Outcomes	• **Read** a review of a book about cities. • **Complete** sentences about cities using adverb clauses. • **Write** sentences about yourself and your city. • **Listen** to a conversation about a tall building. • **Discuss** and **present** a group plan for an ideal city. • **Find** and **edit** errors with adverb clauses.
Lesson Vocabulary	(adj.) diverse (v.) exchange (n.) public service (n.) species (n.) triumph (n.) emission (v.) inhabit (n.) resident (n.) skyscraper (v.) underestimate

EXPLORE

1 READ, page 334   15 min.

- Use the photo to teach vocabulary such as *skyscraper* and *resident*.
- Have students use the context to guess the meaning of new words (e.g., *diverse, emission, exchange inhabit, species,* and *underestimate*).

Be the Expert

Edward Glaeser is a professor of economics at Harvard University. He is interested in the way that living close to other people helps with the spread of ideas and innovation. He believes skyscrapers are architecturally interesting, greener than other buildings, and more likely to foster creativity. His book *Triumph of the City* was published in 2011.

- **Expansion Tip:** Have students reread the article and list all of the advantages Glaeser mentions for cities and for skyscrapers in particular. Have students discuss in pairs which of Glaeser's points they agree with.

2 CHECK, page 335   5 min.

1. ~~About one third~~ More than half of the world's population lives in cities.
2. Cities today are ~~decreasing~~ increasing in size.
3. According to Glaeser, cities ~~cause~~ reduce pollution.
4. ~~Eighty-six percent~~ Fewer than a third of New York City residents drive to work.
5. The reviewer ~~agrees~~ does not agree with all of Glaeser's ideas.

- **Tip:** Have students identify where in the article they found the answers to exercise **2**.

3 DISCOVER, page 335   5 min.

A 1. Whenever   4. because
      2. Since   5. Although
      3. so that

B 1. although   3. because, since
      2. so that   4. whenever

- **Tip:** Have students work in pairs to write a sentence using each word in exercise **B**.

LEARN

Chart 12.1, page 336   10 min.

- **Note:** Students have already worked with adverb clauses of time when they used time clauses with *before, after, when,* and *while*. Adverb clauses of time answer the question *when*. Focus on the meanings of the new expressions as you review and reinforce students' understanding of how time clauses work.

4 page 336   5 min.

As you fly over Singapore, you'll see enormous skyscrapers. Five million people live there in just 270 square miles (700 sq. km), so most people live in tall buildings. Whenever people think of skyscrapers, they usually think of crowded spaces. However, this is not true of the Pinnacle@Duxton in Singapore. The Pinnacle is a huge skyscraper with 1800 apartments. You'll be amazed as you walk around it. As soon as you reach the 20th floor, you'll see a 2625-foot (800-m) jogging track. You'll feel like you're running in the clouds whenever you go there to exercise. The skyscrapers in Singapore look like something from a science fiction movie. They're truly amazing works of architecture. You'll remember them as long as you live!

112   ADVERB CLAUSES

5 page 337 5 min.

1. whenever
2. As soon as
3. just as
4. Whenever
5. Whenever
6. As
7. as long as
8. just as
9. as soon as
10. Whenever

Chart 12.2, page 337 10 min.

- **Notes:** *Though* is used more frequently in conversation than in writing, even in informal writing. Point out that *although* is one word and *even though* is two.
- **Tip:** Provide students with main clauses and elicit adverb clauses of contrast (e.g., *She got an A on the test . . . , We had a great time at the party . . . , I've got a cold . . . , Our plants died. . .*).

6 pages 338–339 5 min.

1. a. Singapore has a population of five miillion although it is only 270 square miles (700 sq km) wide. (no comma)
2. b. Even though Chicago is a large city, it has a lot of of parks and gardens.
3. b. Some of the world's oldest cities are in Egypt although there are many ancient cities and towns in China. (no comma)
4. a. Toronto is the largest city in Canada although it is not the country's capital. (no comma)
5. a. Although Yamoussoukro is the capital city of the Ivory Coast, it began as a very small village.
6. a. Even though many ancient cities had walls around them, the walls did not always stop invaders.

- **Expansion Tip:** Put students in pairs and have them write five sentences about cities they know, giving surprising or unexpected information. Have volunteers write sentences on the board.

Chart 12.3, page 339 10 min.

- **Notes 1 & 2:** Students have already used *because* in sentences, so focus on how *since* can be both similar and different in meaning. Provide examples of *since* used both ways (time and reason) and elicit its meaning.
- **Note 3:** Provide examples of sentences using *because . . . now* (e.g., *I bought a new car because I earn more money now.*) and have students rewrite them using *now that*.

> **REAL ENGLISH, page 339**
>
> *So* used as a coordinating conjunction indicates result (e.g., *She didn't study, so she failed*). *So that* indicates purpose (e.g., *We're going to leave early so that we can avoid traffic*). *So* can also be an adverb (e.g., *It was so cold yesterday*). Suggest that students listen to English language television or radio programs and collect examples of the use of *so*. Ask them to give examples of *so* and explain how it was is used.

7 page 339 5 min.

1. Because
2. Since
3. now that
4. so that
5. because
6. Now that
7. Since
8. so that

8 page 340 5 min.

1. because/since
2. so that
3. so that
4. because/since
5. now that
6. because/since

PRACTICE

9 page 340 5 min.

1. so that
2. Because
3. Even though
4. since
5. as
6. Although
7. Even though
8. Whenever

10 pages 341–342 5 min.

1. Because Curitiba has historic buildings and beautiful woods around it, it is an attractive city./Curitiba is an attractive city because it has historic buildings and beautiful woods around it.
2. Curitiba has a diverse population since immigrants from Europe and Japan have made it their home./Since immigrants from Europe and Japan have made it their home, Curitiba has a diverse population.
3. As the population began to grow rapidly, Curitiba's mayor tried to reduce crowding./Curitiba's mayor tried to reduce crowding as the population began to grow rapidly.

4. Because there are no cars on "The Street of Flowers," it's a nice place to walk and shop./ "The Street of Flowers" is a nice place to walk and shop because there are no cars on it.

5. Although many people own cars in Curitiba, two million people take public transportation every day./Two million people take public transportation every day although many people own cars in Curitiba.

6. Curitiba developed a good recycling program so that it could keep the city clean./So that it could keep the city clean, Curitiba developed a good recycling program.

7. Whenever children bring cans and bottles to recycling centers, they receive small gifts./ Children receive small gifts whenever they bring cans and bottles to recycling centers.

8. Though not all of the city's garbage is recycled in Curitiba, seventy percent of it is./Seventy percent of the city's garbage in Curitiba is recycled though not all of it is.

- **Expansion Tip:** Have students research other cities that are "green"—ones that use different strategies to reduce fuel consumption, trash, and so on. In small groups, have students share what they found out.

11 WRITE & SPEAK, pages 342–343   15 min.

A 1. although/even though/though
   2. Because/Since
   3. so that
   4. Although/Even though/Though
   5. Whenever
   6. so that
   7. Because/Since
   8. because/since
   9. Whenever

B Answers will vary.
C Answers will vary.

12 LISTEN & SPEAK, pages 343–344   10 min.

A 1. Rome's first residential skyscraper
   2. in Rome
   3. negative

B 1. a
   2. b
   3. a
   4. a
   5. b
   6. b

13 EDIT, page 344   5 min.

Even though a lot of people who work in cities would prefer to live closer to their jobs, not all can afford to do so. Although Since/Because the cost of housing in cities is usually very high, a lot of people have to live outside of the city in the suburbs and commute to work. The spread of cities into outside areas is called urban sprawl. Unfortunately, urban sprawl can have serious consequences. For example, in Mexico City, developers built new buildings as fast as possible so that they could make money. They also built new housing, but it was far away from the city center. It can take two to five hours to get to work every day, so a number of people have moved in with family members who live in the city. Since Although/Even though/Though they are now more crowded, they are closer to their jobs. Even though Because/Now that many people have moved back to Mexico City, there are now a great number of empty homes in the suburbs. It will take time and careful planning to solve this problem. People will have to be patient just as urban planners try to solve this problem.

14 APPLY, page 344   15 min.

A Answers will vary.
B Answers will vary.

- **Alternative Writing:** Have students write one page on their ideal city plan. It should have at least five adverb clauses. Then, put students in pairs to exchange and edit papers.

114   ADVERB CLAUSES

LESSON 2	**Reduced Adverb Clauses**

Student Learning Outcomes	• **Read** an article about cycling in Amsterdam. • **Rewrite** sentences using reduced adverb clauses. • **Write** sentences about cities. • **Find** and **edit** errors with reduced adverb clauses. • **Speak** and **write** about city maps.
Lesson Vocabulary	(v.) accommodate (n.) cyclist (adj.) lasting (adj.) outraged (n.) smart card (adj.) apart (adj.) digital (n.) official (n.) protest (adj.) walkable

EXPLORE

1 READ, page 345   15 min.

- Have students look at the photo and read the title. Ask, *Why do you think Amsterdam is a cyclist's dream?*
- Have students use context clues to guess the meaning of new words (e.g., *smart card, accommodate, outraged, protest,* and *official*).

Be the Expert

- Amsterdam has 4000 km (2480 miles) of bike paths and lanes. Bike rentals cost about 12 euros per day or 2.50 for an hour. There are about a million bicycles in the city and 50,000 are stolen every year. Other cities that are very bicycle friendly include Copenhagen, Seville, Antwerp, Berlin, Dublin, Tokyo, and Montreal.
- **Expansion Tip:** In Lesson 1, students worked in groups to plan an ideal city. Now, have them work in pairs or groups to plan an ideal city for cyclists using ideas from the reading, their own ideas, and adverb clauses.

2 CHECK, page 346   5 min.

   1. F   2. F   3. T   4. F   5. T

- **Expansion Tip:** Have students correct the false statements and identify where they found the answers.

3 DISCOVER, page 346   5 min.

A 1. While finishing his coffee
    2. After unlocking the bike with a smart card
    3. Having had a long tradition of cycling
    4. Hoping to solve the problem quickly

B 1. 1, 2   3. while, after
    2. 3, 4   4. no

- **Tip:** Write the first sentence from exercise **A** on the board. Ask students to rewrite the beginning using a full adverb clause. By working backwards, this will help them see how adverb clauses are reduced.

LEARN

Chart 12.4, page 347   10 min.

- **Tip:** Write the two sentences from the chart and from Note 1 on the board before students look at the Notes. Elicit how the adverb clause was reduced. (The subject and *be* were omitted in the first sentence, the subject was omitted in the second sentence and the *–ing* form was used.)

- **Notes:** Reduced adverb clauses are also called adverbial phrases or reductions. One of the more frequent mistakes that students make is using a main clause with a subject that is not the subject of the reduced clause (e.g., *After spending three hours preparing the meal, none of the guests ate the food.*). Provide other examples of sentences with adverb clauses of time that students can practice. Include sentences where the subjects of the clauses are not the same, so students also practice identifying those that can be reduced.

4 pages 347–348   5 min.

1. Since starting a bike-share program,
2. After closing the downtown area to cars,
3. before getting their driver's licenses
4. After getting a bike diploma,
5. While taking a road test,
6. before exiting the car
7. While turning to open their doors,
8. After improving its road safety,

UNIT 12   LESSON 2   **115**

Chart 12.5, page 348 — 10 min.

- **Note 1:** Point out that when the main verb is *be*, there may be other ways to express the same idea (e.g., *As an only child, she was often lonely.*)
- **Note 2:** Point out that the verbs in reduced clauses have one of two forms: the *–ing* form of the main verb or *having* + the past participle of the main verb. The second form is used with perfect tenses.

5 pages 348–349 — 5 min.

1. Having 316 miles of track
2. Running every two minutes during rush hour
3. Providing digital maps and schedules
4. Having heard complaints about high subway fares
5. Having heated seats
6. Having opened a lot of new stations
7. Offering free Wi-Fi in stations and on subway cars
8. Having read about it

- **Expansion Tip:** Suggest that students work in pairs to write five sentences with adverb clauses of reason. Then, have each pair exchange sentences with another pair to reduce the clauses to adverbial phrases.

PRACTICE

6 WRITE & SPEAK, page 349 — 10 min.

- **Tip:** Suggest that students circle the subjects in each clause to help them identify those that can be reduced.

A Statements 1, 2, 4, 5, 8, 9, and 10 can be reduced.

B
1. After arriving in London, Pam and Emily took a bus to their hotel.
2. After having spent a year in Mexico, Matt spoke Spanish fluently.
4. After seeing the pyramids outside Cairo, Ed wanted to learn more about them.
5. Before moving to Istanbul, Jackie learned some Turkish.
8. Being an art history major, Tanya really enjoyed her trip to Florence.
9. After leaving Lisbon, Scott went to Madrid.
10. Having never been to Iceland, Anita was excited to spend a day there on her way to Moscow.

C Answers will vary.

- **Alternative Writing:** Have students work individually to write one or more paragraphs about a city they have visited. They should use as many adverb clauses as they can. Have students exchange paragraphs with a partner to rewrite using as many reduced adverb clauses as they can.

7 page 350 — 10 min.

1. Having driven everywhere for years, Ella wanted to move to a more walkable neighborhood.
2. Before making a decision, Ella looked for a website about walkability.
3. While doing some research online, Ella found a "walkability" website.
4. After considering factors such as walking distance to stores and public transportation, the website gives a walkability score.
5. Having gotten bad walkability scores, some communities made changes to improve their scores.
6. Having everything nearby, Ella's family is happy in their new home.
7. While walking home from school, Ella's children can stop at a park and play.
8. Having been dependent on a car for years, Ella is happy that she doesn't need one now.

8 EDIT, page 350 — 10 min.

After ~~grow~~ growing up in the suburbs, many young people in the United States are choosing to live in cities. ~~Have~~ Having attended college in lively cities, a lot of young people don't want to give up their urban lifestyles after they graduate. Cities offer a variety of interesting things to do plus the convenience of having everything nearby. After ~~experience~~ experiencing city life, many young people find living in the suburbs boring. Transportation is another factor that makes cities attractive to them. Having spent their early years riding around in the family car, a lot of young people prefer to get around on public transportation, by bike, or on foot. These forms of transportation give them more independence. ~~Being~~ Because they are more independent, their parents are proud of them. There are other benefits, too. For example, walking can be a social activity. While friends are walking together, they can have a conversation or stop and have coffee. Since there are sidewalks, bike lanes, and public transportation, there's no need to have a car in many cities. Not ~~own~~ owning cars, young people don't have to spend money on parking and gas.

Whenever they want to leave the city, they can rent a car or take a bus or train. Cities offer everything that many young people want these days.

9 APPLY, page 351 — 20 min.

- **Tip:** Ask students questions about the map (e.g., *Where is Fisherman's Wharf? How far is it from Coit Tower?*).

A *Answers may vary. Possible answers:*

1. After leaving the Transamerica Pyramid, you will need about 20 minutes to walk to Coit Tower.
2. After leaving Union Square, you can get to Fisherman's Wharf quickly by taking Powell Street.
3. While traveling from Union Square to Fisherman's Wharf, you will see Chinatown and North Beach.
4. While walking from Powell Street to Telegraph Hill, you will cross Grant Avenue and Montgomery.
5. Before arriving in Chinatown, you will see the Transamerica Pyramid.
6. Yes, before having dinner at Pier 39, you should spend some time shopping there.

B *Answers will vary.*

C *Answers will vary.*

- **Alternative Writing/Speaking:** Have students choose any means of transportation to get around their city or hometown to visit interesting places. Tell them to write five to ten sentences using adverb clauses or reductions. Then, have them tell a partner about such a tour. (E.g., *Traveling by bike, you can see a great deal of the city.*)

Review the Grammar UNIT 12

1 page 352 5 min.

1. <u>Although Pontevedra has only around 85,000 people</u>, traffic congestion used to be a problem.
2. (Being the major city in the region), it has attracted a lot of commuters.
3. <u>Since it now has a free bike-lending service</u>, the city has set a new lower speed limit for cars.
4. The city council designed a special map with walking times <u>so that the city would become more walkable</u>.
5. People can leave their cars in one of the free parking lots <u>whenever they visit the city</u>.
6. <u>Though people disliked the new policies at first</u>, they now support them.
7. (Being a small city), Pontevedra was never very well known outside of the region.
8. <u>Now that it is such a walkable city</u>, it has become popular with urban planners.

2 page 352 5 min.

1. so that
2. Whenever
3. Just as
4. Though
5. so that
6. Having spent
7. Since
8. Although

3 LISTEN & SPEAK, pages 352–353 15 min.

A Amsterdam, Dubai, Stockholm, Yokohama

B 1. b
2. b
3. a
4. b
5. a

C *Answers will vary.*

4 EDIT, page 353 5 min.

Even ~~though~~ Sydney is more famous, Melbourne, Australia is one of the most livable cities in the world. What makes a city livable? Excellent education, quality health care, good roads, and public transportation are essential. People need to feel safe **so** that they can walk around day or night without feeling afraid. ~~Even though~~ Because/Since it has a great tram system, people can get around Melbourne easily. Having so many restaurants, unique shops, and music festivals, Melbourne offers a wide variety of leisure activities. ~~Although~~ Because/Since it's located on the beautiful Yarra River, it's perfect for water sports. Melbourne has great weather, too. Whenever they are in the mood**,** residents can go to the beach. ~~Though~~ Because/Since Melbourne has so much to offer, it has visitors from all over the world. After ~~come~~ coming to the city, people don't want to leave.

5 SPEAK & WRITE, page 353 10 min.

Answers will vary.

118 ADVERB CLAUSES

Connect the Grammar to Writing

1 READ & NOTICE THE GRAMMAR,
pages 354–355   20 min.

A *Answers will vary.*

B *Answers will vary. Possible answers:*

Reduced Adverb Clauses	Changed into Full Adverb Clauses
Having lived near the highway at that time . . .	Because I lived near the highway at that time . . .
Seeing the greenery and flowing stream . . .	When I see the greenery and flowing stream . . .
Having brought beautiful scenery to Seoul . . .	Because it brought beautiful scenery to Seoul . . .

C *Answers will vary.*

2 BEFORE YOU WRITE, page 355   15 min.

3 WRITE, page 355   15 min.

> **WRITING FOCUS, page 355**
>
> Have students choose one of the cities discussed in the unit and write three sentences comparing that city with another one they know well. Each sentence should use *like*. (e.g., *Like Rome, Athens has a lot of ancient buildings.*) Have students share their sentences in pairs.

- **Alternative Writing:** Have students imagine they are writing a tourist guide for a city they know well. Tell them to choose one neighborhood and list the positive and negative features of that neighborhood. Then, have them write a review using full and reduced adverb clauses. (e.g., *If you're planning a trip to Washington, D.C., you should visit the National Mall. Running from the Capitol to the Lincoln Memorial, you can see the Washington Monument, the Reflecting Pool, and many other memorials.*)

UNIT 12   CONNECT THE GRAMMAR TO WRITING   119

UNIT 13 Choices

Conditionals

Unit Opener

Photo: Have students look at the photo and read the caption. Ask, *What do you see?*

Location: People trying to decide which way to go in the middle of multiple waterfalls (Plitvice Lakes National Park, Croatia)

Theme: This unit is about choices. It provides information on decision making, a debate on extinct animals, and a man's walk around the world. Have students look at the photos and titles on pages 358, 366, and 377. Ask, *How do the photos relate to the theme?*

Page	Lesson	Grammar	Examples
358	1	Present and Future Real Conditionals	**If I eat late at night,** I don't sleep well. He won't graduate **unless he passes all of his classes.**
366	2	Present and Future Unreal Conditionals; *Wish*	**If I lived in Rio de Janeiro,** I'd go to the beach every day. **If you didn't have to work,** you could go with us. We wish we **lived** in a nicer place.
377	3	Past Unreal Conditionals; *Wish*	**If he had gone to class,** he would have seen her. I wish **I had studied** harder for last week's test.
385	**Review the Grammar**		
388	**Connect the Grammar to Writing**		

Unit Grammar Terms

conditional: a structure used to express an activity or event that depends on something else.
➢ ***If the weather is nice on Sunday**, we'll go to the beach.*

future conditional: expresses something that we believe will happen in the future based on certain conditions; the *if*-clause + simple present gives the condition, and *will* or *be going to* + the base form of the verb gives the result.
➢ ***If you don't go to practice, the coach will not let you play in the game.***

if clause: a clause that begins with *if* that expresses a condition.
➢ ***If you drive too fast,** you will get a ticket.*

unreal: used to describe situations that are contrary to fact, impossible, or unlikely to happen.
➢ *If I **weren't learning** English, I **would have** more free time.*
➢ *I **wish I had** a million dollars.*

120

LESSON 1 Present and Future Real Conditionals

Student Learning Outcomes	• **Read** an article about making decisions. • **Make** sentences with conditionals. • **Write** and **speak** about careers. • **Listen** to a talk about making decisions. • **Discuss** and **write** about decisions. • **Find** and **edit** errors with conditionals.
Lesson Vocabulary	(n.) brand (adj.) costly (n.) influence (v.) perceive (adj.) rational (n.) candidate (adj.) efficient (n.) non-profit (n.) rate (n.) workaholic

EXPLORE

1 READ, page 358 — 15 min.

- Have students look at the photo. Ask, *Where are the people? What are they doing? What images do you see?*
- Have students use context to guess the meaning of new words (e.g., *efficient, influence, reaction, perceive, candidate, rational*).

Be the Expert

- A study conducted at Arizona State University found that voters often preferred candidates who are physically attractive.

2 CHECK, page 359 — 5 min.

1. F   2. T   3. F   4. T   5. F

- **Expansion Tip:** Have students work in pairs to discuss their reasons for decisions they have made in the last week. Ask, *What influenced your decision? What information did you consider?* After reading the article, do you think your decision was rational?

3 DISCOVER, page 359 — 5 min.

A 1. <u>If you are</u> like most people, you will probably choose Flyright.

2. However, <u>if you stop and think,</u> you will find no difference between the two flight records.

3. . . . <u>if an option is presented</u> in a positive way, people usually prefer it.

4. <u>Even if we think</u> our decisions are completely rational, they are not.

5. <u>if we know this,</u> we will be able to do something about it in the future.

B 1. Sentence b   2. Sentence a   3. b

LEARN

Chart 13.1, page 360 — 10 min.

- **Note:** Real conditionals describe conditions and results that actually happen. Explain that conditionals, like other adverb clauses, can come before or after the main clause with no change in meaning.
- **Expansion Tip:** Write three main clauses on the board and have students write three conditional clauses for each, using *if, unless,* and *even if*. On the board, have volunteers write sentences that connect the *if* clause and the main clause.

4 pages 360–361 — 10 min.

A 1. a   2. a   3. a   4. b

B 1. drive; want   5. needs; thinks
2. has; go   6. buy; return
3. see; am not   7. have; ask
4. makes; tries   8. shop; don't make

5 page 361 — 5 min.

A 1. If   3. when   5. if   7. Unless
2. even if   4. even if   6. If   8. even if

B SPEAK

Answers will vary.

Chart 13.2, page 362 — 10 min.

- **Note:** Point out that any present verb forms can be used in the *if* clause, including modals, simple present, and present continuous. A common mistake students make with future real conditionals is to use a future verb in the conditional clause.

6 page 362 — 5 min.

A 1. make; will choose/might choose
2. make; will hurt/can hurt/may hurt

UNIT 13   LESSON 1   121

3. worries; will not be/may not be
4. thinks; may have/will have/might have
5. don't sleep; will be/can be/may be
6. ask; will get/may get/might get
7. are; won't try/might not try/may not try
8. keeps; will learn/may learn

B SPEAK

Answers will vary.

7 page 363   5 min.

1. If Paulo takes the internship, he will/may/might get some useful job experience.
2. He will be interested if his coworkers teach him new skills.
3. If he does the internship, it will be good for his resume.
4. If he accepts the position, he will/may/might make some professional connections.
5. He won't get in shape unless the work is physically demanding.
6. He won't be able to pay his bills unless he has a paying job.
7. He won't/might not/may not accept the offer if his work hours are 7:00 a.m. to 7:00 p.m.
8. If he enjoys the internship, he will/may/might apply for the job.

B *Answers will vary.*

PRACTICE

8 pages 363–364   10 min.

1. If you choose a career that matches your talents, your job will be more enjoyable. OR Your job will be more enjoyable if you choose a career that matches your talents.
2. Even if we don't realize it, we each have a personal work style.
3. If you don't like a set schedule, you will be happier in a job that has flexible hours.
4. If you don't like to be away from home, don't take a job that requires travel.
5. A stressful job might be good for you if a lot of pressure helps you to succeed.
6. Don't choose a low-paying career if making a lot of money is important to you.
7. The interviewer won't be interested in you unless you seem excited about the job.
8. It is hard to make a decision unless you know all your career possibilities.

9 WRITE & SPEAK, page 364   10 min.

Answers will vary.

10 EDIT, page 364   10 min.

If ~~Even~~ you don't want to work in an office every day, you should consider starting your own business. That's right, you can be your own boss! If you have a hobby that you are very good at, you might be able to earn a living doing it. For example, if you ~~will~~ have a talent for web design, you could sell your services to small companies. To get started, choose a company that you know about and show them some examples of web pages you've designed. ~~Unless~~ If they like your work, offer to design a web page for them for a small fee. If you ~~will~~ do a good job the first time, they will probably hire you again. They may also recommend you to other businesses. Soon you'll have a lot of customers contacting you, and you'll be running your own business. ~~If~~ Even if you don't make a lot of money, you'll feel satisfied and successful. You will also be doing something you love. Running your own business can be a lot of work, but it's worth it. If people ~~will~~ enjoy their jobs, they are usually happier. You won't know for sure unless you ~~are going to~~ try.

11 WRITE & SPEAK, page 365   10 min.

A *Answers will vary. Answers may include:*

1. If you have your own business, you can be your own boss.
2. You will/may/might work 60–80 hours a week if you have your own business.
3. You will not have much free time if you have your own business.
4. If you have your own business, you will not have any paid vacation time.
5. If you have your own business, you will do something you love.
6. You will take risks if you have your own business.

B *Answers will vary.*

- **Alternative Writing/Speaking:** Have students list three things they love to do. Then, have them talk in pairs about complementary careers (e.g., *love to hike—lead hiking trips, work for the park service*). Have students list advantages and disadvantages of one job, and write sentences using conditionals. Call on students to share their ideas with the class.

12 LISTEN, page 365   10 min.

the time of day, eating, too many choices, language

B 1. T   2. F   3. T   4. F   5. F

13 APPLY, page 365   15 min.

A & B *Answers will vary.*

LESSON 2   Present and Future Unreal Conditionals; *Wish*

Student Learning Outcomes
- **Read** an article about animal extinction.
- **Write** sentences about people's wishes.
- **Write** and **talk** about personal wishes.
- **Give** opinions on issues.
- **Discuss** hypothetical situations.
- **Find** and **edit** errors with conditionals and *wish*.

Lesson Vocabulary

| (n.) contribution | (adj.) extinct | (v.) permit | (n.) resource | (n.) tundra |
| (n./v.) debate | (n.) habitat | (v.) release | (v.) revive | (n.) vegetarian |

EXPLORE

1 READ, page 366 — 15 min.
- Have students look at the photo. Ask them to describe what they see. Ask them what other animals have become extinct.
- Have students use context clues to guess the meaning of new words (e.g., *revive, tundra, habitat,* and *debate*).

Be the Expert
- Mammoths originated in Africa three to four million years ago but spread to Europe, Asia, and North America when sea levels were low. The bones of extinct mammoths were first found and described about 300 years ago.
- In May 2013, scientists in Siberia discovered a very well-preserved mammoth in a chunk of ice in the Arctic Sea. They have been able to extract DNA. They think that they can clone a mammoth some day.
- **Expansion Tip:** Have students research other extinct species to answer these questions: *Does DNA from this species exist? What would be the advantage of bringing the species back? How would a revival of the species affect other animals including people?* Have students discuss their findings in small groups.

2 CHECK, page 367 — 5 min.
1. They are all extinct species.
2. They are becoming extinct.
3. It has turned into tundra.
4. They might be harmed by hunting, or pollution, or die out again.

3 DISCOVER, page 367 — 5 min.

A 1. T   2. F   3. T   4. T

B 1. T   2. F   3. F   4. F

LEARN

Chart 13.3, page 368 — 10 min.
- **Note 3:** The simple past form indicates that the situation is unreal, not that the action occurred in the past.
- **Expansion Tip:** Write example sentences containing errors on the board. Have students correct the errors.

4 pages 368–369 — 10 min.
1. If extinct animals *were* brought back to life, there *would be* consequences.
2. Most people *would not believe* it if they *saw* a dinosaur.
3. Animals that have gone extinct *would cause* problems if they *were* revived.
4. What *would happen* if woolly mammoths *lived* in Siberia now?
5. *Would* it *improve* the land if woolly mammoths *were* alive today?
6. If my government *spent* money on reviving extinct species, I *would be* unhappy.
7. If I *were* a scientist, I *would* be interested in researching extinct species.
8. I *would major* in biology if I *got* into a good program.
9. *Would* fewer species go extinct if people *took* better care of the environment?
10. It *would be* better for the environment if scientists *spent* their energy on living species, not extinct species.

Chart 13.4, page 369 — 10 min.

- **Notes 1 & 5:** Make sure students understand that *wish* is talking about a situation that does not and will not exist. *Hope* is used for things that are possible.
- **Expansion Tip:** Have students write five sentences about existing situations that they are not happy about. (e.g., *My sister can't come to visit this weekend.*) Then, have them exchange their sentences with a partner so that the partner can write corresponding sentences with *wish*. (e.g., *Mara wishes her sister could come to visit this weekend.*)

5 page 369 — 5 min.

A
1. were
2. am helping
3. did
4. can find
5. could work
6. were sitting
7. lived
8. called
9. had
10. give

B SPEAK

Answers will vary.

PRACTICE

6 page 370 — 10 min.

- **Tip:** Before students do exercise **6**, have them look at photo and caption. Ask, *Would you like an owl as a pet? Why, or why not? What other unusual animals do people sometimes have as pets? What problems do unusual pets cause?*

1. understood
2. would change
3. realized
4. would think
5. knew
6. would not be able to
7. would change
8. were
9. stopped
10. would help

7 page 371 — 5 min.

Answers will vary. Answers may include:

1. Kate wishes she had a pet owl.
2. Len wishes he knew how to help it.
3. Josh wishes he had his cell phone with him.
4. Molly wishes the cars wouldn't drive so fast down her street.
5. Jenny wishes her parents would let her go to Australia.
6. Meg wishes her neighbors wouldn't play loud music every night./Meg wishes she could sleep.
7. Anna wishes her sister wouldn't borrow her clothes without asking first./Anna wishes her sister would ask her before she borrows her clothes.
8. Roland wishes his roommate would clean their apartment.

- **Alternative Writing:** To use as prompts, bring in photos that show people and action. Using *wish*, have students write sentences about the people. Call on students to read their sentences aloud, or ask volunteers to write sentences on the board.

8 WRITE & SPEAK, page 371 — 10 min.

Answers will vary.

9 WRITE & SPEAK, page 372 — 15 min.

Answers will vary.

> **REAL ENGLISH,** page 372
>
> Write two or three sentences on the board that give advice. (e.g., *You should call your mother and apologize. You ought to study more for the next test. Why don't you try exercising in the morning?*) Have students rewrite the advice using *If I were you* and the appropriate completion. (e.g., *If I were you, I'd call your mother and apologize.*)

- **Expansion Tip:** Have students stand and walk around the room to talk to their classmates, taking turns to share a problem and give advice. This will help students become much more fluent in using *If I were you* to give advice.

10 PRONUNCIATION, page 373 — 10 min.

A
1. it would
2. It wouldn't
3. they wouldn't
4. I would not
5. I would
6. I would not
7. We would
8. It would

B *Answers will vary.*

11 WRITE & SPEAK, page 373 — 10 min.

A *Answers will vary. Answers may include:*
1. would be/wouldn't be
2. wouldn't survive
3. wouldn't wear
4. wouldn't buy
5. would live
6. wouldn't keep
7. would be
8. would help

B *Answers will vary.*

12 WRITE & SPEAK, page 374 — 10 min.

A
1. If people understood the consequences, they would not to keep wild animals as pets./People wouldn't want to keep wild animals as pets if they understood the consequences.
2. If my sister were not allergic to dogs, we could get one./We could get a dog if my sister were not allergic to them.
3. If I didn't have to work late, I could go to the movies tonight./I could go to the movies tonight if I didn't have to work late.
4. If Nick had the time, he would take guitar lessons./Nick would take guitar lessons if he had the time.
5. If I lived near my office, I would walk to work every day./I would walk to work every day if I lived near my office.
6. If Lila were in shape, she would run in the race./Lila would run in the race if she were in shape.
7. If Tom and Sarah needed a car, they would buy one./Tom and Sarah would buy a car if they needed one.
8. If I felt well, I would go to the gym this afternoon./I would go to the gym this afternoon if I felt well.

B *Answers will vary.*

C *Answers will vary.*

13 EDIT, page 375 — 10 min.

A: If someone on the street offered you money, ~~you would~~ would you take it?

B: No, I ~~don't~~ wouldn't.

A: Why not? I often wish a stranger would give me money.

B: I guess I don't trust strangers. If a stranger ~~tries~~ tried to give me money, I'd think it was a trick. Nobody just gives money away without a reason.

A: What would you do if money ~~would fall~~ fell out of a window?

B: That would never happen either.

A: I guess you're right. I wish things like that ~~happen~~ happened, but they never do.

B: I know. I wish making money ~~is~~ were that easy, but it's not.

14 READ & LISTEN, page 375 — 10 min.

A *Answers will vary.*

B No.

C
1. would give
2. had to share
3. were
4. would be
5. wouldn't
6. would be
7. didn't split
8. would stop

15 WRITE & SPEAK, page 376 — 10 min.

A
1. Would you talk to a stranger if he or she stopped you on the street?
2. If a stranger offered you money, would you take it?/Would you take money if a stranger offered it?
3. If you got some money from a stranger, would you share it?/Would you share it if you got some money from a stranger?
4. Would it be fair if you kept all the money for yourself?/If you kept all the money for yourself, would it be fair?
5. Would you get angry if your friend didn't share the money with you?/If your friend didn't share the money with you, would you get angry?
6. Would you be annoyed if the stranger took the money back?/If the stranger took the money back, would you be annoyed?

B *Answers will vary.*

16 APPLY, page 376 — 20 min.

Answers will vary.

LESSON 3 | Past Unreal Conditionals; *Wish*

Student Learning Outcomes
- **Read** an article about a man's walk around the world.
- **Write** and **speak** about wishes regarding the past.
- **Rewrite** sentences using past unreal conditionals.
- **Listen** to sentences with reduced forms.
- **Write** about and **discuss** life-changing decisions.

Lesson Vocabulary

| (n.) container | (n.) life raft | (n.) migration | (n.) pace | (adj.) skillful |
| (adj.) harsh | (v.) measure | (adj.) overpowering | (adj.) scarce | (v.) strengthen |

EXPLORE

1 READ, page 377 — 15 min.
- Have students look at the photo. Ask, *Why do you think he is doing this? Why is this unusual?*
- Have students use context to guess the meaning of new words (e.g., *pace, migration, scarce, overpowering, harsh,* and *commitment*).

Be the Expert
- The Afar Triangle is also known as the Afar Depression and is home to 12 active volcanoes. Magma swirls beneath the surface, erupting occasionally and swallowing land features. It includes the lowest point in Africa. Because of the low elevation, it has been repeatedly flooded by the Red Sea, which has left behind layers of salt. Scientists go to the Afar Triangle to study the geologic processes.
- Paul Salopek is an American journalist who grew up in Mexico. He has won two Pulitzer Prizes. He has reported on mountain gorillas, the Human Genome Project, and border issues, among other things. He plans to walk from Africa through the Middle East and Asia, and then cross over to North America and continue south to the tip of South America.
- **Expansion Tip:** Put students in pairs to discuss these questions: *How is traveling on foot different from traveling in other ways? Why would someone want to travel this way? As a journalist, how might the kind of stories he or she reports on be affected by the form of travel used?*

2 CHECK, page 378 — 5 min.
1. Salopek is walking to follow the path of ~~animal~~ human migration out of Africa.
2. Salopek walked across Ethiopia ~~alone~~ with guides.
3. People can follow Salopek's journey by reading his ~~newspaper articles~~ website.
4. Salopek sometimes feels lonely during his journey ~~and~~ but this ~~may~~ will not stop his future travels.

3 DISCOVER, page 378 — 5 min.

A 1. a 2. b 3. b 4. a

B 1. a 2. c 3. b 4. c

- **Tip:** Ask students to try to write rules for past unreal conditionals. Then, have them check their ideas against Chart 13.5.

LEARN

Chart 13.5, page 379 — 15 min.
- **Notes 1–5:** To focus on form, write on the board: *If* + subject + *had* + past participle and subject + *would/could/might have* + past participle. Leave this on the board as students work through the exercises in this lesson.
- **Expansion Tip:** Write sentences on the board that express facts in the past. (e.g., *I didn't study. I failed the test. // Ana missed her flight. She was late.*) Have students work in pairs to write sentences using past unreal conditionals.

4 page 379 — 10 min.

A
1. had invited
2. had asked
3. wouldn't have been
4. would have kept
5. might have gotten
6. had gone
7. had been
8. have worn

126 CONDITIONALS

B SPEAK

Answers will vary.

5 page 380 — 10 min.

1. hadn't chosen; wouldn't have raised/might not have raised/couldn't have raised
2. would have been/might have been/could have been; hadn't rained
3. wouldn't have been able/might not have been able; hadn't been
4. hadn't had; would have had/might have had/could have had
5. would have gotten/might have gotten/could have gotten; hadn't drunk
6. hadn't used; wouldn't have been/might not have been/couldn't have been

Chart 13.6, page 380 — 10 min.

- **Note:** Point out that the clause that follows *wish* is similar to the *if* clause in structure.
- **Expansion Tip:** Write sentences with errors on the board and have students correct them.

6 SPEAK & WRITE, pages 380–381 — 5 min.

A
1. had walked
2. had done
3. had gone
4. had brought
5. hadn't given
6. had spent
7. hadn't moved
8. had worn

B SPEAK

Answers will vary.

PRACTICE

7 READ & WRITE, pages 381–382 — 15 min.

- **Tip:** Point out that we use the verb *catch* with *fire* when we are talking about something that starts to burn.

B
1. If the boat hadn't hit the large container, water wouldn't have gotten into the boat./Water wouldn't have gotten into the boat if the boat hadn't hit the large container.
2. If he hadn't been skillful, he would not have been able to fix the hole./He would not have been able to fix the hole if he hadn't been skillful.
3. If he had not gotten into the life raft, he would not have survived./He would not have survived if he had not gotten into the life raft.
4. If the people on the other ships had seen him, they would have rescued him./The people on the other ships would have rescued him if they had seen him.
5. If he had controlled the fire, the life raft wouldn't have caught fire./The life raft wouldn't have caught fire if he had controlled the fire.
6. If the man hadn't gone out on his boat, he wouldn't have had this terrible experience./The man wouldn't have had this terrible experience if he hadn't gone out on his boat.

C
1. He wishes the shipping container hadn't hit his boat.
2. He wishes the weather had been good.
3. He wishes the people on the other ships had noticed him.
4. He wishes he had taken more food and water from his boat before it sank.
5. He wishes he could have put out the fire on the life raft.
6. He wishes he had stayed home.

- **Alternative Writing/Speaking:** Brainstorm a list of movies, books, or real-life news stories in which a number of events have gone wrong (e.g., *Guardians of the Galaxy, the Amazing Race,* an attempt to swim to Cuba, etc.). Put students in pairs to choose a story and write a paragraph describing what went wrong and the results. Then, have students write sentences using past unreal conditionals.

8 PRONUNCIATION, page 383 — 10 min.

A
1. would not have gotten
2. would have reached
3. would have been
4. would not have survived
5. would have been
6. would not have started

9 WRITE & SPEAK, pages 383–384 — 15 min.

Answers will vary.

- **Expansion Tip:** Have students find new partners and describe their first partner's wishes and regrets.

10 APPLY, page 384 — 15 min.

A *Answers will vary.*

UNIT 13 LESSON 3 127

Review the Grammar UNIT 13

1 page 385 5 min.

1. f   5. b
2. a   6. c
3. h   7. e
4. g   8. d

2 WRITE, page 385 5 min.

Answers will vary.

3 pages 385–386 5 min.

1. moved   5. would arrive
2. had told   6. had been able
3. had known   7. hadn't seen
4. were   8. didn't have to read it

4 EDIT & SPEAK, pages 386–387 5 min.

A Some people wish it ~~is~~ were possible to travel back into the past. If it were possible, they ~~can~~ could go back to any time they wanted. At least, that's what they think. Actually, this isn't true, but it's easy to get the wrong idea. When you ~~will see~~ see movies about time travel, you don't always get the full story. In fact, you can only go back to the time when your time machine was created. For example, if your time machine was built on January 1 and you traveled in it six months later, then you ~~can't~~ couldn't travel back in time any earlier than January 1.

Why is time travel such an attractive idea? We all have done things in the past that we wish we hadn't done. We wish things had happened differently. For example, if I ~~didn't go~~ hadn't gone to the store the day of my car accident, the accident wouldn't have happened. I wouldn't have gotten hurt if it ~~didn't happen~~ hadn't happened. If time travel allowed us to go back in time, it ~~will~~ would be possible to prevent bad experiences. Wouldn't we all want to do that if we could? It's too bad we can't.

Future time travel, however, is possible. If scientists figure out how to do it, people will be able to see their lives 20 or 30 years into the future. If you could travel 20 or 30 years into the future, ~~will~~ would you want to do it?

B Answers will vary.

5 LISTEN & SPEAK, page 387 15 min.

A

1. Why did young Mallett want to go back in time?	His father died.
2. What did he read that made him think about making a time machine?	He read H. G. Wells's science fiction novel, *The Time Machine*.
3. What could Mallett do if he had a time machine?	He could go back into the past and do something to prevent his father's death.
4. Why did Mallett keep his work a secret?	If he had shown his work to other scientists, they would have thought he was crazy.
5. What does Mallett believe will happen if he keeps making progress?	If his work keeps progressing, he will be successful.
6. How could time machines be helpful?	They can warn people of coming disasters.

B Answers will vary. Answers may include:

1. If his father hadn't died, Mallett wouldn't have wanted to go back in time./Mallett wouldn't have wanted to go back in time if his father hadn't died.
2. If Mallett hadn't read H. G. Wells's science fiction novel, *The Time Machine*, he wouldn't have thought about making a time machine./Mallett wouldn't have thought about making a time machine if he hadn't read H. G. Wells's science fiction novel, *The Time Machine*.
3. If Mallett had a time machine, he could go back into the past and do something to prevent his father's death./Mallett could go back and do something to prevent his father's death if he had a time machine.
4. Mallett believes that if his work keeps progressing, he will be successful./Mallett believes that he will be successful if his work keeps progressing.
5. If we had time machines, they could help warn people of coming disasters./Time machines could help warn people of coming disasters if we had them.

6 WRITE & SPEAK, page 387 10 min.

Answers will vary.

128 CONDITIONALS

Connect the Grammar to Writing

1 READ & NOTICE THE GRAMMAR,
pages 388–389   20 min.

A Answers will vary.

B

After all, <u>if you have money</u>[R], you have fewer financial worries.

I think that people who dislike their jobs are not truly happy <u>even if they are wealthy</u>[R].

<u>Unless I made enough money to retire early</u>[U], I would not choose a job that I disliked.

I want to enjoy my work <u>even if it means I will make less money</u>[R].

<u>If I had no time for my kids</u>[U], I would be very unhappy.

They may not care if the work they do is interesting, <u>as long as it pays very well</u>[R].

C **REASON 1:** People who choose a job for the money may not like it.

REASON 2: High-paying jobs require long hours and keep you away from your family.

2 BEFORE YOU WRITE, page 389   15 min.

3 WRITE, page 389   15 min.

> **WRITING FOCUS, page 389**
>
> If possible, use students' past writing assignments as a source for sentence fragments. Write or display the examples on the board and have students correct them. If you have not saved examples of student writing, write some correct and some incorrect sentences on the board. Have students identify and edit the fragments.

- **Alternative Writing:** Have students write about where they would like to live. First, put them in small groups to discuss the following: *Where would you like to live and why?* Then, have students complete a chart like the one in exercise **1C** before they write their essays. After students have written their essays, have them exchange papers and edit the classmate's essay focusing on correcting fragments.

UNIT 13 CONNECT THE GRAMMAR TO WRITING **129**

UNIT 14 Food

Noun Clauses and Reported Speech

Unit Opener

Photo: Have students look at the photo and read the caption. Ask, *What do you see?*

Location: With more than 14 million people, Istanbul is the largest city in Turkey. The city covers more than 2000 square miles (5000 square kilometers). It has also been known as Byzantium and Constantinople and has served as the capital of the Roman, Byzantine, Latin, and Ottoman empires.

Theme: This unit is about food. It includes information about the relationship between food and the brain, research on food and the senses, and a cooking class in Italy. Have students look at the photos and titles on pages 392, 403, and 412. Ask, *How do the photos relate to the theme?*

Page	Lesson	Grammar	Examples
392	1	Noun Clauses	Gina discovered **that her refrigerator was broken**. Did you know **that it's supposed to snow**? Please explain **why you missed the deadline**.
403	2	Reported Speech: Part 1	Troy told me **that he wasn't ready**. She said **that they couldn't leave early**. Ben asked **if the car was going to be safe**.
412	3	Reported Speech: Part 2	The chef **told me to stir the soup**. Bob said he'd be out of the office **that** afternoon.
419	**Review the Grammar**		
422	**Connect the Grammar to Writing**		

Unit Grammar Terms

direct quote: a statement of a speaker's exact words using quotation marks.
➤ *Our teacher said, "Do exercises 5 and 6 for homework."*

imperative: a sentence that gives an instruction or command.
➤ ***Turn** left at the light.*
➤ ***Don't use** the elevator.*

noun clause: a kind of dependent clause. A noun clause can be used in place of a noun, a noun phrase, or a pronoun.
➤ *Could you tell me **where the bank is**?*

reported speech: part of a sentence (a noun clause or infinitive phrase) that reports what someone has said.
➤ *They said **that they would be late**.*
➤ *They told **us not to wait**.*
➤ *Sandra said, "I missed class **today**." When I saw Sandra, she said that she had missed class **yesterday**.*

LESSON 1	Noun Clauses
Student Learning Outcomes	• **Read** an article about the relationship between food and the brain. • **Ask** and **answer** questions about diets. • **Discuss** places that have experienced a famine. • **Listen** to a radio show about solar cooking and **answer** questions. • **Find** and **edit** errors with noun clauses. • **Speak** about food and diets.
Lesson Vocabulary	(adj.) allergic (n.) anthropologist (adj.) concerned (n.) neuroscientist (adj.) raw (n.) ancestor (adj.) beneficial (n.) neuron (n.) nutrient (adj.) significant

EXPLORE

1 READ, page 392   15 min.

- Have students look at the photo. Ask, *What do you see in this house? Who do you think lived there? How did they stay warm? How did they cook? What did they probably eat?*
- Have students use context to guess the meaning of new words (e.g., *neuron, biological anthropologist, digest, raw, theory, evidence, neuroscientist*).

Be the Expert

- Richard Wrangham is a primatologist and studies all kinds of primates. He is the cofounder of the Kibale Chimpanzee Project in Uganda. He is interested in primate social systems and has focused on aggression and more recently, on cooking.
- Suzana Herculano-Houzel is a professor at the Federal University in Rio de Janeiro, Brazil. She has written six books on the neuroscience of everyday life. She discusses her research on how cooking has affected the human brain on a TED talk.

- **Expansion Tip:** Have students watch the TED talk online and take notes. Have them answer these questions: *What is special about the human brain? How does Suzana Herculano-Houzel count neurons? How do other large apes afford or support their number of neurons? What does cooking do to food?*

2 CHECK, page 393   5 min.

1. One advantage of cooking food is that it makes it easier and faster for humans to digest food and gain energy for the brain and body.
2. A raw-food diet doesn't support brain growth because it provides less energy.
3. Some scientists doubt the cooking theory because there is no evidence of fire being used for food preparation until much later.

- **Expansion Tip:** Put students in small groups to discuss diets they are familiar with (e.g., raw food, vegan, Paleo). Have them list the pros and cons of each. Then, call on students to share their ideas with the class.

3 DISCOVER, page 393   5 min.

A   1. that   3. if
    2. why   4. whether or not
B   c

LEARN

Chart 14.1, page 394   10 min.

- **Note 1:** Give a brief overview of clauses to help students understand the role of a noun clause. Review the two major types of clauses (main or independent and dependent). Tell them that dependent clauses can be relative (or adjective) clauses, adverb clauses, or noun clauses.

4 page 394   10 min.

   Some people feel <u>that we should eat the way our ancestors did</u>. In other words, they believe <u>that eating raw food is healthier for human beings</u>. People that think like this eat only raw food, including some meats. Often they believe <u>that a raw-food diet is better for the environment</u>. Some hope <u>they will lose weight by eating only raw food</u>. But not everyone agrees.

   "If you're healthy, this is a terrible idea," said neuroscientist Suzana Herculano-Houzel. The problem is <u>that humans have to eat lots of raw food to get all the necessary nutrients</u>. That takes a lot of time. Also, people forget <u>that our bodies have changed over time</u>. Thus, we may not be able to eat exactly as our ancestors did. However, it is true <u>that many diets of the past were healthier</u>. We probably should try to eat more simply as our

UNIT 14   LESSON 1   **131**

ancestors did. For example, we can avoid food that is processed. Most people agree <u>that we should eat more vegetables</u>. Some people are also certain <u>that a diet of different-colored foods (red radishes, green spinach, blueberries) is especially beneficial</u>.

5 WRITE & SPEAK, page 395   5 min.

A *Answers will vary.*

B *Answers will vary.*

Chart 14.2, page 395   10 min.

- **Note:** Students often use question order rather than statement order in noun clauses. This is especially common with the question words in Chart 14.3. It is a good time to emphasize word order.

- **Expansion Tip:** To focus on common problem areas with *whether* and *if*, write sentences containing targeted errors on the board. (e.g., *I don't know whether are they home. She isn't sure if or not the dinner was ready. I hadn't thought about if people should eat raw food.*) Have students correct the errors and identify the note they referred to.

6 pages 395–396   5 min.

A 1. it's a good idea to eat different-colored foods?
2. people should drink more water.
3. a salt-free diet benefits everyone?
4. most people eat a lot of carbs.
5. coffee is good for your health?
6. most people follow a specific diet.
7. I've had an allergic reaction to food.
8. artificial colors in food are harmful?

B SPEAK

Answers will vary.

Chart 14.3, page 396   10 min.

- **Note:** Remind students about statement vs. question word order. Point out that the word order of the noun clause is always S + V whether the main clause is a statement or a question.

7 page 397   5 min.

1. I should do next.
2. this lasagna is made
3. I've ever eaten
4. you have added
5. you were given
6. foods I prefer
7. some people don't like
8. cooking is

> **REAL ENGLISH,** page 397
>
> Write common questions on the board: *What is the professor's name? Where is the closest bank? When does the movie end? How can we get to the post office? Who is in charge?* Have students ask each other polite questions using *Could you tell me* or *Can I ask* and the questions above in exercise **7**.

8 page 397   5 min.

1. how much longer we have to wait?
2. who our server is?
3. how this salad is made?
4. what *stew* means?
5. what vegetables are in the soup.
6. where there is an ATM machine?
7. how much a half order costs?
8. why my table isn't ready.

PRACTICE

9 page 398   10 min.

1. that
2. that
3. that
4. if/whether
5. whether
6. that
7. that
8. if/whether

10 pages 398–399   10 min.

1. Do you know where potatoes were first grown?
2. I think that potatoes originally came from Ireland.
3. I'm afraid that you're wrong.
4. I never realized that potatoes came from South America.
5. I wonder how many varieties are grown there.
6. I heard that they hold a special ceremony after the potato harvest.
7. Can you tell me what we covered?
8. Did you learn what caused the famine?
9. I believe that a harmful fungus destroyed the potatoes.
10. I'm not sure what a fungus is.
11. Do you know where they went?
12. I think that over one million people emigrated to the United States.

132   NOUN CLAUSES AND REPORTED SPEECH

- **Alternative Writing/Speaking:** Have students go online (suggest using the term "worst famines") to research a particular famine and answer these questions: *When and where was the famine? What was the cause? What were the effects?* Have students share their findings with other students who researched the same famine to add more information and clarify their ideas. Then have students write paragraphs about their famine and read their paragraphs to partners or small groups who researched another topic.

11 page 400   10 min.

A
1. that people cooked over open fires in prehistoric times?
2. if the first cast-iron stoves were built by the French?
3. how people cooked in China before cast-iron stoves were invented?
4. where the first wood-burning stove was invented.
5. when gas stoves were invented.
6. what country the gas stove was invented in?
7. that/if/whether people in America used ovens shaped like beehives.
8. if/whether people cooked first with gas or electricity.
9. when people started using microwave ovens in their homes?
10. where people started using solar ovens?

B SPEAK

Answers will vary. Answers may include:
1. Yes, the timeline shows that people cooked over open fires in prehistoric times.
2. I believe they were built by the Chinese.
3. No, the timeline doesn't give that information.
4. I think that was in France.
5. I think that gas stoves were invented in the 1800s.
6. I think that it was England.
7. Yes, they did.
8. Yes, it looks like people cooked first with gas.
9. I believe it was in the 1960s.
10. California, of course!

12 LISTEN & SPEAK, page 401   20 min.

A inexpensive, healthy, safe, convenient, easy

B
1. Molly is making
2. food tastes better with solar cooking or not
3. solar cooking is
4. solar cooking works
5. a solar oven works
6. more people aren't cooking
7. it's slowly becoming
8. solar cooking is

C Answers will vary.

13 EDIT, page 402   10 min.

Researchers have found ~~if~~ that ancient Europeans were cooking with garlic mustard seeds over 5000 years ago. The findings come from archaeological sites in Denmark and Germany, where the seeds were found inside pieces of pottery. Archaeologists think people used the seeds in their cooking. Because the seeds have no nutritional value, archaeologists are convinced that they were used to add flavor to other foods.

The researchers have explained why ~~are their findings~~ their findings are important. Although other examples of ancient spices ~~had~~ have been found, the mustard seeds are the first to be linked to cooking. In earlier studies, scientists weren't sure ~~if~~ whether or not these spices had been used in cooking. Experts believed that prehistoric people simply ate food for energy without caring about its taste. Until the garlic mustard seed discovery, they had no idea how much ~~did early humans thought~~ early humans thought about their food preparation. Now scientists realize that flavor was important to people long ago. In the future, researchers would like to find out what other spices early humans ~~did~~ used, but it won't be an easy task.

14 APPLY, page 402   15 min.

A Answers will vary.
B Answers will vary.

UNIT 14   LESSON 1   133

LESSON 2   Reported Speech: Part 1

Student Learning Outcomes	• **Read** a web page about food and the senses. • **Write** sentences using reported speech. • **Find** and **edit** errors with reported speech. • **Write** and **talk** about a survey. • **Discuss** how to choose a restaurant. • **Report** on a partner's opinions.
Lesson Vocabulary	(n.) atmosphere (n.) critic (adj.) homemade (v.) process (adj.) upbeat (adj.) bitter (adj.) culinary (n.) loaf (n.) senses (n.) vendor

EXPLORE

1 READ, page 403   15 min.

- Have students look at the photo. Ask, *Would you like to eat one of these? Why? What is appealing about the food in the photo?*
- Have students use context clues to guess the meaning of new words (e.g., *perception, sense, bitter*).

Be the Expert

Charles Spence is interested in how senses affect each other. One particular interest is in how vision, odor, taste, and even sound influence our perception of food. He is also interested in how the indoor environment affects our mood and performance. His research shows that the person who orders first in a restaurant enjoys his or her meal more, and that we eat more food with each additional person at the meal. With one other person, we eat 35 percent more, and with three, we eat 75 percent more. Spence consults with big food companies on how to make food taste better with less sugar, salt, and fat.

- **Expansion Tip:** Put students in pairs or small groups to discuss these questions: *Why do you think dessert tastes sweeter on a white plate? How does the size of a plate affect your eating? Why do you think people eat more when they are with more people? Do you like to listen to music when you eat? If so, what kind and why?* Call on students to share their ideas with the class.

2 CHECK, page 404   5 min.

1. Charles Spence does some of his research in restaurants.
2. Charles Spence uses seeing and tasting in his experiments./Sight/Seeing and taste/tasting play a big part in the experiment.
3. The brain processes all of the information around us while we eat./The brain uses information from one sense, such as hearing, to inform another sense—taste.
4. Spence thinks a chef can make a dessert taste sweeter by serving it on a white plate.

3 DISCOVER, page 404   5 min.

A
1. said
2. told his server
3. said,
4. has said,

B The true statements are sentences 2 and 3.

LEARN

Chart 14.4, page 405   10 min.

- **Note 1:** To check understanding of the term "reporting verb," elicit examples (e.g., *say, tell, ask, report*).
- **Note 2:** In addition to pronouns, other words may change: *here* to *there*, *this* to *that*, *now* to *then*, *yesterday* to *the day before*.
- **Note 3:** Write several more direct quotes on the board that use a variety of tenses and elicit the change necessary in reported speech.

4 pages 405–406   5 min.

1. was applying
2. wanted
3. had been studying
4. they had gained
5. taught
6. was taking
7. had offered
8. were having; had

134   NOUN CLAUSES AND REPORTED SPEECH

5 page 406   5 min.

1. she needed
2. she felt
3. he was; she was feeling
4. he wanted
5. she didn't mind; she had her; she didn't need
6. she needed; she got

- **Expansion Tip:** Model the activity. Describe what you did last night. Call on students to report what you said. Put students in pairs to talk about what they did last night. Then, have students find new partners and report on what their first partner said.

Chart 14.5, page 407   10 min.

- **Expansion Tip:** Have students write three sentences using *will, can, must,* or *may*. Then, put them in pairs to say their sentences as their partners report back what they said. (e.g., *I can swim. – You said you could swim.*)

6 page 407   5 min.

1. should go
2. might bake
3. would bring
4. could drive
5. might need
6. would be
7. could go
8. might bring

Chart 14.6, page 408   10 min.

- **Note:** Remind students that just as noun clauses with questions words and *whether* and *if* use statement order, so do reported questions. This is because reported speech is a kind of noun clause.

- **Expansion Tip:** Elicit three questions from the class and write them on the board. (e.g., *Where did you go on vacation last summer? Is Kate Middleton married? Can we take the test on Tuesday?*) Have students work in pairs to rewrite the questions as reported speech. (e.g., *Keiko asked where the teacher/you went on vacation last summer. Marina asked if Kate Middleton was married. Ahmed asked whether we could take the test on Tuesday.*) Go over the answers with the class. Have students identify which note they used to make the changes.

7 page 408   10 min.

1. if there was a food I hated
2. if anyone could learn to be a great chef
3. if I would be opening my restaurant soon
4. how I thought people's eating habits had changed
5. how big my garden was
6. if there is/was anything people should eat for their health
7. if I cooked for my family, too
8. if I could share one of my favorite recipes
9. if he was going to post our interview on his blog
10. what time the photo shoot was

PRACTICE

8 page 409   10 min.

- **Tip:** Before students do exercise **8**, have them look at the photo and caption. Ask, *Have you had dim sum? What kinds of dishes are included? What Chinese food do you like? What foods in your country are similar to dumplings?* Then, ask two students to read the conversation in exercise **8** aloud.

1. were
2. (that) he didn't know
3. wouldn't make him
4. (that) everyone loved
5. if she could try
6. (that) she was going to love
7. if she wanted
8. (that) she didn't think
9. what she thought
10. (that) she thought they were

9 page 410   5 min.

A 1. e   2. d   3. b   4. c   5. a

B WRITE

1. Kate asked Tony if he was going to have the dumplings. Tony told her he might try one or two.
2. Rudy asked Elsie how the rice was. Elsie said (that) it tasted delicious.
3. Luke asked Dena if she had tried the spicy sauce yet. Dena told him that she had had some on Sunday.
4. Rosa asked Yuri where the spices came from. Yuri told her (that) they grow wild in the Himalayas.
5. Dave asked Jenny how many of the dishes were Nepalese. Jenny told him that all of them were.

- **Expansion Tip:** As an out-of-class assignment, have students listen to or watch an interview on the radio, TV, or online. Instruct them to write five sentences about the interview using reported speech. Put students in pairs to report on the interview.

10 EDIT, page 410 10 min.

Last week, I called Catherine and asked her what ~~was she~~ she was doing. She said that she and some friends ~~are~~ were going out. I asked her whether I ~~can~~ could go with them. She said that I was welcome to come along. We met at a bakery. Catherine ordered a funny looking cake. She asked me ~~had I~~ if I had ever tried that kind of cake. I hadn't, so she ordered me a piece. I took a bite and bit something hard. She laughed and said that there ~~is~~ was a toy inside. She told me that I ~~am~~ was eating a special cake for French holidays. I told her that ~~you~~ she should have told me before. I thought maybe I had broken my tooth. She apologized and asked me ~~that~~ if I forgave her. I said that I did.

11 READ, WRITE & SPEAK, pages 410–411 10 min.

A *Answers will vary. Answers may include:*

The survey shows that more people said they chose a restaurant based on recommendations from friends, family, or coworkers.

B *Answers will vary slightly. Answers may include:*

Nearly 49 percent said they followed the recommendations of relatives, friends, and coworkers.

Almost 23 percent said that they paid attention to consumer reviews online.

Nearly 10 percent said that they looked at recommendations in food blogs.

Only 7.6 reported that they read reviews in newspapers.

Only 4.4 percent said that they did a Google search.

Only 1.7 percent reported that they watched TV shows to help them decide.

- **Alternative Writing/Speaking:** Have students work in pairs to write five questions for a survey about food and/or eating habits. Have each student survey five classmates and report their findings. Instruct the pairs to write a paragraph explaining their results, and then have students present their paragraphs to the class.

12 APPLY, page 411 20 min.

Answers will vary.

LESSON 3   Reported Speech: Part 2

Student Learning Outcomes	• **Read** an article about a cooking class. • **Report** on a conversation. • **Rewrite** a conversation between a health inspector and restaurant owner. • **Listen** to a conversation in a hotel restaurant. • **Write** about and **discuss** advice people have given.
Lesson Vocabulary	(n.) crust (adj.) fabulous (n.) inspector (n.) pastry (n.) security (n.) dough (n.) flight attendant (v.) knead (n.) recipe (n.) toppings

EXPLORE

1 READ, page 412   15 min.

- Have students look at the photo. Ask, *Where is this? What kind of food is Italy known for?*
- Have students use context to guess the meaning of new words (e.g., *knead, dough, sticky, fabulous, toppings, paddles, slide, crust*).

Be the Expert

- Ravello is a town of about 2500 residents on the Amalfi coast in Italy. It is a UNESCO World Heritage Site. Tourists come to see the churches, villas, and gardens. Musicians, artists, and writers have spent time in Ravello including Richard Wagner, Joan Miro, D. H. Lawrence, and George Eliot.
- Culinary, or food, tourism is becoming more popular. People travel to different regions of the world to experience the food and drink of other cultures.

2 CHECK, page 413   5 min.

   1. F   2. T   3. F   4. T   5. F

3 DISCOVER, page 413   5 min.

A 1. to knead

    2. not to stop

    3. to explain

    4. not to get

B b

- **Tip:** For the first two sentences in exercise **A**, ask students to write Francesco's exact words (e.g., *"Knead the dough."* and *"Don't stop until it is smooth and sticky."*). Then, have students write a rule about imperatives in reported speech.

LEARN

Chart 14.7, page 414   10 min.

- **Note:** Have students compare the rule they wrote in the previous activity to the first note.
- **Expansion Tip:** Write other examples of commands, advice, and requests on the board, both affirmative and negative. Have students work in pairs to write them as reported speech. Have volunteers write the sentences on the board.

4 pages 414–415   10 min.

  1. her to show me how to do it

  2. him to stand away from the oven

  3. her to move it to a cooler spot

  4. him to stop mixing the dough

  5. her to explain step 3

  6. him to weigh the sugar on the scale first

  7. him not to continue until he had washed his hands

  8. her to tell me how to prepare it

Chart 14.8, page 415   10 min.

- **Expansion Tip:** Use examples from the news or famous events to illustrate the reason for the changes in reported speech. Give the facts including day/date, place, speaker, and the situation (e.g., Abraham Lincoln, the Gettysburg Address in Gettysburg, PA, during the American Civil War in 1863), and the actual words (*Now we are engaged in a great civil war . . .*). Walk through each change explaining or eliciting the reason for the change.

UNIT 14   LESSON 3   **137**

5 pages 415–416 10 min.

1. the week before
2. the following week
3. there
4. those
5. that
6. the next day
7. the following year
8. then

PRACTICE

6 page 416 5 min.

1. to get the freezer fixed
2. to have ten days to get the freezer fixed
3. to give all employees a food safety training the next day
4. to put labels on the food before closing time that evening
5. not to leave any boxes on the floor anymore
6. to come back later that afternoon
7. to get the door fixed by the following week
8. to show him the inspection report the following day

7 LISTEN, page 417 15 min.

A coffee, continental breakfast, delivery, garbage, orange juice

B
1. to come over
2. to go
3. to throw away
4. to go
5. to check; see
6. to ask

8 READ, WRITE & SPEAK, pages 417–418 10 min.

A   It was another stressful day at LaGuardia Airport. Everyone was in a hurry. The lines were extremely slow because there weren't enough security guards on duty that day. Passengers were furious that the lines were slow. They yelled, "Hurry! We're going to miss our flight." One airline attendant was saying to passengers, "Calm down! Don't panic!" Another attendant ran to the gate. He yelled, "Wait!" at the crew. An announcer said, "Everyone flying to Brazil should get in the express line." The passengers lined up. We began taking their food orders. Some customers were worried that the food wouldn't come. We said, "Don't worry about the food."

B
1. to hurry
2. to calm down and not to panic
3. to wait
4. to get in the express line
5. to be patient

C Answers will vary.

- **Alternative Writing/Speaking:** Put students in small groups to create a role play in a workplace or situation they know well where one or more people typically give commands or make requests. Have the small groups perform their role plays as their classmates take notes. After each role play, call on students to report what they heard.

9 APPLY, page 418 15 min.

A Answers will vary.
B Answers will vary.
C Answers will vary.

- **Expansion Tip:** Put students in pairs to tell each other the advice they plan to give to children, partners, parents, or someone else in the future (e.g., *I will tell my children to follow their dreams. I'll tell them not to be afraid of new things*).

UNIT 14 Review the Grammar

1 page 419   5 min.
1. the chef was
2. whether
3. is?
4. not to borrow
5. had seen; the day before
6. not to
7. she was
8. she
9. could
10. made
11. would; .
12. had to

2 LISTEN & WRITE, pages 419–420   5 min.

A
1. T
2. F
3. F
4. T
5. F
6. F

B
1. was your trip
2. what it was
3. experienced anything
4. who thought of
5. what; will be
6. it will be

C
1. He asked her how her trip to London was/had been.
2. He asked her to tell him what it was like/had been like.
3. She told him (that) she had never experienced anything like it.
4. He told her he would like to know who had thought of that crazy idea.
5. He asked her if she had any idea what their next project would be.
5. She told him (that) she was sure it would be pretty outrageous.

3 EDIT, page 421   5 min.

I can't remember ~~if~~ whether or not I've had any extraordinary experiences with food, but I'm certain that I have had some unusual cooking experiences. The funniest was when I was about 12 years old. Before then, I had asked my mother many times ~~when would I~~ when I would be allowed to cook dinner. Finally, one Thursday night, she told me I could make roast chicken ~~tomorrow~~ the following day. She told me to wash the chicken first. I asked if I was supposed to wash only the skin of the chicken. She said that I should wash the inside, too. She also told me ~~don't~~ not to forget to put salt and pepper on the chicken before putting it in the oven. I wrote down exactly what my mother ~~did tell~~ told me to do. The next day, I took the chicken out of the fridge and went over to the sink. I turned on the water and put soap all over the inside and the outside of the chicken. When my brother came in, he asked what ~~was I~~ I was doing. I told him that Mom had said I could make chicken for dinner. He asked where the chicken ~~is~~ was. He said all he saw was soap. I said that Mom had told me to wash the chicken. He told me he would never eat it. Then, he called my mother to tell her what I had done. I was so embarrassed. It was years before I ever cooked chicken again.

4 SPEAK & WRITE, page 421   15 min.
Answers will vary.

UNIT 14   REVIEW THE GRAMMAR   139

Connect the Grammar to Writing

1 READ & NOTICE THE GRAMMAR,
page 422   20 min.

B   Everyone knows how useful online restaurant reviews are, but you can also get great suggestions from your friends. You trust them, and they know what you like and dislike. I surveyed three of my classmates—Nayma, Esra, and Oscar—because I wanted to know where I could go to get some really delicious food.

They each had different opinions. First of all, Nayma is crazy about desserts, so she told me to go to a place called the Chocolate Room. She said that a dessert called "Death by Chocolate" would change my life. Unlike Nayma, Esra is very health conscious. She asked me if I liked salads. When I said that I pretty much liked everything, she told me to try a place called Omer's Garden. According to her, no one else in the world makes such delicious salad. Finally, Oscar likes to eat meat. He asked me if I had ever eaten Brazilian barbecue. When I told him that I had not, he said that I absolutely had to try the Brasilia Grill. I asked him why it was so great. He described how the waiters walk around with freshly grilled meats and slice them directly onto your plate.

All my friends' suggestions sounded terrific. Which place will I try first? Like Nayma, I really love desserts, so I think I will try the Chocolate Room first. I hope that I get a chance to try the other places soon, too. I can't wait to tell my classmates what I think of their recommendations!

C

Restaurant	Recommended Food & Why
Chocolate Room	dessert called Death by Chocolate; will change your life
Omer's Garden	salad; most delicious salads
Brasilia Grill	grilled meat; very fresh

2 BEFORE YOU WRITE, page 423   15 min.

3 WRITE, page 423   15 min.

WRITING FOCUS, page 423

Have students write five sentences that begin with *According to X*, and continue with that person's opinion, advice, instructions about food. For example, *According to Richard Wrangham, cooking made it easier for people to digest food.*

- **Alternative Writing:** Have students conduct online research to answer this question: *What are the most significant changes in restaurant cooking in the last 20 years?* Instruct students to use quotes from chefs, researchers, or culinary critics in their descriptions.

UNIT 15 Learning

Combining Ideas

Unit Opener

Photo: Have students look at the photo and read the caption. Ask, *What is in this photo? What do you know about the Titanic?*

Location: Denver is the capital and largest city in Colorado. One of the well-known passengers on the Titanic, Molly Brown, was from Denver. The ship sank on April 14, 1912, after hitting an iceberg. Molly Brown survived, but 1500 passengers died in the disaster.

Theme: This unit is about learning. It includes information on motivating people to learn about astronomy and about a learning experiment. Have students look at the photos and titles throughout the unit. Ask, *How do they relate to the theme?*

Page	Lesson	Grammar	Examples
426	1	Transition Words	It can be cold in April in New York. **However,** it doesn't snow very often. The exam was long. **Therefore,** it was tiring. An essay should be clear and well organized. **In addition,** it should be interesting.
436	2	Prepositional Phrases: Cause and Effect, Contrast	She will get good grades **as a result of** her hard work. Jonathan was **so** funny **that** people were crying. Some people did well on the test **despite** the pressure.
446	**Review the Grammar**		
450	**Connect the Grammar to Writing**		

Unit Grammar Term

transition word: a word or phrase that connects ideas between sentences.
  ➢ *I'd like to go. **However,** I have too much work to do.*

141

LESSON 1	**Transition Words**
Student Learning Outcomes	• **Read** an article about motivating people to learn about astronomy. • **Write** sentences using transition words. • **Listen** to a conversation and **connect** ideas. • **Speak** and **write** about learning tools. • **Edit** and **find** errors with phrases of cause and effect, contrast, and result.
Lesson Vocabulary	(n.) astrobiologist (n.) astronomy (n.) drawback (n.) planetarium (n.) social media (n.) astronaut (v.) captivate (v.) motivate (v.) sign up (n.) universe

EXPLORE

1 READ, page 426   15 min.

- Have students look at the photo. Ask, *What are the people doing? Where can you go to see the stars?*
- Have students use context to guess the meaning of new words (e.g., *aliens, talented*).

Be the Expert

Brendan Mullan teaches at Penn State. In 2012 he won the FameLab competition, which judges how well scientists communicate their work to the public. The competitors have to explain complex ideas in just three minutes. In his research, Mullan studies how stars form when galaxies collide.

- **Expansion Tip:** Conduct a similar competition with your class. Tell students they will have three minutes to explain a complicated subject. They can choose something they already know a lot about, or something they research. Judging will be based on how well they communicate the ideas in a fun and engaging way.

2 CHECK, page 427   5 min.

   1. F   2. F   3. T   4. F   5. T

3 DISCOVER, page 427   5 min.

A   1. Nevertheless,   3. In addition,
     2. , however,   4. As a result,

B   1. However   2. As a result   3. In addition

LEARN

Chart 15.1, page 428   10 min.

- **Note 1:** Transition words help readers and listeners follow the connections between ideas. Students have a tendency to overuse transition words. Point out that in an extended text, writers will use transition words, conjunctions, and subordinating conjunctions such as *because, when,* and *although*.

- **Notes 3 & 4:** Emphasize the difference between *however/nevertheless* and *on the other hand*. Use your hands to demonstrate. Present one idea or point of view as you gesture with one hand, and then contrast that with a second idea with the second hand.

4 pages 428–429   5 min.

   1. a   3. a   5. b   7. a
   2. a   4. b   6. a   8. b

5 page 429   5 min.

1. However, they need to make their expectations clear.
2. On the other hand, they shouldn't ask questions that are too personal.
3. However, they must work alone during the exam.
4. However, they must not hurt anyone's feelings.
5. On the other hand, reading is better for visual learners.
6. Nevertheless, many students still prefer traditional classes.

Chart 15.2, page 430   10 min.

- **Expansion Tip:** To focus on placement of the three transition words/phrases, write several sentences with *so* on the board. (e.g., *Jack has trouble studying in his dorm room, so he goes to the library every night.*) Have students rewrite the sentences using all the transition words in the chart. They should also use the transition words in different places in the sentenses if possible. Ask volunteers to write sentences on the board.

6 pages 430–431   10 min.

1. Digital learning is increasing. As a result, teachers' roles are changing.
2. Digital learning gives students more control. Thus, they become more active learners.
3. Digital learning gives students more responsibility. As a result, they become more independent.
4. We can often both see and hear online content. Therefore, it is more interactive.
5. That course is very popular. Therefore, it fills up quickly.
6. Our university has an excellent biology department. Thus, many students major in biology.
7. The final exam was very difficult. As a result, many students didn't pass.
8. Professor Chen is well known in her field. Therefore, a lot of students want to take her classes.

Chart 15.3, page 431   10 min.

- **Note:** Point out that transition words often sound more formal than conjunctions.
- **Expansion Tip:** To focus on the differences in meaning across the transition words in the three charts, write sentences on the board that show one of these relationships: contrast, result, or addition. (e.g., *I have always loved ice cream. It turns out that I am allergic to dairy products.*) Have students work in pairs to add transition words.

7 pages 431–432   10 min.

- **Expansion Tip:** Before students complete the activity, direct their attention to the photo on page 432. Ask, *How do people use video chats for personal, professional, or educational purposes?*

1. With video chat apps, you can talk online for free. In addition, they're easy to use.
2. Video chat apps allow you to make phone calls. In addition, they let you have group chats.
3. These apps make it easy for you to talk to your classmates. Moreover, they connect you to other students.
4. Teachers can give feedback with these apps. In addition, students can comment on each other's work.
5. During video chats, students can watch artists at work. Moreover, they can learn about the artists' techniques.
6. You can learn about foreign countries through video chats. Moreover, you can find a language partner.
7. With video chatting, students can hear authors read their work. In addition, they can talk to the authors.
8. Students can use these apps to go on virtual field trips. In addition, they can give presentations.

PRACTICE

- **Alternative Writing/Speaking:** Before students begin the Practice activities, put them in pairs to list positive and negative aspects of social media. Then, have students write five sentences combining their ideas using transition words from the lesson. Have students complete exercise **8** and compare their ideas to those in the article.

8 page 433   5 min.

1. In addition,
2. As a result,
3. Moreover,
4. On the other hand,
5. As a result,
6. In addition,
7. Therefore,
8. However,

9 page 433   5 min.

1. However,
2. In addition,
3. Therefore,
4. As a result,
5. Nevertheless,
6. Moreover,

10 page 434   5 min.

1. In addition,; However,
2. Therefore,
3. Nevertheless,; therefore,
4. However,; Therefore,
5. In addition,

11 SPEAK & WRITE, pages 434–435   10 min.

Answers will vary.

12 LISTEN & WRITE, page 435   10 min.

A 1. T   2. T   3. F   4. F
B 1. b   2. d   3. f   4. e   5. c   6. a
C *Answers will vary.*

13 APPLY, page 435   15 min.

A & B *Answers will vary.*

- **Expansion Tip:** Write this question on the board: *How does using digital technology affect learning?* Put students in small groups to discuss the pros and cons of using technology.

UNIT 15　LESSON 1　143

LESSON 2 Prepositional Phrases: Cause and Effect, Contrast

Student Learning Outcomes
- **Read** an article about a learning experiment.
- **Complete** sentences with prepositional phrases.
- **Find** and **edit** errors with phrases of cause and effect, contrast, and result.
- **Write** and **speak** about personal experiences.
- **Speak** for one minute about learning to do something.
- **Edit** and **find** errors with phrases of cause and effect, contrast, and result.

Lesson Vocabulary
(n.) biotechnology	(v.) download	(v.) excel	(n.) inexperience	(v.) strike
(v.) browse	(n.) entrepreneur	(n.) formal education	(n.) rhythm	(n.) style

EXPLORE

1 READ, page 436 — 15 min.

- Have students look at the photo. Ask, *Do you think children in this neighborhood usually have computers? Do people everywhere have the same access to computers? Why, or why not? How does this affect their education?*
- Have students use context clues to guess the meaning of new words (e.g., *formal education, browse*).

Be the Expert

Sugata Mitra is Professor of Educational Technology at the School of Education, Communication and Language Sciences at Newcastle University, UK. His experiment with the computer in New Delhi was called the "Hole in the Wall" experiment and was conducted in 1999. The movie *Slumdog Millionaire* was based on a novel written by Vikas Swarup after he read about Mitra's experiment. In 2013, Mitra won the $1 million TED prize to help build The School in the Cloud, where children from all over the world can gather in an online creative space to answer big questions.

- **Expansion Tip:** Have students go online to watch one of Mitra's TED talks: *Kids Can Teach Themselves, The Child-Driven Education,* or *Build a School in the Cloud.* You may want to divide students into three groups to watch one of each of the videos. Have students take notes and then compare their notes with others who watched the same talk. Put students in groups of three, in which each member has watched a different TED talk, and have them share what they learned.

2 CHECK, page 437 — 5 min.

1. F   2. F   3. T   4. T

3 DISCOVER, page 437 — 5 min.

A
1. Despite
2. As a result of
3. so, that
4. due to
5. such, that

B   1. b   2. a   3. a

LEARN

Chart 15.4, page 438 — 10 min.

- **Note 1:** To reinforce the meaning of these prepositional phrases, ask students to say the sentences in the chart using conjunctions or transition words with the same meaning instead. (e.g., *She will get good grades because she works hard. She works hard. Therefore, she will get good grades.*)
- **Notes 2–5:** Write sentences on the board containing errors discussed in Notes 2, 3, and 5. Have students rewrite the sentences to correct the errors. Then, have volunteers write the corrected sentences on the board and identify the note that they used for the correction.

4 pages 438–439 — 5 min.

1. because of
2. Because/Due to the fact that
3. because
4. Due to
5. because of
6. As a result of
7. As a result,
8. due to
9. due to the fact that
10. due to

144   COMBINING IDEAS

5 page 439 — 5 min.

1. Because of the teacher's strike,
2. as a result of their low test scores
3. because of the noise
4. Due to the class website,
5. Due to the spread of the flu
6. as a result of the fire

- **Expansion Tip:** Have students look at the photo on page 439. Have them talk in pairs about what students can learn from researchers in space. Suggest that they discuss these questions: *What kinds of research do astronauts do? Why is it important to do experiments in space? What kinds of questions do you think children have for astronauts?*

Chart 15.5, page 440 — 10 min.

- **Note:** Emphasize the unusual structure of this kind of transition: *so* or *such* is separated from *that* by an adjective or noun phrase.
- **Expansion Tip:** Write five sentence starters on the board giving causes. Have students complete the sentences with the effects, and then compare the complete sentences in pairs.

6 page 440 — 5 min.

1. so
2. so
3. so many
4. so much
5. such
6. so
7. so many
8. such a

7 pages 440–441 — 5 min.

1. so many
2. such
3. so much
4. so
5. so many
6. so
7. so little
8. such

Chart 15.6, page 441 — 10 min.

- **Expansion Tip:** To recycle earlier lessons/units, have students rewrite the sentences in the chart and notes using conjunctions or transition words. (e.g., *There was a lot of pressure. However, some people did well on the test.*) Ask volunteers to write their sentences on the board.

8 pages 441–442 — 5 min.

1. I took lessons as child,
2. I didn't know anything about music,
3. my parents' threats of punishment
4. my fear of failure
5. I don't play the guitar well now,
6. my dreams of being a musician,
7. my lack of singing talent,
8. my inexperience singing on stage,

- **Expansion Tip:** Model the activity. Say a sentence about learning something. (e.g., *I learned to juggle when I was 12.*) Elicit ideas from the class on difficulties you had to overcome. (e.g., *Despite my lack of physical ability, . . . ; In spite of the fact that I have only one hand, . . .*) Encourage students to be creative. Have students write five sentences about a personal experience learning how to do something. The experience can be real or imaginary. Then, have them exchange sentences with a partner and add a contrasting idea.

PRACTICE

9 page 442 — 10 min.

- **Tip:** Before students do exercise **8**, have them look at the painting. Ask, *How would you describe this painting? What do you like about it? How is it different from other painters' work?*

1. Despite
2. Despite the fact that
3. As a result,
4. despite the fact that
5. as a result of
6. As a result of
7. so much
8. so much
9. Because of
10. Despite

- **Expansion Tip:** Have students go online and search for the terms "famous self-taught." This will show famous self-taught artists, guitarists, musicians, and so on. Have them choose one person to research. Then, have them share what they learned in small groups.

10 page 443 — 10 min.

1. In spite of Kate's fear of heights, she learned to ski./Kate learned to ski in spite of her fear of heights.

UNIT 15 LESSON 2

2. Despite the fact that Margaret is an excellent dancer, she was not chosen by the dance company./Margaret was not chosen by the dance company despite the fact that she is an excellent dancer.

3. Due to Josh's passion for winter sports, he learned to snowboard./Josh learned to snowboard due to his passion for winter sports.

4. In spite of the fact that Maya worked on a farm, she never learned how to grow vegetables./Maya never learned how to grow vegetables in spite of the fact that she worked on a farm.

5. As a result of Mark's natural musical talent, he learned to play the violin by himself./Mark learned to play violin by himself as a result of his natural musical talent.

6. Ben is so impatient that he stopped taking art lessons after just one month.

7. Because of Henry's good computer skills, he was able to build his own website without any help./Henry was able to build his own website without any help because of his good computer skills.

8. Tomas is such a wonderful pianist that his friends love to hear him play.

11 WRITE & SPEAK, page 444   10 min.

Answers will vary.

- **Alternative Speaking:** Put students in pairs to write five to ten questions for an interview on a difficult learning experience. Questions might include: *What is something difficult that you learned to do? What made it difficult?* Have students find new partners and take turns asking and answering the questions. Call on students to report on their partner's answers.

12 EDIT, page 444   10 min.

Watching a friend compete in a dance contest was ~~so~~ such a great experience that I decided to learn how to dance. I watched ~~such~~ so many YouTube videos that I started to dream about dancing. However, I got very frustrated. It was so hard for me to learn from the videos that I almost gave up. Then, my friend told me about a dance class. I signed up, but the first time I went I was so shy that I couldn't move. In spite of my fear, I kept going. I had so ~~few~~ little free time that I couldn't practice a lot. But a half hour before dinner every night, I put on music and practiced the steps I had learned in class. Because of the teacher's patience, I eventually learned to dance. I'm such a good dancer now that I'm going to be my friend's partner in a dance contest. As a result of my experience, I am convinced that a person can learn just about anything. All you need is the desire and an effective way to learn.

13 APPLY, page 445   20 min.

Answers will vary.

- **Alternative Writing:** Have students use their ideas from exercise **13B** and the model in exercise **12** to write a paragraph about their experience of learning to do something. Have students exchange paragraphs with a partner to edit.

UNIT 15 Review the Grammar

1 page 446 — 5 min.
1. However,
2. As a result of
3. Due to
4. Despite the fact that
5. Because of
6. Due to
7. so

2 WRITE, page 446 — 5 min.
1. Zooniverse is a web portal. In addition, it is a citizen science project.
2. Despite the fact that non-scientists are welcome in many science projects, they can't always be included.
3. Some sciences require specific advanced knowledge. However, other sciences are more accessible.
4. Most scientists of the past were professionally trained. On the other hand, Isaac Newton was a citizen scientist.

3 READ & WRITE, pages 447–448 — 10 min.
Answers will vary. Answers may include:
1. , there are many plants and animals right in our own backyard
2. , they look for mammals, fish, birds, and insects
3. species found are usually known
4. , they have a lot of fun
5. fun that
6. , you need to wear layers of clothing
7. , you will need sunglasses, sunscreen, and a hat
8. the weather

4 LISTEN, page 448 — 10 min.
A bats, birds, owls, spiders, turtles
B 1. Despite the fact that
2. In addition,
3. Therefore,
4. such, that
5. due to
6. As a result of
7. However, because of
8. so many; that

5 EDIT, page 449 — 10 min.

On our first day in Mongolia, we saw ~~such~~ so many amazing mountains that I didn't know what to photograph first. We came for the Eagle Festival. Later, our guide gave a talk about eagles and life in Mongolia. We learned that because of Western influences, many young people in Mongolia move to the cities. ~~Despite~~ Because of this, traditional life in Mongolia is threatened.

We saw Kazakhs training their eagles. They do ~~so~~ such a good job that the eagles will hunt for them. We spent time on horseback with the Kazakhs. In fact, we spent ~~such~~ so much time on the horses that I was in a lot of pain later. After the Eagle Festival, we visited with a Kazakh family. ~~Despite~~ In spite of the fact that I was very tired, I was very interested in learning about their lives. ~~However,~~ As a result, I stayed up very late talking to them.

We have been ~~such~~ so busy that I have hardly had time to think about home, though I do miss my family. ~~Therefore,~~ However, I'm having a wonderful time.

6 WRITE & SPEAK, page 449 — 10 min.
Answers will vary.

Connect the Grammar to Writing

1 READ & NOTICE THE GRAMMAR,
pages 450–451   20 min.

B *Answers may vary. Answers may include:*

Transition words:

Thus, the student body is much more diverse than in a traditional classroom. (effect)

On the other hand, you learn from experts from all over the world. (contrast)

Prepositional phrases:

As a result of these high rates, many people can't afford a traditional college education. (cause)

Due to the exciting opportunities that MOOCs offer, I think that the traditional college classroom will have a difficult time competing. (cause)

C *Answers may vary. Answers may include:*   10 min.

| Traditional College Classroom ||
Advantages	Disadvantages
direct contact with professor	expensive
meet with classmates face to face	less flexible

| Online Learning or MOOC ||
Advantages	Disadvantages
diverse student body	no face-to-face contact with classmates
learn from experts all over the world	little direct contact with professor
free	offer certificates, not degrees

2 BEFORE YOU WRITE, page 451   15 min.

3 WRITE, page 451   15 min.

> **WRITING FOCUS, page 451**
>
> Have students look through the texts in the unit to find five pairs of sentences joined by transition words. Then, have them rewrite the sentences using semicolons.

- **Alternative Writing:** Have students write about the use of digital tools (online reading, tablets, digital note taking) vs. traditional print/paper and pencil for reading, writing, and note taking. Have them complete charts like the ones on page 451 to gather and organize their ideas before writing.

148   COMBINING IDEAS

AUDIO SCRIPTS

UNIT 1

LESSON 1

1 READ, page 4   CD1–Track 2

11A, page 10   CD1–Track 3

Leyla: Oh, is that a photo of your family?
Julia: Yeah, it's of all of us at my grandmother's 90th birthday.
Leyla: 90? That's amazing. Is she your dad's mom?
Julia: Yes. And *that's* my dad.
Leyla: Wow. They look alike.
Julia: I know. That's what everyone says.
Leyla: Does she live with your dad?
Julia: No, she lives in her own apartment, and she still drives, too.
Leyla: Good for her.
Julia: Yeah. But she doesn't drive very far now and she never drives at night . . .
Leyla: Hmmm . . . And that's your mom on the sofa?
Julia: Yeah, that's my mom.
Leyla: She's pretty. . . . Who's standing next to you, in the black dress? Is that your sister?
Julia: Yeah, that's my twin sister, Ana.
Leyla: You have a twin? I didn't know that. You don't look alike.
Julia: I know. And we have completely different interests and personalities, too. She's a musician. She's in an orchestra.
Leyla: Really? What instrument does she play?
Julia: The cello. And she practices all the time, day and night. I love to go to the concerts when the orchestra's in town.
Leyla: Does she travel a lot with the orchestra?
Julia: All the time . . . about eight months a year.
Leyla: Wow. Where are they playing now?
Julia: Hmmm . . . You know, I'm not sure, but last week they were in Budapest.
Leyla: Interesting. I'd love to go to Budapest. . . . And those must be your brothers.
Julia: Yes. The taller one standing next to my Dad is Alex. He's my younger brother. We don't see him too often now because he's studying in Scotland.
Leyla: Really? What's he studying?
Julia: Sports management.
Leyla: Sports management . . . that's different. What courses do people take for that major?
Julia: All kinds. Right now he's taking a course in sports law and another in sports marketing.
Leyla: Does he play any sports?
Julia: He plays just about every sport! He's very athletic, unlike me! But he's really a great soccer player and he's also on the college basketball team.
Leyla: Cool. And what about your other brother?
Julia: Lucas lives in New York City. He's a computer software engineer.
Leyla: Wow. So with all of you in so many different places, how often does the whole family get together?
Julia: Not very often. My parents are often away on business trips, too. It's nice when we have times like this . . . like my grandmother's birthday celebration.

LESSON 2

1 READ, page 12   CD1–Track 4

10, page 17   CD1–Track 5

Some aspects of family life among Antarctica's emperor penguins seem strange to people. For example, the female lays one egg, and then she leaves. She isn't being a bad mother. She simply needs to find food, and she is depending on the male to keep the egg warm. In about two months, the female returns and the egg hatches.

The chick resembles its parents, but it doesn't have black and white feathers. It has grey ones. Also, it is much smaller, and it weighs much less than the average 75-pound adult. The parents teach the chick how to take care of itself, but there's one thing the chick doesn't need to learn: how to swim! When a penguin sees water, it knows exactly what to do. Emperor penguins are excellent swimmers!

LESSON 3

1 READ, page 18   CD1–Track 6

7A and 7B, pages 24 and 25   CD1–Track 7

One day, I was cleaning out a desk drawer when I found a copy of my family tree. While I was looking at it, my mother came into the room. When she saw it, she became quiet. That's when she told me the family secret.

It turns out that Grandma's name wasn't really Maria. Her real name was Marina. Many years ago back in Russia, my grandmother's sister planned to marry an American when she turned 20. But while she was packing to go to America, she started to cry. She didn't want to go anymore, but her sister Marina did. The two sisters looked alike, so when Maria's passport and boat ticket arrived, Marina took them and traveled all the way from Russia to America.

While my mother was growing up, no one, not even my grandfather, knew the secret. Of course they were shocked when they found out. I certainly was!

AUDIO SCRIPTS   **A1**

AUDIO SCRIPTS

REVIEW THE GRAMMAR

3A and 3B, page 27   CD1–Track 8

Louise: From GRX, I'm Louise Lontano and this is *Time to Talk*. Brothers and sisters . . . they can drive us crazy. But they're there for us when we need them, and they share memories with us that nobody else does. Sometimes we love them to death; other times we don't. Today on *Time to Talk* we are looking at the relationship between siblings and how they shape the people we become. With us we have Richard Stedman, the author of the new book *Brothers and Sisters: The Good, the Bad, and the Ugly*. Welcome Richard Stedman. Thank you for joining us.

Richard: Thanks for having me, Louise.

Louise: So what is it about brother-sister relationships that make them distinct, different from any other relationship?

Richard: Well, when you think about it, brothers and sisters, they're the only ones who are with us all of our lives. Parents die before we grow old. Husbands and wives, our children . . . they don't enter the scene for many years. But brothers and sisters . . . they're there from the start, from when we're babies, and they're still there when we're old and at the end of our lives. They know us in a way that no one else does.

Louise: Our siblings know us differently from the way our adult friends know us because our siblings knew us when we were children.

Richard: Right. You and your siblings were together throughout your childhood.

Louise: And they know us as adults.

Richard: Of course, yes. The relationship is constantly changing. We feel differently, and of course we interact differently, when we're children and when we're adults.

Louise: Let's start off with what your research tells us about the sibling relationship with young children. Siblings are not all the same.

Richard: No, things are never always the same. Gender plays a role and so does age difference, as does the number of children in a family. And I also have to clarify. I'm not talking about sibling relationships all over the world. My research doesn't cover that. Family relationships vary greatly in different parts of the world. So what my research looks at are the relationships in this society.

Louise: Yes. Good to point out. When I was reading the book, one of the first things that struck me was the data you collected on fights between children. It was fascinating, the number and the frequency. I don't have children myself. And my brother is ten years older than I am so we didn't fight. I guess that's why I was shocked to see how often young children fight.

Richard: Yes, I mean if you ask parents how often their children fight, a lot of them will say, "My children are always fighting." It sounds like an exaggeration, but in fact, the research studies showed that children between the ages of three and seven fought about 3.5 times per hour. That means they had more than one fight—one fight with words, or with pushing and shoving, or with both—every 17 minutes.

Louise: And just what do children fight about?

Richard: What do they fight about? It appears that they're fighting about a toy, about the chocolate ice cream. But what siblings are really fighting for is something more important to them: They're fighting for the time, the love, and the attention of their parents.

Louise: Stand by, Richard Stedman if you will. We have to take a short break.

Richard: Sure.

Louise: The book is *Brothers and Sisters: The Good, the Bad, and the Ugly*. I'm Louise Lontano, and you're listening to *Time to Talk*.

UNIT 2

LESSON 1

1 READ, page 32   CD1–Track 9

8, page 37   CD1–Track 10

Lisa has just arrived.
[*Lisa's*] just arrived.
Most people have already left.
Most [*people've*] already left.
Who has she talked to?
[*Who's*] she talked to?
What have you done?
[*What've*] you done?

8A and 8B, page 37   CD1–Track 11

1. [*Lee's*] always loved animals.
2. Our neighbors have adopted many animals over the years.
3. [*Who's*] taken care of an animal before?
4. [*We've*] faced many challenges with our cats.
5. [*Kara's*] taken her dog to the park every day for years.
6. Tyrone has volunteered at the animal shelter since 2012.
7. Our [*landlords#'ve*] made a rule about owning pets.
8. [*What've*] you learned from working with animals?

9B, page 39   CD1–Track 12

Sara: How long have you been a snake catcher, Tim?

Tim: I've had this job for over ten years.

Sara: When did you become interested in snakes?

Tim: When I was a kid, and snakes have fascinated me ever since then. When I was in middle school, I didn't read much about any other subject. During my high school years, I often volunteered at the local zoo, and then in college I majored in herpetology—the study of reptiles.

Sara: And after college you spent a few years in Thailand. Isn't that right?

Tim: Yes, I was working with Thai snake experts. I really enjoyed my time with them.

Sara: Have you ever experienced any life-threatening situations since you started working with snakes?

Tim: I've worked with many poisonous snakes over the years, but only one has bitten me. That was scary! Since that time, I've paid more attention to the snakes' behavior.

Sara: Why do you love your job?

Tim: Because I've been able to live my childhood dream.

LESSON 2

1 READ, page 41   CD1–Track 13

8A and 8C, page 46   CD1–Track 14

Interviewer: How did your life lead you to this career choice?

Barton Seaver: It all started from when I was a child. My parents taught me the importance of healthy eating. My father was a fantastic cook and the way I ate as a child is very similar to how I eat today. And seafood has always been a part of that. I learned to love food and what it represents—health and joy and family. And seafood, in particular, has influenced my career choices.

Interviewer: You have worked as a chef in a variety of restaurants and you have owned some.

Barton Seaver: Yes, and that's how the oceans have become so important in my life. I've learned that they are the basic source of our life on earth, and that we need to protect them. This understanding has led me to participate in a variety of food-related businesses *and* organizations, but over the years I have been shifting my focus away from the restaurant business, and concentrating more on teaching people about protecting oceans and healthy living.

Interviewer: How do you make such a goal real?

Barton Seaver: Different ways. For example, I've developed a list of ocean-friendly substitutes for popular kinds of fish that we've been eating too much of, and I've been testing recipes that people can use in their own kitchens.

Interviewer: I understand that you have been doing some writing and lecturing as well.

Barton Seaver: Yes, I've been giving talks about oceans and I've written some articles. I've also written a couple of cookbooks featuring seafood and vegetable recipes.

Interviewer: Vegetables?

Barton Seaver: Of course, vegetables! We should eat fish, too, but we must do so carefully, so that there will always be enough of them in our oceans. We must not eat large portions of seafood. Instead we should be eating smaller portions of seafood with *large* amounts of delicious vegetables. Mothers have always been right when they said, "Eat your vegetables."

Interviewer: Barton Seaver, thank you for being here today, and thank you for working so hard to improve our relationship to the oceans.

Barton Seaver: Thank you.

LESSON 3

1 READ, page 48   CD1–Track 15

10A and 10B, pages 55 and 56   CD1–Track 16

Interviewer: Good evening, and thanks for listening to the *History Show.* Our guest tonight is Susan Carter.

Susan: Thanks very much, Bill.

Interviewer: Susan, can you tell us a little about your new book, *What Went Wrong: Franklin's Failed Expedition?*

Susan: Sure. It's about Sir John Franklin's 1845 expedition to find the Northwest Passage, which is a water route through the Canadian Arctic from the Atlantic Ocean to the Pacific Ocean. Many explorers had tried to find it, but they had not been successful. Sir John Franklin took two powerful ships and 128 men to find it. It was the biggest expedition that had ever gone to the Arctic.

Interviewer: That sounds like a risky journey.

Susan: It was, but everyone was confident that Franklin would succeed.

Interviewer: And did he?

Susan: No. The summers of 1846 and 1847 passed, and no one had heard anything from Franklin. England sent dozens of rescue teams to the Canadian Arctic to look for him.

Interviewer: Did they find anything?

Susan: Yes, but not until 1850. One team found where Franklin and his men had camped and the graves of three men who had died. Then in 1859, another team found a short written message with very little detail.

Interviewer: What did it say?

Susan: The message said that the men abandoned their ships, which were frozen in the ice. It also said that Sir John Franklin and several other men had died.

Interviewer: So what do historians think happened?

Susan: Some people think Franklin's men starved to death because they had refused to eat the local sea animals—seal and walrus. We now have additional new research that shows that the men died from several different causes. First, of course, were the freezing temperatures and the lack of food. Another was disease, such as tuberculosis. Still others were poisoned from canned food they ate. They may have also died because they did not get enough vitamin C.

Interviewer: It sounds like a deadly trip.

Susan: Yes, it was. Even the ships on the Franklin Expedition had deadly names.

Interviewer: What were they called?

Susan: One ship was called Erebus, which means deep darkness. The second ship was called Terror. . . . And the ships have never been found.

AUDIO SCRIPTS

REVIEW THE GRAMMAR

3A, page 59   CD1-Track 17

A: I've been reading about China's national hero, Liu Yang.

B: Who is that? I've never heard that name.

A: She's the first female astronaut that China has ever sent into space. Over 50 women astronauts from other countries have traveled in space, but Liu is the first from China.

B: That's interesting. So what has she done to prepare?

A: Well, she's already had a wide range of experience. She trained to be a pilot at China's Air Force College, and then she joined the Air Force. She's flown five different types of aircraft, and she's done 1680 hours of flight time. She's also participated in military exercises and emergency rescues. After nine years in the Air Force, Liu started training to be an astronaut. And that training was really hard! In fact, she had never experienced anything so challenging. In order to qualify for the space mission, she had to finish 14 years' worth of course work in just two years!

3B, page 59   CD1-Track 18

B: She sounds amazing! Had she always wanted to travel in space, even as a young child? Was this her lifelong dream?

A: No. She had never imagined herself as an astronaut. It had never occurred to her that someday she would be an important part of her country's space program. But it has turned out to be the perfect job for her!

B: It must be amazing to see planet Earth from such a distance. I've always wanted to do that. But it takes a very special kind of person to succeed. I wonder what Liu Yang is like.

A: Well, her co-workers have described her as smart, calm, and very friendly. She's also a good public speaker. And she must be very brave!

B: Wow! She sounds great . . . and busy! Do you think she has any free time?

A: She does work hard, but according to the article, she's been enjoying life's pleasures, too. She likes to spend time with her family and read novels, and she's a fantastic cook!

UNIT 3

LESSON 1

1 READ, page 64   CD1-Track 19

6, page 68   CD1-Track 20

Kesha: Steve, hi! Hey, are you going to the Robotics Club party at Chris and Pat's place next Saturday?

Steve: I don't know yet. I'm playing basketball that afternoon.

Kesha: You'll have plenty of time. The party is at eight o'clock.

Steve: Chris and Pat's house is really far away. The bus will take a long time.

Kesha: I'm going to borrow my brother's car. I've already asked him, and he said OK. So, I'll drive you.

Steve: Great. Thanks. . . . Hey, watch out! That guy on the bicycle is going to hit you.

Kesha: Wow! Thanks. I didn't see him!

9A, page 69   CD1-Track 21

1. **Chris:** Hey, someone's at the door.
   Pat: I'll get it.
2. **Pat:** Come on in and take off your boots. You can leave them here.
   Kesha: Thanks. It's freezing out there. I think it's going to snow tonight.
3. **Kesha:** That coffee smells great!
   Chris: Do you want some? I'll pour you a cup.
4. **Pat:** Hey Steve, I heard you're organizing the technology fair this year. I'm interested in helping out.
   Steve: That's right. Will you help me set up the exhibits? It's a big job, and I can't do it myself.
5. **Pat:** Sure. No problem. By the way, did Chris tell you about my new invention? It's a machine that dusts furniture.
   Steve: That's great! Are you showing it at the tech fair next week? I didn't see your name on the schedule.
6. **Chris:** Oh, is Pat talking about his invention again? He's always talking about that thing.
   Pat: OK, I'll keep quiet about it from now on. I promise.
7. **Ken:** Pat, our final planning meeting is tomorrow at my house. Why don't you come?
   Pat: I'm really busy tomorrow, but I can try. What time are you meeting?
8. **Chris:** Luisa, you're leaving already?
   Luisa: Sorry, but the last bus leaves at 10:30. I don't want to miss it.

9B, page 69   CD1-Track 22

Chris: Hey, someone's at the door.

Pat: I'll get it. Come on in and take off your boots. You can leave them here.

Kesha: Thanks. It's freezing out there. I think it's going to snow tonight. . . . That coffee smells great!

Chris: Do you want some? I'll pour you a cup.

Pat: Hey Steve, I heard you're organizing the technology fair this year. I'm interested in helping out.

Steve: That's right. Will you help me set up the exhibits? It's a big job, and I can't do it myself.

Pat: Sure. No problem. By the way, did Chris tell you about my new invention? It's a machine that dusts furniture.

Steve: That's great! Are you showing it at the tech fair next week? I didn't see your name on the schedule.

Chris: Oh, is Pat talking about his invention again? He's always talking about that thing.

Pat: OK, I'll keep quiet about it from now on. I promise.

Ken: Pat, our final planning meeting is tomorrow at my house. Why don't you come?

Pat: I'm really busy tomorrow, but I can try. What time are you meeting?

Chris: Luisa, you're leaving already?

Luisa: Sorry, but the last bus leaves at 10:30. I don't want to miss it.

10A and 10B, page 70   CD1–Track 23

I'm graduating from high school next year, and one thing is clear about my future: I want to work in Robotics. When I have some time, I'm going to do some research on engineering programs. I won't apply to schools until I find a really good one. Also, I'm planning to read as much as I can about robot projects, such as HERB at Carnegie Mellon University. HERB is terrific! He can do a lot of useful things. When the engineers are finished, HERB and robots like him will be a big help in people's homes. They will take care of the elderly and physically challenged people as well.

Maybe I'll design robots someday. I want to create a robot that will respond to human needs. For example, if a person says, "I'm thirsty," my robot will say, "No problem; I'll get you a drink." And if the trash can is full, my robot will notice and take out the trash right away. What am I going to name him? I don't know yet, but I do know that my robot will be amazing!

LESSON 2

1 READ, page 71   CD1–Track 24

10A, page 77   CD1–Track 25

Ari: My first day has been great. My boss introduced me to a lot of people. I don't know how I'll remember all the names and faces. I have a great work space, but it's in a big open room with a lot of other designers. I'm not used to working that way. I hope I'll be able to concentrate on my work. I started to read the documents that my boss gave me, but there's a lot of information and it's hard to understand. I'm worried that this job will be too hard for me!

11A, page 77   CD1–Track 26

Janet: I'm finally going to study abroad, just as I've always dreamed! I'm so happy the college accepted me, but now that I am packed and almost ready to go, I'm becoming a little afraid. Will I understand the teachers? They will only speak in French. Who will I ask for help when I don't understand? Also, as I say goodbye to my friends and family, I'm worried that I'm going to miss them! How will I make friends when I don't speak the language fluently? I can read and write, but I can't speak very well. I'm worried I'll be lonely.

LESSON 3

1 READ, page 78   CD1–Track 27

9B, page 85   CD1–Track 28

As a designer of office space, it is my job to learn as much as possible about how workplaces will be changing in the future. I want to know answers to questions like these: By the year 2050, for example, how will office work have changed? Will people be using office space differently from the way they do now? Will offices look different? Let me share with you some future trends that experts are predicting.

- Large numbers of people won't be working in offices in the years to come. They're going to be working from home instead. That means that fewer people will be using company office space.
- Over the next few decades, more and more workers will be having video conferences instead of face-to-face meetings. When people do want to meet in person, they will need to reserve office space in advance.
- Desktop phones and desktop computers will have disappeared from offices by the middle of the twenty-first century, or maybe even sooner. By then, almost everyone will be communicating with mobile phones and wireless computers.
- By 2050, most companies will have been rethinking office space for many years. For example, some will already have replaced regular walls with electronic walls so that many people can share information in electronic form at the same time.

These are just a few of the trends that people in my profession are paying close attention to. It seems very clear that the office of tomorrow is going to be taking a very different shape from the office of today.

REVIEW THE GRAMMAR

2C, page 87   CD1–Track 29

Jamal: Hi Sara, how's it going?

Sara: Fine, thanks. It's great to hear from you! What's happening?

Jamal: Things are pretty busy right now. I'm trying to finish my application for graduate school. I'll need to send it in by the end of May. I haven't written the essay yet, but I'm planning to work on it this weekend.

Sara: Do you know what you're going to say?

Jamal: Yeah, I've thought a lot about it. I'm going to explain how a Master's degree in urban planning will help me do what I've always wanted to do.

Sara: And what is that?

Jamal: Well, I've always been interested in cities and how they deal with the huge challenges facing them. Think about it . . . there are so many problems.

Sara: You're right . . . the traffic, the noise, air pollution, and so many people!

AUDIO SCRIPTS

Jamal: And how about the future? When I think about how much the population of cities is going to grow, it seems to me that the problems are only going to get worse.

Sara: True. Yeah, I see. And without good planning, cities will be in big trouble. . . So what else will you need to do to prepare?

Jamal: I'll need to get some experience, so in June I'll be starting a seven-month internship at a big urban planning firm. I'm also going to take an advanced economics class in the evenings.

Sara: Wow! You'll be very busy. And when will you hear about your application?

Jamal: Apparently, I won't hear about my application until the admissions office gets back to me next November. But by then I'll have made some good contacts and gotten some good hands-on experience. If I'm accepted, I'll be in school for the next three years, starting in January.

Sara: I really hope it works out.

Jamal: Thanks. . . . Hey, I've been talking about myself the whole time. How about you? What are your plans?

Sara: Well, I think I'm going to take a year off after I graduate. I'm planning to get a part-time job and spend the rest of my time writing. I'm actually working on a short story now.

Jamal: Really? That's great. Can I read it?

Sara: Sure, that is, if I ever finish it.

Jamal: So, do you think you'll be writing full-time in ten-years-time?

Sara: That's my hope. We'll see what happens. How about you? What do you think you'll be doing in ten years?

Jamal: Well, my hope is that in ten years, I'll be managing a small urban planning company of my own.

Sara: Great! And in fifteen years?

Jamal: Hmm. I'm not sure. But I hope that by that time, I'll have worked on a lot of projects that will make city life better for a whole lot of people.

UNIT 4

LESSON 1

1 READ, page 92   CD1–Track 30

4C, page 95   CD1–Track 31

1. **A:** Wasn't the first person in space American?
   B: No, it was a Russian named Yuri Gagarin.
2. **A:** Didn't space travel begin in the 1960s?
   B: No, it actually began in the 1950s.
3. **A:** Didn't the first astronaut step on the moon in 1969?
   B: Yes, it was on July 21, 1969.
4. **A:** Haven't there been trips to Mars already?
   B: No, nobody has gone there yet.
5. **A:** Isn't space travel expensive?
   B: Yes, it's extremely expensive.
6. **A:** Aren't all objects weightless in space?
   B: Yes, they float around in the air.
7. **A:** Doesn't life in a space station seem exciting?
   B: Yes, it seems amazing.
8. **A:** Doesn't everyone want to travel to the moon?
   B: No, I don't think so.

5A, page 96   CD1–Track 32

1. There's a Mars research station on Earth?
2. The training at the station isn't for everyone.
3. There are people who specialize in space psychology?
4. Astronauts haven't gone to Mars yet?
5. It will take years for humans to travel to Mars.
6. It takes longer to travel to Mars than to the moon?
7. We aren't going to read about other planets?
8. We have to learn all this information about Mars?

5B, page 96   CD1–Track 33

A: There's a Mars research station on Earth?
B: Yes. It's located in a desert.
A: There are people who specialize in space psychology?
B: Yes, but there aren't many.
A: Astronauts haven't gone to Mars yet?
B: No. No humans have gone there yet.
A: It takes longer to travel to Mars than to the moon?
B: Yes, the moon is much closer to Earth.
A: We aren't going to read about other planets?
B: No, not this semester.
A: We have to learn all this information about Mars?
B: Yes, but I'm sure you'll find it interesting.

6B, page 97   CD1–Track 34

Reporter: You traveled all that distance in a canoe. You weren't afraid?

Explorer: Not really. I had done a lot of training before the journey.

Reporter: Yes, I think I read about that. Didn't you train for months to get ready?

Explorer: Yes, I did. I had to be in excellent physical condition.

Reporter: Right. It would not be possible otherwise. But still . . . Wasn't it hard?

Explorer: Yes, it sure was. This kind of trip is not for everybody. Some people get lonely.

Reporter: What about for you? It didn't get lonely?

Explorer: No, not for me. It was quiet, and I had a lot of time to think.

Reporter: How about the weather? Were there storms?

Explorer: Sometimes, but I was ready for them.

Reporter: Weren't you ever afraid?

Explorer: Not really. I had some good maps so I knew what I was doing. I can't wait to go out again.

Reporter: You're planning another trip already?

Explorer: Yes, I am. In fact, I'm training for it now.

Reporter: You're kidding. Aren't you tired of the ocean by now?

Explorer: No, I'm not. I love it.

8A, page 99   CD1–Track 35

1. Polynesian explorers traveled across the Pacific Ocean over a thousand years ago?
2. Didn't the Polynesians have big ships?
3. Didn't they need a lot of wind in order to travel?
4. Weren't the stars important to the Polynesians?
5. Modern-day scientists didn't follow the Polynesians' route in sailboats?
6. Don't scientists have proof that the Polynesians were in Hawaii?
7. Isn't Hawaii two or three hundred miles from Tahiti?
8. Didn't the Polynesians ever get lost?

8B, page 99   CD1–Track 36

1. **A:** Polynesian explorers traveled across the Pacific Ocean over a thousand years ago?
   B: Yes, that's what the research shows.
2. **A:** Didn't the Polynesians have big ships?
   B: No, they didn't. They had smaller boats called canoes.
3. **A:** Didn't they need a lot of wind in order to travel?
   B: Yes. They waited for strong winds before they began their journeys.
4. **A:** Weren't the stars important to the Polynesians?
   B: Yes. They used the stars to find their way.
5. **A:** Modern-day scientists didn't follow the Polynesians' route in sailboats?
   B: No. They traveled in canoes.
6. **A:** Don't scientists have proof that the Polynesians were in Hawaii?
   B: Yes. The proof is ancient Polynesian tools in Hawaii.
7. **A:** Isn't Hawaii two or three hundred miles from Tahiti?
   B: No. Hawaii is thousands of miles from Tahiti.
8. **A:** Didn't the Polynesians ever get lost?
   B: No, they never had trouble.

LESSON 2

1 READ, page 101   CD1–Track 37

7, page 105   CD1–Track 38

A: This is a terrific party, isn't it?
B: Yeah. It's great!

A: You invited Paul to the party, didn't you?
B: No, I forgot. Sorry.

7A, page 106   CD1–Track 39

1. It's very hot in the Maya caves, isn't it?
2. The Maya lived thousands of years ago, didn't they?
3. There were many interesting things in the caves, weren't there?
4. The cave paintings are unusual, aren't they?
5. We can learn a lot about the Maya from the paintings, can't we?
6. You don't know the meaning of the symbols on the walls, do you?
7. You needed the help of the local people to find the caves, didn't you?
8. There isn't a lot of information about Maya cave traditions, is there?

7B, page 106   CD1–Track 40

1. **A:** It's very hot in the Maya caves, isn't it?
   B: No, actually the temperature is very comfortable.
2. **A:** The Maya lived thousands of years ago, didn't they?
   B: Yes, and there are Maya people today who live in southern Mexico and parts of Central America.
3. **A:** There were many interesting things in the caves, weren't there?
   B: Yes, many amazing things.
4. **A:** The cave paintings are unusual, aren't they?
   B: Yes, they're very unusual.
5. **A:** We can learn a lot about the Maya from the paintings, can't we?
   B: Yes, the artwork is full of information about how the Maya lived.
6. **A:** You don't know the meaning of the symbols on the walls, do you?
   B: No, not yet. We hope to figure out the meaning soon.
7. **A:** You needed the help of the local people to find the caves, didn't you?
   B: Yes, of course. They know the area very well.
8. **A:** There isn't a lot of information about Maya cave traditions, is there?
   B: In fact, there is quite a lot. There are many books on the subject.

8B, page 107   CD1–Track 41

1. **A:** Rock climbing seems dangerous, doesn't it?
   B: That's why I don't want to do it.
2. **A:** The view is beautiful, isn't it?
   B: It's gorgeous.
3. **A:** We start the hike tomorrow at eight o'clock, don't we?
   B: No, eight-thirty.

AUDIO SCRIPTS

4. A: The climb was hard, wasn't it?
  B: Yeah, unbelievably hard.
5. A: There's plenty of water, isn't there?
  B: Let me check.
6. A: We're going to stop at four o'clock, aren't we?
  B: I'm not sure, but we stopped at four o'clock last time.

REVIEW THE GRAMMAR

2A, page 110   CD1–Track 42

Moderator: Good afternoon, ladies and gentlemen. Welcome to the fifth annual meeting of the *University Explorers Club*. We have an exciting program and some terrific speakers, so let's get started right away. Our first guests are doing some very interesting work. Please join me in welcoming them . . . Thanks for being with us today. I know you're both involved in a fascinating project. You're working on Dr. Albert Lin's project, aren't you?

A: Yes, that's right. We're working on the *Valley of the Khans* project. It's really the most interesting work we've ever done.

Moderator: Could you tell us a little about the project?

B: Sure. Dr. Lin is trying to identify the burial site of Genghis Khan. No one knows exactly where it is. But this project is very different from a typical archeological search. Normally when people study cultures of the past, they look for the remains of old buildings, tools, and other objects by digging deep into the earth. Dr. Lin's goals are the same, but his methods are different. He collects information about ancient Mongolian structures and objects, but he uses modern technology instead of shovels, so he never disturbs the earth.

Moderator: The use of technology is especially important in Mongolia, isn't it?

A: Yes, absolutely. Most Mongolian people have great respect for Genghis Khan. They consider him to be the founder of their nation. Many Mongolians believe that it would bring bad luck to damage the land around the area where Genghis Khan might be buried.

Moderator: So Lin's team of explorers never disturbs the ground?

B: That's right. It works like this: Lin and his team take satellite photos of huge areas of Mongolia. They show these images to volunteers like us. We examine the photos and look for things that might be old roads, buildings, or objects, and we report what we see.

Moderator: And you do this right from your home computers?

A: Yes, but we're not alone. There are thousands of volunteers just like us around the world, who look at the photos and report back.

Moderator: Well, that makes sense. There must be hundreds of thousands of miles to cover. Isn't Mongolia enormous?

A: Yes, it's huge. It covers about 600,000 square miles of land. And there are about 85,000 photos to look at.

Moderator: What happens next?

B: Well, Lin takes a group of explorers to Mongolia to do on-the-ground research. They follow up on the volunteers' reports and try to locate the areas that have been identified on the photos. Lin's team uses sensors to explore the land. These instruments allow the researchers to collect information about structures and objects without ever touching them or disturbing the earth.

A: That's how they get an idea of what the ancient land looked like and where Genghis Khan's tomb might be.

Moderator: So similar methods could be used in a wide range of exploration projects, couldn't they?

A: Yes, definitely. The technology is useful for anyone who is trying to learn about ancient times and people's cultural traditions. That's an important part of Dr. Lin's work.

Moderator: Well, thank you so much for sharing your experiences. We look forward to following the . . .

2C and 2D, page 110   CD2–Track 43

1. Moderator: Thanks for being with us today. I know you're both involved in a fascinating project. You're working on Dr. Albert Lin's project, aren't you?

A: Yes, that's right. We're working on the *Valley of the Khans* project. It's really the most interesting work we've ever done.

2. Moderator: The use of technology is especially important in Mongolia, isn't it?

A: Yes, absolutely. Most Mongolian people have great respect for Genghis Khan. They consider him to be the founder of their nation. Many Mongolians believe that it would bring bad luck to damage the land around the area where Genghis Khan might be buried.

3. Moderator: So Lin's team of explorers never disturbs the ground?

B: That's right. It works like this: Lin and his team take satellite photos of huge areas of Mongolia. They show these images to volunteers like us. We examine the photos and look for things that might be old roads, buildings, or objects, and we report what we see.

4. Moderator: And you do this right from your home computers?

A: Yes, but we're not alone. There are thousands of volunteers just like us around the world, who look at the photos and report back.

5. Moderator: Well, that makes sense. There must be hundreds of thousands of miles to cover. Isn't Mongolia enormous?

A: Yes, it's huge. It covers about 600,000 square miles of land. And there are about 85,000 photos to look at.

UNIT 5

LESSON 1

1 READ, page 116   CD2–Track 2

LESSON 2

1 READ, page 124   CD2–Track 3

7, page 128   CD2–Track 4
   the book, the question, the difficult exercise
   the exercise, the answer, the easy question

7A and 7B, page 129   CD2–Track 5
1. Do you like the flowers I just bought?
2. They're for the annual party.
3. The other day Ling baked some delicious cookies.
4. Is he going to the celebration, too?
5. Mia made the most amazing dress.
6. Do you know where the holiday dinner is?
7. Bring the address so we don't get lost.
8. Twenty years old—that's the age I want to be.

9A and 9B, page 130   CD2–Track 6
   What do David Dicks, Zac Sunderland, and Laura Dekker have in common? When they were in their teens, they all wanted to have a thrilling adventure. They each had a sailboat, and they all wanted to sail around the world alone.
   Seventeen-year-old David Dicks sailed out from his native Australia in his 34-foot (10-meter) boat. He had to face many challenges on the ocean, such as bad weather and problems with his boat, but he successfully completed the difficult trip in nine months.
   Zac Sunderland set out from the west coast of the United States at the age of 16 in a boat called *The Intrepid*. He had bought the boat with money saved from after-school jobs. He sailed around the world in 13 months, completing the trip when he was 17.
   Sixteen-year-old Laura Dekker of the Netherlands could not start her trip right away. At first, government officials were worried that the trip was too dangerous for a young person. Finally, they allowed Dekker to go, and she successfully completed her year-long sail around the world.

LESSON 3

1 READ, page 131   CD2–Track 7

7B and 7C, page 135   CD2–Track 8

Interviewer: Well, Ms. Montero, thank you for agreeing to do this interview today.

Ms. Montero: Oh, you're very welcome. My pleasure.

Interviewer: So, tell me. What are your greatest joys at this stage of your life?

Ms. Montero: Ahhh, well. My greatest joy is my family, being surrounded by my family. It is so heart-warming to be with everyone during special celebrations. I was so happy when everyone was together for my 80th birthday this year.

Interviewer: 80—congratulations!

Ms. Montero: Thank you. It was wonderful. . . . Some of my family lives in Puerto Rico, but my daughters arranged for all of them to come for the celebration. We were all together—all nineteen of us! . . . I had all my children, grandchildren, and great-grandchildren with me. I was so happy. It was just wonderful.

Interviewer: Wow, so you're a great-grandmother?

Ms. Montero: Yes, I have three great-grandchildren.

Interviewer: That's terrific. So you turned 80 this year . . . what have you learned about life over the course of your lifetime?

Ms. Montero: Well, let's see . . . I think my experiences as a mother have taught me to be a better listener and to communicate better with others. . . . That's very important. . . . I don't think as a mother I used to listen to my children—you know, their hopes, their dreams, their fears. . . . I know my children much better now because I listen to them. I talk to them.

Interviewer: Uh-huh.

Ms. Montero: Yeah, I think my children and I have a much better understanding of each other now. Also, I now have more patience as a result of my life experiences.

Interviewer: Well, patience, that's important.

Ms. Montero: Oh, yes, it sure is. . . . before, when I was younger, I had trouble communicating with people outside of my home and family because I was shy. . . . I was really shy, so I didn't have many friends. . . . Friendship is important just like family. I guess what I have learned about life is how important communication is.

Interviewer: Well, that seems like a very valuable lesson.

Ms. Montero: Oh, yes. It certainly is.

Interviewer: So, what advice would you give to the younger generation? What do you think is most important for them to know about?

Ms. Montero: Oh, let's see. . . . I would advise them, as I did with my children and grandchildren, and now do with all my great-grandchildren, to study hard so that they can have a career.

AUDIO SCRIPTS **A9**

AUDIO SCRIPTS

Interviewer: Uh-huh.

Ms. Montero: My husband and I, we didn't have much education. We had few opportunities. . . . But my husband worked hard, and I took care of our home and our children. . . . I made sure they studied hard, and they did. They all went to college and have had successful careers—a teacher, a banker, a head of a corporation.

Interviewer: Wow. That's great.

Ms. Montero: Yes, all of my grandchildren are professionals. I am so proud of them, and think I'm so fortunate because everyone in my family has a good job and a lot of opportunities. . . . Education was the key. It really was. . . . So, that's what I'd like the younger generation to know. . . . Life is very hard if education does not play a big part in it.

Interviewer: Well, thank you very much, Ms. Montero. I appreciate your time today.

Ms. Montero: You're welcome. Thank you.

REVIEW THE GRAMMAR

3B, page 139   CD2–Track 9

Near a Chippewa village was a large lake, and in the lake there lived an enormous turtle. This was no ordinary turtle because he would often come out of his home in that lake and visit with his Indian neighbors. He made most of his visits to the head chief of the tribe, and on these occasions he stayed for hours talking with him.

The chief, seeing that the turtle was very smart and showed great wisdom, took a great fancy to him, and whenever a difficult question came up before the chief, he generally asked Mr. Turtle to help him decide.

One day there was a great misunderstanding between two different groups in the tribe. Each side became so angry that the argument threatened to become a bloody fight. The chief was unable to decide which side was right, so he said, "I will call Mr. Turtle. He will judge for you."

3C, page 139   CD2–Track 10

The chief sent for the turtle. When the turtle arrived, the chief gave up his seat, so that the turtle could sit down, listen to both sides, and decide which side was right. The turtle listened very carefully to both sides, and thought long and hard before he gave his decision. After thinking and studying each side carefully, he came to the conclusion to decide in favor of both. This would not cause any bad feelings. So after his decision, he gave them a long speech and showed them where they were both right, and finished by saying, "You are both right in some ways and wrong in others. Therefore, I will say that you both are equally right."

When the people heard this decision, they saw that the turtle was right, and gave him a long cheer for the wisdom he displayed. The whole tribe saw that without this wise decision, there would have been a lot of bloodshed. So they voted him as their judge, and the chief was so well pleased with the turtle that he . . .

UNIT 6

LESSON 1

1 READ, page 144   CD2–Track 11

8A and 8B, pages 149 and 150   CD2–Track 12

Lose weight without suffering!

Would you enjoy being a few pounds lighter? Do you spend a lot of time trying out special diets? Has losing weight always been difficult for you? Don't worry . . . you're not alone. Many people would like to lose weight, but they don't know how.

There are three key things that you can do to make your weight-loss plan successful. They involve changing the way you eat. A number of medical studies show that how you eat matters as much as what you eat.

Tip 1: Cut your food into small pieces.

Some recent studies show that cutting your food into small pieces may help you eat less. In one experiment, for example, college students were divided into two groups, and each student was given a bagel, a kind of roll. One group of students ate whole, uncut bagels; the other group ate bagels that were cut into four pieces. Then the students were invited to a lunch. Those who had eaten the cut-up bagels ate less than the students who ate whole bagels. Researchers say that eating several small pieces of food may satisfy people more than having one large piece.

Tip 2: Don't eat large meals late in the day.

Some researchers believe that consuming the largest meal of the day in the early afternoon helps people control their weight better than eating late in the day. Why does timing make such a difference? Scientists are not sure. One theory is that when we eat late in the day, it causes our body to have problems falling asleep. This in turn affects the way we use and store food, and may cause us to gain weight.

Tip 3: Eat slowly and stop eating when you are 80 percent full.

Eating slowly gives your body a chance to process food properly. It will also prevent you from overeating. The Japanese know this well. They also say *Hara hachi bunme*, which means "eat only until you are 80 percent full." Limiting the total amount of food you eat helps you avoid gaining weight and other health problems.

LESSON 2

1 READ, page 152　　　　　　　　　　CD2–Track 13

9B, page 159　　　　　　　　　　　　　CD2–Track 14

Can Venom Be Good for You?

While Michael was on vacation in Mexico, he decided to go for a swim. It was very hot, and he wanted to get some cool relief. He jumped into the pool, but instead of relief, all of a sudden he started to feel a burning pain in his leg. He looked down and saw his attacker—a poisonous scorpion. Michael got to a local hospital quickly, and about 30 hours later, the pain seemed to disappear. He was very relieved.

But that isn't the end of the story. Before the scorpion bite, Michael had been suffering from back pain. Doctors had often encouraged him to do regular exercise such as swimming. Surprisingly, days after the scorpion bite, his back pain went away, and it never came back. The scorpion's venom had cured him. Whenever he remembers the suffering from his horrible back pain, he is grateful for that scorpion.

Experts advise people not to go anywhere near scorpions or snakes. But if scorpion researchers stopped working with these creatures, we might not find out more about the medical benefits their venom can provide.

LESSON 3

1 READ, page 161　　　　　　　　　　CD2–Track 15

11A and 11B, pages 168 and 169　　　CD2–Track 16

Interviewer: Tonight our guest speaker is Dr. Margaret Tate. Dr. Tate's specialty is public health. Twenty years ago, she moved to Thailand to study the development of health services there, and she's here to tell us about her research. Please join me in welcoming her.

Dr. Tate: Thank you so much. It's good to be here.

Interviewer: Dr. Tate, can you please give us a general picture of healthcare in Thailand?

Dr. Tate: Yes, certainly. Thailand has been successful in bringing healthcare to its population. In fact, it has been so successful that many countries send officials to Thailand to study its healthcare model. What is especially encouraging is that Thailand was not a wealthy country 20 years ago, but it has brought universal health care to the Thai people in 2002. That is, all citizens of Thailand receive healthcare. In the past, people thought that it would be too difficult for countries without a lot of money to have universal healthcare. But Thailand worked hard to improve its economy and its healthcare system. It does not have as much money as countries such as the United States, yet it manages its healthcare system very well.

Interviewer: I guess that's why countries are studying Thailand in order to improve their own healthcare.

Dr. Tate: Yes, that is correct.

Interviewer: Dr. Tate, you say that Thailand brought healthcare to all of its people. How did it do this and what were the challenges or problems?

Dr. Tate: One very big problem was the rural areas—that is, the countryside. People in those areas lived too far away to get medical treatment in hospitals. The hospitals were in the cities. Around this time, the economy was improving. The government of Thailand decided to spend money on the countryside in order to bring healthcare to the rural areas.

Interviewer: That makes sense.

Dr. Tate: The government could have spent all its money on the hospitals that existed in the cities, but instead it focused on the countryside. This greatly improved the health of people there and it saved the country money, too.

Interviewer: How did it save the country money?

Dr. Tate: People in the rural areas received enough preventative healthcare to stay healthy. That way, they did not need as much emergency treatment, which is very expensive.

Interviewer: I see. What other problems did Thailand have?

Dr. Tate: There was not enough clean water for people to drink. The government worked to improve the drinking water and sanitation. Now Thai people all have access to clean water.

Interviewer: What about transportation? Was that a problem in Thailand in terms of health care?

Dr. Tate: Yes. There were not enough existing highways. That made it difficult to bring medical workers to the countryside. It also made it difficult for someone from the countryside to go to a hospital in the city if they needed to. The solution was that the Thai government improved the infrastructure and built more highways.

Interviewer: Were there problems with the quality of healthcare itself?

Dr. Tate: Yes. Back 20 years ago, there was not enough highly trained medical staff in the countryside. But the government now requires medical graduates to spend three years in the countryside. The government made this requirement so that there will always be enough skilled doctors to serve the rural areas.

Interviewer: Dr. Tate, we're almost out of time, but can you tell us what challenges Thailand still faces for the future with its healthcare system?

Dr. Tate: Yes, there are still some challenges that remain. First, Thailand needs to include foreign workers in the healthcare system. Second, the government needs to make sure that health benefits are more equal. And third, the population of Thailand is aging, so the healthcare system will have to be ready to help meet the needs of the elderly.

Interviewer: Thank you, Dr. Tate. This has been very informative for our audience and for the world medical community.

Dr. Tate: My pleasure. Thank you for having me.

AUDIO SCRIPTS

REVIEW THE GRAMMAR

2A and 2B, pages 170 and 171 CD2–Track 17

Do you find time to go outside every day? Or do you feel that you're just too busy to go outside and enjoy nature? If that's true, you're certainly not alone. In today's world, many people have trouble having outdoor experiences when they have such busy schedules.

Author Richard Louv writes about the benefits of spending time outside and connecting with nature. He feels that these days, too many of us suffer from a loss of that connection. Louv believes that not being outside enough affects our health and general well-being.

Louv's first book, *Last Child in the Woods*, is about children not spending enough time outside. The book became a best-seller, and it encouraged people to start nature programs to get children to go outside.

In an interview, Louv talked about how connecting with nature actually changed one person's life. Juan Martinez grew up in a poor section of Los Angeles, California. He used to get into trouble a lot and he also did poorly in school. Then he got a bad grade in a high school science class . . . and it was the best thing that ever happened to him. Why? Because the school principal gave him a choice: he could fail the class, or join the Eco Club. Martinez was unhappy at first, but he decided to join the club.

First, Martinez grew a chili plant in the club garden and proudly took it home to show his mother. Later, he participated in an Eco Club trip to the Grand Teton Mountains. It was those two things—the chili plant and the experience of nature in the mountains—that changed Martinez's life forever. He realized that children don't have enough opportunities to connect with nature. Martinez later became the head of the Natural Leaders Network, an organization that provides kids with these opportunities.

In his lectures, Martinez emphasizes the importance of getting young people outdoors. He points out that nature can teach everyone skills for life—"communicating, working together, and realizing you can do things that you never thought you could."

The work of Richard Louv and Juan Martinez has been important in recent times to our awareness of having a healthier lifestyle. Being outside makes people feel happier and healthier, and can change lives.

UNIT 7

LESSON 1

1 READ, page 176 CD2–Track 18

8, page 181 CD2–Track 19
We have to help Mom.
We [*hafta*] help Mom.
Nobody has to know.
Nobody [*hasta*] know.
You don't have to pay right away.
You don't [*hafta*] pay right away.
I have got to go now.
I've [*gotta*] go now.
Jack has got to get up.
Jack's [*gotta*] get up.

8A and 8B, page 181 CD2–Track 20
1. We [*hafta*] be there in 20 minutes, or we'll miss the plane.
2. [*Everybody's gotta*] be back on time. We leave at 6 o'clock sharp.
3. You [*hafta*] call us every day.
4. Max [*hasta*] learn some basic Chinese before he goes.
5. I'm sorry that I'm late. I [*hafta*] take an earlier train next time.
6. [*We've gotta*] buy gifts before we go back home.

11, page 183 CD2–Track 21

Coffee drinking is an important part of life in Ethiopia. Preparing the coffee and sharing it with family, friends, and neighbors is a daily event. In fact, in most parts of the country, people have coffee ceremonies in their homes three times a day—morning, noon, and night.

If you're traveling in Ethiopia and someone invites you to a coffee ceremony, you should be very pleased. Such an invitation is a sign of friendship and respect. Before you go, though, there are a few important things to know:

- You must not act like you're in a hurry. A coffee ceremony can take up to two or three hours. The ceremony includes preparation of the coffee beans, eating snacks, and talking with your hosts and the other guests. In order to be polite, you have to stay for the entire ceremony.
- Preparing the coffee is a process with many steps, and the preparation is typically done by a woman. You must remember to praise her several times. You're supposed to comment on the wonderful smell of the beans, the woman's skillful technique, and the excellent taste of the coffee in your cup. It will probably be the best coffee you've ever had!
- The youngest child usually serves the coffee. According to tradition, she's supposed to give the first cup to the oldest person or a special guest at the ceremony.
- Your host will offer you three cups of coffee. You must not refuse any of them even if you're starting to feel the effects of the caffeine. Be polite, and drink all three cups.

Remember, you don't have to speak Amharic, the language of Ethiopia, in order to have a good time. Just sit quietly, smile, drink the coffee, and enjoy the experience.

LESSON 2

1 READ, page 184 — CD2–Track 22

LESSON 3

1 READ, page 191 — CD2–Track 23

8, page 197 — CD2–Track 24

We should have helped them.
We [should've] helped them.
Chris should have for a ride.
Chris [should've] asked for a ride.
I shouldn't have left so early.
I [shouldn've] left so early.
The children shouldn't have gone.
The children [shouldn've] gone.

8A, page 197 — CD2–Track 25

1. I [shouldn've] bought a ticket for her.
2. I [shudəv] taken the bus.
3. We [shouldn've] come early.
4. She [shouldn've] invited her friend.
5. We [shoulda] worn jeans today.
6. He [shouldn've] made a reservation online.
7. They [shoulda] stayed at a hotel on the beach.
8. You [shouldn've] eaten the soup.

10, page 199 — CD2–Track 26

Sally: So, Ben, I understand that you're thinking about making some changes at Sun and Sea Tours, and you need my advice. Your friend Lou told you about us?

Ben: Yes, he did. He said you are very experienced in tourism. I hope you can help us.

Sally: We'll certainly try. Can you tell me about your hotel?

Ben: Yes, it's located in Morocco. Business hasn't been good the last few years, so I've been thinking of ways to get more tourists to our hotel. I'm thinking of making our hotel environmentally friendly to increase tourism.

Sally: Yes, these days more people are looking for an environmentally friendly hotel or tour. They understand that tourism can help to preserve the environment and help local communities.

Ben: Can you suggest how we can become environmentally friendly?

Sally: Yes—well, it's both about the environment and the community. For example, does your hotel employ local people? Do you hire managers from the local area? If so, the hotel is contributing to the development of the community.

Ben: That makes sense. We can start doing that.

Sally: You should also make sure that you buy food that is locally grown. Serving local food at the hotel is a good way to support the local economy.

Ben: I see. And it gives tourists a better experience, too. We'll be sure to check food sources from now on.

Sally: Good. Another thing you should think about is recycling and using water efficiently. That is especially important in countries where water is limited.

Ben: OK, we'll look into it.

Sally: Now let's talk about sightseeing. Your company, in addition to your hotel, has on-site tours?

Ben: Yes, we arrange tours in Fez and Marrakech, but also in natural areas, such as the Atlas Mountains.

Sally: Good. I suggest you use local guides only and make sure that they are careful with the environment. Guides should be careful not to visit the same sites too often. That way they protect it from overuse.

Ben: OK.

Sally: You also ought to ask the guides how they take tourists around. There are different choices in transportation, and some are better for the environment. So ask the guides if they use only cars and trucks, or if they offer walking tours. They might also offer trips on camels, and that is also a good choice. Those are a lot less damaging to the environment and less polluting as well.

Ben: That's important. Tourists love camels, too. We really should have thought about all this before!

Sally: Don't worry, Ben. It's never too late.

REVIEW THE GRAMMAR

2B, page 201 — CD2–Track 27

Mara: . . . OK. So we're going to start at the Lincoln Memorial, right? Everyone says we shouldn't miss that.

Paul: Yeah. It's good to start at the Lincoln Memorial because we'll be able to visit it early in the morning. It's open 24 hours a day.

Mara: Do we have to buy tickets?

Paul: No, it's free.

Mara: Look how clearly you can see the Washington Monument from here. Isn't it a spectacular view?

Paul: It is. Are you ready to walk over there?

Mara: Almost. Let's take pictures of the monument first. Oh, no. The flash isn't working again! I haven't been able to get the flash to work at all on this trip.

Mara: Look at that line of people. Isn't it only a quarter to nine? The monument isn't supposed to open until 9 o'clock. Why are they standing there?

Paul: For tickets. You have to have a ticket to take the elevator. And you have to go to the top to see the view. It's great. You can see the whole city from up there. And the Washington Monument is free. We don't have to spend any money on tickets. It's the same at the Jefferson Memorial.

Mara: That was great. I'm so glad we didn't have to wait in a long line here. One long line a day is enough for me.

AUDIO SCRIPTS **A13**

AUDIO SCRIPTS

2D, page 203   CD2–Track 28

Paul: OK. So how do we get to the Freer Gallery from here?
Mara: First we go up 14th Street. Then we're supposed to make a right.
Mara: I think we turned too soon. The map says we should have turned on Constitution Avenue. This is D Street.
Paul: I think we'd better ask that police officer for directions. I don't want to walk all the way back to 14th Street.
Paul: I'm starving. We should have brought sandwiches with us.
Mara: It's a good thing we didn't. Do you see that sign? People aren't supposed to eat here.
Paul: OK, then we should find a café nearby.

UNIT 8

LESSON 1

1 READ, page 208   CD2–Track 29

10A, page 215   CD2–Track 30

LESSON 2

1 READ, page 216   CD2–Track 31

10, page 224   CD2–Track 32

F: They may have left the house.
M: They [may've] left the house.
F: It might have happened fast.
M: It [might've] happened fast.
F: I could have screamed.
M: I [could've] screamed.
F: She must have known the truth.
M: She [must've] known the truth.
F: You might not have known that.
M: You might [not've] known that.
F: He could not have called my number
M: He [couldnt#'ve] called my number.
F: It might have happened fast.
M: It [mighta] happened fast.

10A, page 225   CD2–Track 33

1. We [may've] forgotten to lock the door.
2. Everybody [might've] been at the game that night.
3. You [could've] dropped your keys on the way home.
4. Max [must've] noticed the footprints in the yard.
5. You [may've] left the window open.
6. We [may#not#'ve] checked the security system last night.
7. You [might#not#'ve] heard the footsteps outside.
8. It [couldnt#'ve] happened yesterday.

13, page 227   CD2–Track 34

For hundreds of years, Roanoke Colony has remained a mystery. There has not been much evidence that would tell us what happened to the colonists at Roanoke. However, many experts have had different ideas or theories to explain what might have happened.

Theory 1: It's possible that Native Americans killed the Roanoke colonists. This might have happened for any of several reasons: different Native American groups were fighting and the colonists may have been friends with the wrong side. Also, the Colonists had had some troubles with the Native Americans. The leader of the colonists had burned the village of Aquascogoc. It is therefore possible that the Native American tribes then later killed the Roanoke colonists.

Theory 2: Some people believe that all the Roanoke colonists got sick and died from a terrible disease. However, this theory is probably incorrect because no one ever found the bodies of the colonists, and their houses had disappeared, too.

Theory 3: Some people think that a terrible storm destroyed Roanoke Colony. This theory explains why both the people and the houses were gone. However, later, some explorers went back to Roanoke Island to investigate, and found a fence still standing. Could a storm have destroyed everything except for one fence? That seems very unlikely.

Theory 4: It's possible that the colonists left Roanoke Island to live with Native American tribes. The Roanoke colonists were friendly with the Croatoan Indian tribe, who lived on Hatteras Island. Also, the Croatoan Indians knew how to find food, so they could help the colonists survive. The Croatoan Indians might also have protected the colonists from unfriendly Native American tribes. Investigators later found the word "Croatoan" carved on a tree where the Roanoke colonists had lived and three letters, C-R-O, on a piece of wood. This shows that the Roanoke colonists and the Native Americans may have lived together.

Theory 5: Some people think the Roanoke colonists moved to a different area on their own. According to this theory, the colonists broke apart their houses, and they used the wood to build a boat or rafts. Then they sailed across the water. In 2012, experts found an ancient map. It showed a possible fort 70 miles away. The colonists at Roanoke may have built this fort and lived there until they died.

With little scientific evidence, we may never know for certain what happened to the colonists of Roanoke.

REVIEW THE GRAMMAR

3A and 3B, page 230 **CD2–Track 35**

Some people used to worry in the year 2012, the world was going to end. Why were these people afraid that this was going to happen? They thought the Maya had predicted it. The Maya were an ancient people who lived in Mexico, Guatemala, and other Central American countries. They had a very advanced civilization, so people believed that their predictions had to be true. However, we are way past 2012 now, and the world hasn't ended yet. So, it seems that there was no reason to worry. In fact, there was never any reason to worry, because the Maya actually never made this prediction.

How do we know this? In 2011, archaeologists made an important archaeological discovery in Xultún, Guatemala. They found murals—images painted on a wall—in a room in an ancient Maya house. The murals showed a king with his advisers and servants. The walls were also filled with mathematical calculations. These calculations measured large amounts of time. They also suggest that the end of the world was not going to happen in 2012. It was going to happen thousands of years later.

Archaeologists believe that this room was the workroom of a Maya scribe. Scribes were important because they wrote down all the information that the king needed. Kings also needed their scribes to make predictions. They wanted to know when times were going to be good—with plenty of food and no wars—and when times were going to be bad. It's possible that the scribes had a unique way of predicting the future. They used past events and math, like the calculations that were found on the walls of the ancient Maya house.

Archaeologists say that the calculations include dates 7000 years in the future. Why? Nobody knows for sure. Experts know that they will probably never understand everything about the murals. But it seems likely that the Maya were worried because their world was changing. They didn't want to be alive when the end of the world happened. If the world ended so many thousands of years in the future, they would be safe. That is probably why they made these future predictions.

UNIT 9

LESSON 1

1 READ, page 236 **CD3–Track 2**

10A and 10B, page 244 **CD3–Track 3**

Narrator: Part 1

M: One night last November, a cruise ship called the *M/S Explorer* was sailing to Antarctica. Suddenly, it hit an iceberg. BANG! All the alarms went off. Frightened passengers ran out of their cabins. Everyone on board got into lifeboats and escaped from the ship. Fortunately, there were two other ships in the area. The next day, they picked up all the passengers from the lifeboats.

10A and 10B, page 244 **CD3–Track 4**

Narrator: Part 2

M: The passengers were very lucky to escape, because the ocean near Antarctica is very cold and icy. It's dangerous to sail in these waters, and it's easy to have an accident. In the past, this was not a serious problem because very few ships came to Antarctica. But now, many more ships are coming. Quite a few of them have accidents and sink. Why are all these ships coming to Antarctica? Many of them are cruise ships, and they are bringing tourists. These tourists want to see the penguins on the Antarctic Peninsula. In fact, over 34,000 tourists visit Antarctica every year.

10A and 10B, page 244 **CD3–Track 5**

Narrator: Part 3

M: Cruise ships cause problems for the environment. Trash and waste water from the ships sometimes pollute the sea and the air. Some tourists have walked all over the delicate plants in Antarctica and damaged them. And some people have bothered animals in order to get a perfect photo. For these reasons, many people think that tours to Antarctica should be stopped. If they can't be stopped, they should at least be limited and controlled so that they do not cause more damage.

10A and 10B, page 244 **CD3–Track 6**

Narrator: Part 4

M: The International Association of Antarctica Tour Operators (IAATO) is an organization for tour companies. It has created guidelines to protect the land. For example, tourists must promise to respect the wildlife. Each tour group can include no more than 100 people. There must also be one tour guide for every 20 people. But are these rules effective? The situation in Antarctica has improved, but many people are still worried. Tour companies are not required to join the IAATO. So, some of them do not join, which means that they don't have to follow its guidelines. In fact, some tour companies don't even know what the guidelines are. Work still needs to be done to protect Antarctica.

LESSON 2

1 READ, page 246 **CD3–Track 7**

10A, page 253 **CD3–Track 8**

M: Did you hear about the repairman who found a 500-pound bear in a basement?

F: No. What happened?

AUDIO SCRIPTS

M: He was working in the basement when he heard some growling noises. He looked up and saw an angry bear in the corner. The repairman ran out of the house as fast as he could.

F: He was lucky the bear didn't bite him. So then what happened?

M: The guy contacted the animal control department. The animal control people came and shot the bear twice with tranquilizers to calm it. But the bear escaped from the house. The animal rescue people chased the bear for nearly 45 minutes before the tranquilizer worked and they caught him. They said they will release the bear into the wild after they give it a medical exam.

LESSON 3

1 READ, page 254   CD3–Track 9

8, page 259   CD3–Track 10

Debra: Hey, Julie, do you want to go camping with me next weekend?

Julie: Hmm. I don't think so, Debra. I'm not going camping anytime soon.

Debra: Why? I thought you liked camping.

Julie: Well, I used to. But I had a bad experience last summer. Didn't I tell you?

Debra: No. What happened?

Julie: I was camping with a couple of friends. We set up our tent at the campsite and cooked dinner. Then we cleaned up and threw the trash away in the campground dumpsters. You have to do that if you don't want to be bothered by animals. Then we talked for a while and went to sleep.

Debra: Sounds pretty normal so far.

Julie: Well, it must have been about 11:30 or so when I got woken up by a scratching sound outside the tent. No one else heard it—my friends were fast asleep. After a minute or so, the noise stopped. I was scared, but I told myself there was probably nothing to worry about, and I tried to go back to sleep. But I wanted to see what the noise was. So I went outside . . . and I saw a small black and white creature. It was headed toward a bag of food scraps. The bag had gotten left under the picnic table by mistake.

Debra: What kind of animal was it?

Julie: Well, at first I thought it was a cat. But then the animal did this odd little dance and stomped its feet. Then I realized it was a skunk!

Debra: Really? How awful! Being sprayed by skunks is a nightmare. Skunk spray smells terrible!

Julie: I know! I tried to keep still, but that didn't help much. I had no idea how to stop the skunk from spraying.

Debra: That's how they protect themselves from predators, right? They spray to avoid getting attacked.

Julie: Yes. The skunk must have thought I wanted to attack it. In a matter of seconds, our entire campsite got sprayed. The smell was so bad that it woke up my friends. We spent hours washing everything with vinegar and water. That helped . . . a little.

Debra: I bet you left that campsite fast!

Julie: We sure did . . . first thing in the morning. But I guess we were lucky not to be visited by an even more dangerous animal!

REVIEW THE GRAMMAR

5A and 5B, page 263   CD3–Track 11

1. Q: Which of the following is a major problem facing the world's oceans?

   A: The correct answer is d. Earth's oceans and the species that live in them are being harmed by overfishing, pollution, and building on the coasts, as well as a number of other problems caused by human activity.

2. Q: Which of the following has been linked to climate change on Earth?

   A: The correct answer is d. Climate change is linked to droughts, floods, and melting ice caps. Rainfall patterns and polar ice have been affected by increasing temperatures. That's why there is too little water in some regions and too much water in others. If warming continues, floods could become more common. So could droughts, which are long periods without rain or snow. Less fresh water will be available.

3. Q: On average, what are your chances of being struck by lightning in any given year?

   A: The correct answer is b. A person's chance of being struck by lightning in a year is about 1 in 700,000. Participating in certain outdoor activities, like golf and mountain climbing, increases your risk of being hit. So does being outside during a thunderstorm.

4. Q: How many pounds of wild fish and shellfish are removed from the ocean every year?

   A: The correct answer is c. More than 170 billion pounds (77.9 million metric tons) are pulled from the ocean every year by fishermen. That's about three times the weight of every man, woman, and child in the United States.

5. Q: How big was the biggest wave that was ever recorded?

   A: The correct answer is d. The biggest wave that has ever been recorded was about 90 feet (27 meters) high. It was higher than a 10-story building. The wave was formed during a hurricane in the Gulf of Mexico in 2004.

UNIT 10

LESSON 1

1 READ, page 268   CD3–Track 12

9, page 274   CD3–Track 13

Dan: Hey Sam. How is your project going for psychology class? Did you get any good ideas?
Sam: Yes. I'm writing about how beauty affects people. My idea is unusual because I'm writing how beauty changed the life of someone I know.
Dan: Really? Whose?
Sam: A friend of my mom's.
Dan: What did he see that was so beautiful?
Sam: The tropic cost of Bahia in Brazil. It made him want to move there.
Dan: He's Brazilian?
Sam: No, this man, Alex Popovkin—is from Russia. When he was at the University of St. Petersburg, he did a work-study program at the Botanical Garden. They had a lot of tropical plants at the Conservatory there. He was fascinated by them.
Dan: But how did he end up in Brazil?
Sam: After college, he emigrated and moved to New York City. But he heard that Brazil had an amazing ecosystem. He wanted to see it. Finally one year later, he went to Brazil for vacation in the northeast. It was so beautiful, he decided he would go back there to live and five years later, he did. He made his dream come true.
Dan: So he moved to Brazil? But how else did it change his life?
Sam: He lives near the coast in the state of Bahia. His life is devoted to nature and plant life there. Every day he photographs and collects samples of plants from the coast. He finds rare species. Sometimes he has other scientists help him identify species. Look at this photo.
Dan: Wow! That's beautiful!
Sam: Yes, he has some terrific photos. His work has been important for the ecosystem of Brazil. He has posted many of his photos on the Internet, and the photos really allow people to experience some beautiful and rare plants they never would see otherwise. He lets people download the photos, too.
Dan: I'll look him up on the Internet, then. I'd like to see more of his work.

LESSON 2

1 READ, page 275   CD3–Track 14

7A, page 280   CD3–Track 15

Lee: Hello Jim. How did it go yesterday?
Jim: You mean the Egyptian exhibit opening?
Lee: Yes . . . was it a success?
Jim: Well, we had a lot of people come, so in that sense it was good. But the preparation was a nightmare.
Lee: What do you mean?
Jim: Well, first of all, the painters never showed up so I had to have staff members paint the gallery. They didn't do such a great job, but at least the walls dried quickly. I got the lighting installers to come two days later.
Lee: How about the set-up of the art?
Jim: That was exhausting. I was going to have two staff members do it, but they called in sick on the 12th and didn't come back until the following Friday. My back is still aching from unpacking all the art and arranging it on the walls and display shelves.
Lee: That's too bad.
Jim: One of the only things that went smoothly was the labeling of the art. I had the labels prepared by a very reliable company, and they were ready and delivered to me on time. Then I had my assistant carefully label each piece.
Lee: And the photography?
Jim: Another problem! The photographer who was supposed to be at the opening was delayed at another job. Thankfully, I didn't have to get out my old camera. We have a staff member who is a talented photographer, so I got her to take the pictures at the opening.
Lee: Great.
Jim: Then the designing and the printing of the tickets was the last task we had to do. I used a new software program to design and print the exhibition tickets, and it worked perfectly.
Lee: Well, that's good. Sounds like you had a lot of headaches, but the exhibit looks great now. Congratulations!

LESSON 3

1 READ, page 282   CD3–Track 16

REVIEW THE GRAMMAR

3, page 291   CD3–Track 17

Salesperson: Good afternoon. May I help you?
Customer: Yes, please. I've been invited to a costume party. The problem is I don't have a clue about what to wear.
S: Well, you've come to the right place. Let's see what we can do. Does the party have a theme?
C: Sort of. Here, take a look at the invitation. It says, "Wear something that will totally change how you feel.
S: Ok, that's a good start. Let me show you our selection of masks. That's the most important part of any costume. A great mask is the first thing people will notice. Please step right over here.
C: OK, sure . . .
S: Here are our Venetian masks. They're copies of the ones that people wear at the masquerade balls in Venice. This

AUDIO SCRIPTS

one would look great on you. And look—it has a lot of room around the mouth so it allows you to eat, drink, and talk without ever showing your face.

C: Uh, I don't know. I think I'd like something a little more, um, delicate.

S: Good idea. How do you like this beauty?

C: I do like the feathers, but it might be just a little too dramatic. What do you think?

S: I think it's perfect. You'll definitely feel like a movie star! There's no doubt about it. Everyone will be wondering who you are.

C: I'm not sure.

S: Wait. I've got it. This is really the perfect one. This tiger mask is one of a kind. It's simple, but elegant. Here, try it on.

C: Hmm. Maybe. I think I'd feel comfortable wearing that one. How much is it?

S: It's your lucky day! We're having a sale today—20 percent off all animal masks. Give me a minute and I'll tell you the price. (...) OK, so this mask comes to forty-nine ninety-nine, including the tax.

C: That seems reasonable. OK, I'll take it.

S: Great. Now how about the rest of the costume? Would you like to look at a full costume to go with the mask?

C: Actually, I think I have a black cloak at home that will go perfectly with it, so I think I'll just get the mask.

S: All right, fine. Jim doesn't have a customer now. I'll see if he can wrap that up for you. And just so you can see some of our full costumes, in case you change your mind, I will bring some out for you.

C: Sure, thanks. I wouldn't mind taking a look.

UNIT 11

LESSON 1

1 READ, page 296 CD3–Track 18

13, page 305 CD3–Track 19

Colors, which affect our feelings, are important in photography.

Black and white, which are not colors but tones, are important for contrast.

13A, page 305 CD3–Track 20

1. The contest, which is held once a year, has a $5000 cash prize.
2. Many people who have won the prize have gone on to become successful photographers.
3. The judges, who are professional photographers, consider the creativity of each photo.
4. The judges, who do not always agree, have a difficult task.
5. The contestant whose photo gets the highest score is the winner.
6. The photo which won last year's prize was taken by a 15-year old.

14A and 14B, pages 306 and 307 CD3–Track 21

Judge 1: This is going to be a tough choice, Katya.

Judge 2: I agree, Bill. These are both interesting shots with some excellent qualities. So let's take a closer look. This photo that shows the buildings and the sea. . . . Where was it taken?

Judge 1: The photographer who submitted it says it's a picture of Malé, which is the capital city of the Republic of Maldives.

Judge 2: Where is the Republic of Maldives exactly?

Judge 1: In the Indian Ocean. Apparently the Maldives is made up of almost 2000 islands.

Judge 2: Well, the color is certainly rich.

Judge 1: Mm-hmm. Yes, the color is strong, but maybe a little too bright. Do you think it looks real?

Judge 2: Yes, I do. I think the color works. But the part that's bothering me is the composition. It seems a little cluttered, doesn't it? I don't know where to look.

Judge 1: Maybe it's because the buildings take up so much of the space. I think the photographer should have shown more of the sea, which might have provided the viewer with a better perspective.

Judge 2: You might be right. But the photo is still very powerful. For me, the picture is warm and lively.

Judge 1: True. Well let's set that one aside for the moment and talk about the photo that was taken in a Mexican town.

Judge 2: This one is a little mysterious. I can't quite figure it out. We see a hand that is holding something. We don't know whose hand it is. What is it? Is it a picture? Or a small model building?

Judge 1: I'm not sure. That doesn't bother me, though. In fact, the hand adds to the mysterious atmosphere. There is no one there, just the buildings and the hand holding a building or a picture of a building. You can feel the emptiness of the town.

Judge 2: Yes. You also feel that emptiness when you look at the picture, because the photo makes you look to the right down that empty street. It gives a deep perspective.

Judge 1: You're right. The photographer has excellent technical abilities and a composition that captures the viewer's attention.

Judge 2: I couldn't agree with you more. I think we have a winner!

14C, page 307 CD3–Track 22

1. The photo that shows the buildings and the sea was taken in Malé.
2. Malé, which is the capital of the Republic of Maldives, is located in the Indian Ocean.
3. Let's talk about the photo that was taken in a small Mexican town.
4. We see a hand that is holding something.
5. The photographer has excellent technical abilities and a composition that captures the viewer's attention.

LESSON 2

1 READ, page 308   CD3–Track 23

10B, page 316   CD3–Track 24

Professor: During the next few classes, we're going to take a look at some well-known photographers and see what we can learn from them. Today I'd like to discuss Joel Sartore, a longtime photographer for *National Geographic Magazine*. Sartore is known for his ability to tell compelling stories about a wide range of topics. The subjects he's photographed include many topics, but he is most passionate about wildlife. In addition to his magazine assignments, which Sartore has traveled all over the world for, he has initiated a few projects of his own. His current project—and perhaps his most ambitious—is the Photo Ark. Is anyone familiar with this work?

Student 1: Yes, isn't it about animals that are in danger of extinction?

Professor: Right. Sartore believes that half of the world's plant and animal species will face the threat of extinction by the turn of the next century. As a result, he is taking pictures of them so people will understand the problem. So far, he has photographed thousands of species, many of which are endangered already. Now, the Photo Ark project, which he's deeply committed to, shows people animals they may never see. The idea is to make people care about animals through the pictures.

    I'd like to share a few things that Sartore has said about his work. This will give you an even better idea of the man and his mission: He says that many of the animals he is photographing are down to just a few now. In other words, some species have nearly been killed by pollution, climate change, poaching or loss of habitat. He says, "If you think about the stuff I'm photographing here, . . . from tigers to rhinos to some frog species, many are down to just a few individuals left, and that's really kind of tragic.."

Student 2: Wow, that's pretty powerful . . . and depressing. But I don't understand why Sartore sets up most of the photos in a studio. Why isn't he out taking photos in the wild to get his message across?

Professor: Um. hmm. I wondered about that, too. But Sartore explains that some of the species can't be found in the wild anymore. The few that are left are in zoos or nature preserves.

    Before the next class, I'd like you to take a good look at some of Sartore's photos online. Choose a few and be prepared to discuss what makes them so impressive. I think you'll begin to appreciate the great passion he has for animals.

LESSON 3

1 READ, page 318   CD3–Track 25

REVIEW THE GRAMMAR

4A and 4B, page 329   CD3–Track 26

    Do you know of a fruit that can provide you with a health drink, a sweet topping for your desserts, and a mailing container all in one? It's the wonderful coconut, of course! This tropical fruit, which humans have been using for about half a million years, is a great source of iron and other minerals for your diet.

    Have you ever tried coconut water? Anyone who has had a glass will tell you how delicious it is. It's the perfect drink for people needing refreshment on a hot summer day. Just take one sip and you'll be transported to a beautiful tropical land where you'll see coconut palm trees everywhere you look. An 8-ounce glass of coconut water will have you dreaming of the sunny beaches of the Philippines or Indonesia or maybe Sri Lanka.

    And that's not all. Order 5 pounds of coconuts and we'll send you a free gift: a set of instructions about how to turn the hard brown shell into a "coconut postcard." That's right! Just ask the staff at the Hoolehua post office in Hawaii, which ships about 3,000 of these postcards each year.

    So don't delay. Order your coconuts right away. And why not send some to your friends, who will be delighted with such a tasty and unusual gift.

    Offer is good as long as supplies last. Check out our website for quantities and prices. www.thefabulouscoconut.grex.

UNIT 12

LESSON 1

1 READ, page 334   CD3–Track 27

12A and 12B, pages 343 and 344   CD3–Track 28

Anna: What's the matter, Sergio? You look upset.

Sergio: Oh, it's nothing. I'm just annoyed about the Eurosky tower. . . . Rome's first residential *skyscraper*.

Anna: You're not thinking about *that* again, are you? . . . Why?

Sergio: Well, it was in the news again today . . . and you know me, whenever I see it, I get annoyed.

Anna: I don't understand why you're so bothered by it. Just forget about it, Sergio. OK?

Sergio: Well, it's hard for me, Anna. I mean, I'm an *architect*, after all. . . . Remember how they refused to build the hotel I'd designed a few years ago because it was too tall for Rome. . . . And then they go and build the Eurosky tower, which is *enormous*.

AUDIO SCRIPTS

Anna: I know, but then they decided to build it after all because it would be more efficient than the old buildings there, right?

Sergio: Not everyone agrees with that idea.

Anna: I know, but they used green technology when they built it so that it won't use much energy . . . It uses solar energy . . . and that's a good thing, isn't it? . . . Anyway, I think you're just mad because someone *else* built the Eurosky tower.

Sergio: No. . . . That's not it. . . . It's too *tall*. There shouldn't be any huge skyscrapers like that in Rome because it ruins the visual landscape. . . . I think it would be fine in someplace like Dubai, but not Rome.

Anna: Well, at least it's not near the old city, right? It's in in the business and residential district, south of Rome. They built it so that they could provide more housing for people.

Sergio: I don't believe that. . . . Even though they say that, I think that most of the people who'll live in that tower will be wealthy businesspeople. . . . Remember the Pyramide tower in Paris? . . . Who lives in that skyscraper? Rich businesspeople. . . . The same thing is happening in a lot of old cities. First Paris, now Rome. . . . Too many skyscrapers are going up these days. . . . It's too bad. I think skyscrapers are fine, but only if they fit the city.

Anna: OK, Sergio, I think you've made your point. . . . Now can we eat?

LESSON 2

1 READ, page 345   CD3–Track 29

REVIEW THE GRAMMAR

3A and 3B, pages 352 and 353   CD3–Track 30
Smart Cities

We've all heard of smartphones, and chances are you own one and use it every day. They're superior to regular phones because they have so many features: texting, Internet, taking pictures, sharing files . . . Smartphones use smart technology. . . . Now, even though you may not have heard of the term before, there are also smart cities. . . . That's right. . . . These include Amsterdam, Dubai, Cairo, and Yokohama.

So what makes a city *smart*? . . . It's an interesting question . . . and although people argue over the answer, they usually agree that all smart cities have certain things in common, such as an emphasis on new information communication technologies, a good quality of life for the residents, and competitiveness. . . . They're competitive.

Whenever a city invests enough money in its information and communication and technology and its people, it creates more jobs and a better quality of life. When a city provides job opportunities and a good quality of life overall, more skilled and creative professionals want to move there. . . . Because these smart cities are "business-friendly," more and more businesses want to move to them or open offices in them. . . . This makes these cities competitive. . . . An example of a competitive city is Stockholm, Sweden. . . . Stockholm is competitive since it offers high quality education, and because there are a lot of technology jobs there. . . . As a result, it is one of the highest ranking cities when it comes to quality of life. . . . This of course means that Stockholm is a smart city.

People move to cities like Stockholm so that they can earn more money and make a better life for themselves. . . . There are more businesses in smart cities, better jobs, better workers, and better pay.

Even though business is very important to smart cities, natural resources are also a priority. . . . These cities use a lot of new communication technologies, which enables them to use energy more wisely and efficiently. . . . For example, thanks to smart technology they will know when their parks need water, or when there is too much pollution. . . . Smart cities realize that our natural resources such as water are limited, and that we need to use them carefully. They understand that if we don't do this, they run out. . . . And that would be a problem for everyone.

So, in conclusion, more cities today are becoming *smart* cities so that people will want to live and work in them. Having smart technologies and goals, these cities are friendly to businesses, and offer a great quality of life.

UNIT 13

LESSON 1

1 READ, page 358   CD4–Track 2

12A and 12B, page 365   CD4–Track 3

We make hundreds of decisions every day. Should I wear the blue shirt or the white one? Do I want a salad for lunch or a bowl of soup? It takes us a second to decide. But if the decision is about something more serious—should I get married, do I really want to move away from home—it takes us much more than a second to decide. And so it should. The problem is that if the process of deciding takes too long, we may not be able to decide anything at all. If that's your problem, these research findings may help you:

If you have to make a big decision, try to do it in the morning. The more choices you have to make during the day, the more tiring it is for the brain. But if you have to make an important decision in the afternoon, it's a good idea to take a relaxing break first. The more well rested you are, the better your decisions will be.

Eating helps the decision-making process, too. Eating raises the glucose levels in the body, giving us more energy. The brain needs this energy to perform well. If we eat before we have to make a decision, we will be able to focus on the issues better and make better choices.

And here is something that may surprise you. We often think of having choices as a good thing, but research has found that too many choices can make decisions harder. It can also prevent us from making any decision at all if we keep looking for the perfect choice. So the next time you have to make a decision, focus on the most important choices and forget about the others.

Here's something for those of you who speak a foreign language. If you have to make a decision that involves a lot of emotions, try thinking about the issues in the foreign language. Researchers have found that we are more likely to think more rationally in a foreign language and less likely to let emotions influence our choices.

If you'd like to learn more, be sure to check out my blog at www.gooddecisions.grex.

LESSON 2

1 READ, page 366   CD4–Track 4

10, page 373   CD4–Track 5

M: I would get a dog if I could.
F: I'd get a dog if I could.
M: You would like him if you knew him.
F: You'd like him if you knew him.
M: I would not open the door if I were you.
F: I wouldn't open the door if I were you.
M: I would not read it even if I had the time.
F: I wouldn't read it even if I had the time.
M: It would be nice if you came.
F: It'd be nice if you came.

10A, page 373   CD4–Track 6

1. If scientists could revive extinct animals, it'd be interesting to see them.
2. It wouldn't help the environment if all species were preserved.
3. If extinct animals were brought back to life, they wouldn't be happy.
4. I wouldn't want to put more creatures on the planet if it were possible.
5. I'd be selfish if I wanted to see all the extinct animals revived.
6. If someone asked me to support a de-extinction project, I wouldn't do it.
7. We'd help the environment more if we used fewer natural resources.
8. It'd be good for society if people shared more.

14B and 14C, page 375   CD4–Track 7

Mike: Do you want to get some coffee?
Jack: OK. Let's go to that place on the corner.
Woman: Excuse me. Can I talk to you for a minute?
Mike: Uh . . . sure. Do you . . . uh, need directions or something?
Woman: No, I'd like to give you twenty dollars. Here are 20 one-dollar bills.
Mike: What? You want to give me 20 dollars? I don't understand.
Jack: She wants to give you 20 bucks, Mike.
Mike: I know. But why?
Woman: Just consider this your lucky day. But listen. I want you to keep some of the money and offer some to your friend.
Jack: Sounds good to me!
Woman: You decide how much to offer, but if your friend doesn't accept the amount you give him, then you get nothing.
Mike: Huh! OK. . . . Jack, I'll give you five dollars.
Jack: Only five? Why not ten, Mike? That's what I would give you if I had to divide the money with you.
Mike: That's crazy. The woman gave me the money, not you. If I were in your shoes, I'd be happy with five dollars.
Jack: No, you wouldn't. You'd be upset if I didn't split it in half.
Mike: I wish you would stop arguing with me.
Woman: Excuse me, gentlemen. I see your friend refused your offer, so I'll take the money back. Thank you. Goodbye.
Jack: Thanks *a lot*, Mike.
Mike: Don't mention it, Jack.

LESSON 3

1 READ, page 377   CD4–Track 8

8, page 383   CD4–Track 9

M: If Meg had known, she would have called.
F: If Meg had known, she [would've] called.
M: If I had seen her, I would have told you.
F: If I'd seen her, I [would've] told you.
M: If you had stayed, Ray would not have left.
F: If you'd stayed, Ray [wouldnt#ve] left.
M: If it had been cold, we would not have gone.
F: If it'd been cold, we [wouldnt#ve] gone.
M: If you had asked me, I would have helped you.
F: If you'd asked me, I [woulda] helped you.

8A, page 383   CD4–Track 10

1. If the weather hadn't gotten so bad, the ship [wouldnt#ve] gotten stuck in ice.
2. The ship [would've] reached its destination if it hadn't gotten stuck.
3. If a helicopter hadn't rescued the people, they [would've] been in danger.
4. The people [wouldn't#ve] survived if the ship hadn't had plenty of food.
5. If there hadn't been Internet connection, the people [wouldn't#ve] been able to communicate with the outside world.
6. If they had stayed much longer, many people [would've] started to worry.

AUDIO SCRIPTS   **A21**

AUDIO SCRIPTS

REVIEW THE GRAMMAR

5A, page 387   CD4–Track 11

If it were possible to go back to the past and prevent an event from happening, what event would you want to prevent?

If you asked Ronald Mallett this question, he would answer right away. Mallett would go back to the day when his much loved father died unexpectedly. The boy was only 10 years old at the time. His whole world collapsed, and he became deeply depressed. He could not face the fact that he would never see his father again.

Fortunately, Mallett loved to read, and it was a book that saved him: H. G. Wells's science fiction novel, *The Time Machine*. If Mallett hadn't come across this book, he would have been lost. The novel showed him that time travel was possible, at least in fiction. He learned that time is a kind of space in which we can move backward and forward. Mallett was thrilled. If he could build a time machine, he could go back into the past and do something to prevent his father's death.

That was just the beginning of Mallett's lifelong project. Basing his ideas on Einstein's theories, he began to develop mathematical formulas showing how a time machine could work. It was a secret project, though. Although he was a well-respected professor of physics, if he had shown his work to other scientists at that time, they would have thought he was crazy.

Today things are different. There are other scientists who also believe that time travel might be possible, and some of them are working with Mallett. If his work keeps progressing as it has so far, Mallett believes that eventually he will be successful. Because of the limitations of any possible time machine, Mallett knows that he will not be able to travel back to the day his father died—a time machine could only go back as far as the date it was built. However, he believes there would be practical uses for time machines in the future. According to Mallett, if we create working time machines, they can be used to warn people of coming disasters. For example, if we know about an earthquake in our time, we can send that information back and warn people ahead of time. Then they can prepare themselves appropriately. That's part of the reason Mallett remains so committed to his work.

If his time machine succeeds, the little boy who lost his father will become one of the most famous scientists of our time.

UNIT 14

LESSON 1

1 READ, page 392   CD4–Track 12

12A, page 401   CD4–Track 13

Host: Hi, everyone. Today we're discussing a new way of cooking: solar cooking. You may have never heard of it before, but solar cooking is an excellent way to cook, save energy, and help the environment. The benefits are many. First of all, solar cooking is inexpensive. You don't have to buy fuel. The energy is all there, in the sun. Second, it's healthy. Solar cooking is smoke-free! Third, it's safe. Cooking fires can get out of control, but solar cooking is fire-free. It is also convenient and easy.

12B, page 401   CD4–Track 14

Host: Now that we've heard the benefits of solar cooking, we're going to speak to some people who are making solar cooking a part of their lives. We are bringing you our show from the backyard of Molly Cohen in sunny California. Right now Molly is cooking dinner, and she's using the heat of the sun to do it. . . . Mmm. That smells great, Molly. Can you tell me what you're making?

Molly: Sure, Jack. This is a fish and rice dish. It'll be done in just a few minutes.

Host: I understand that you've been cooking on a solar oven for quite a long time.

Molly: Yes, I have. It's been about 20 years. I'm not sure whether food tastes better this way or not, but I know that solar cooking is a terrific way to save energy.

Host: Right. And solar energy is clean energy, isn't it?

Molly: Yes. There's absolutely no need for fuel . . . no electricity, no gas, no coal, no wood.

Host: Let me ask you something else. I've always wondered if solar cooking works only on a warm day.

Molly: Actually, bright sun is much more important than hot air temperature. I know it's surprising, but you can even cook on a cold day when it's very sunny.

Host: Amazing! Molly, could you explain how a solar oven works?

Molly: Well, it's pretty simple. You'll notice that I use a dark pot for the food. The metal directs sunlight onto the pot. The pot absorbs the sunlight, and the energy from the light changes into heat energy. That's all there is to it.

Host: It sounds great. I can't understand why more people aren't cooking with solar energy.

Molly: I think it's slowly becoming more popular. Have you heard of Solar Cookers International? What they do is really great. This organization is introducing solar cooking in developing countries throughout the world.

Host: I know that the smoke from open wood fires is very unhealthy, especially for people who spend many hours around the fire.

Molly: Absolutely. Solar cooking not only saves energy, it's a very healthy way to cook.

LESSON 2

1 READ, page 403   CD4–Track 15

LESSON 3

1 READ, page 412   CD4–Track 16

7A and 7B, page 417   CD4–Track 17

Lin: Hi, Jimmy. How's your first day on the job so far?
Jim: It's fine, thanks.
Lin: Good. Can you come over here? I'm going to explain what you need to do for the hotel guests.
Jim: Sure. OK.
Lin: First, you need to go to every floor of the hotel. On each floor we keep a pot of coffee for the guests in the lounge. Make sure that the coffee is fresh and that we have enough cups. If you need more cups, there are extras under the counter.
Jim: OK.
Lin: When you go to each floor, if you see any garbage or newspapers outside the rooms, please throw them away.
Jim: All right.
Lin: The next thing you have to do is prepare the continental breakfast. The first thing you do is go to the kitchenette. You need to make several gallons of orange juice. Take out three cans of frozen orange juice concentrate from the freezer and mix them with water. Then store it in the refrigerator.
Jim: All right.
Lin: Next, you will get the donuts and rolls. They're delivered at five a.m. Go to the side entrance to pick them up. Do you know where that is?
Jim: Yes.
Lin: Good. When the delivery arrives, count the donuts. There should be 36. Make sure there's a variety. Then take them to the second floor. That's where the main lounge is. Set out the donuts and the rolls with the orange juice on the center table. You also need to make two fresh pots of coffee. Breakfast opens to the guests at six a.m.
Jim: OK.
Lin: Do you have any questions?
Jim: No, I think I understand.

Lin: Great. I'm leaving now, but if you have any questions tonight, you can ask the night auditor at the hotel front desk. Have a good night.
Jim: You, too.

REVIEW THE GRAMMAR

2A and 2B, pages 419 and 420   CD4–Track 18

Dennis: Great to see you, Nedra. How was your trip to London?
Nedra: It was fantastic! I was there for New Year's Eve, and I went to the most incredible celebration on the banks of the Thames River.
Dennis: Sounds exciting. Tell me what it was it like.
Nedra: Well, the fireworks began at midnight. They were noisy and colorful as usual. But believe it or not, they were flavored, too.
Dennis: You're kidding.
Nedra: No, really. When the fireworks went off, you could smell all different fruit flavors in the air—strawberry, orange, peach, banana. I've never experienced anything like it.
Dennis: I'd like to know who thought of this crazy idea.
Nedra: I found out about it online. Apparently, the inventors of the fireworks—their names are Sam Bompas and Harry Parr—have been food artists for some time. They say that they specialize in creating "flavor-based" experiences.
Dennis: Hey, wait a minute. I've heard of them before. They must be the same guys who built a chocolate waterfall. That was in London, too. I heard that visitors to the exhibit could walk right through it. Hmmm. I wonder if they carried umbrellas.
Nedra: They did! I read about that project, too. What a cool idea.
Dennis: Do you have any idea what their next project will be?
Nedra: No, but whatever it is, I'm sure it will be pretty outrageous.

UNIT 15

LESSON 1

1 READ, page 426   CD4–Track 19

12A and 12B, page 435   CD4–Track 20

Jayden: Hey Sarah. I hear you're taking an online class.
Sarah: That's right. I'm taking a MOOC.
Jayden: A what?
Sarah: A MOOC. M-O-O-C. It stands for Massive Open Online Course. My MOOC is in World History.

AUDIO SCRIPTS   **A23**

AUDIO SCRIPTS

Jayden: So how does it work?

Sarah: Well, it's pretty simple. You sign up for a course that interests you. There are no requirements and you don't have to take any tests before, so anyone can do it. Then you watch a couple of short videotaped lectures every week. They're given by university professors.

Jayden: How much does it cost?

Sarah: Nothing! It's free.

Jayden: Really? Do you get college credit?

Sarah: No, you can't get credit. But if you do all the work, you can get a certificate of completion at the end.

Jayden: Is there a lot of work?

Sarah: I'm putting in about five hours a week. The lectures and the readings take a few hours, and then we have to post comments on a discussion question once a week. We also have to write a short essay every other week.

Jayden: Do you get grades?

Sarah: We grade and comment on each other's essays. That way, you always get feedback.

Jayden: It seems like a lot of work for no credit, and you don't get to talk with the professor. But you seem really happy with the course.

Sarah: Well, the subject is really interesting, the lectures are great, and the students' comments are usually thoughtful. Also, the schedule is very flexible. I can watch the lectures anytime during the week as long as I get my posts and essays done on time. Plus, there are no final exams to worry about.

Jayden: Would you ever take another MOOC?

Sarah: Definitely. In fact, I've already signed up for one that starts next month.

LESSON 2

1 READ, page 436   CD4–Track 21

REVIEW THE GRAMMAR

4A and 4B, page 448   CD4–Track 22

On a mid-August afternoon in New York City, over 500 people participated in a bioblitz in Central Park. They included many students from the City University of New York. Their job was to identify as many examples of plant and animal life as they could.

Despite the fact that the people had only 24 hours to work, they were able to find a great variety of wildlife. At least seven species of turtles and over twenty bird species were found. In addition, insect experts were pleased to find 44 beetle species and 31 types of spiders. There were also some surprising new discoveries, such as a catfish in one of the lakes and a bird that had never been seen in the park before.

Some of the creatures in the park are active only at night. Therefore, during a bioblitz, nighttime is especially important. Participants were able to identify many different species of animals in the dark, such as owls and bats. There is such a variety of species in Central Park that scientists are trying to find out why. Many believe that it is due to the conservation work that has been going on for years. As a result of the improvements in the land and water, a large number of living things are now living happily there.

Being able to see all this life in the park was, for many of the students, a new experience. Before the event, most of them thought of the city as a place of tall buildings, noise, and traffic. However, because of their bioblitz work, they now realize that there's a lot of natural beauty as well. In fact, they saw so many new things that they will never think of New York City in quite the same way again.